Social Network Analysis

SAGE was founded in 1965 by Sara Miller McCune to support the dissemination of usable knowledge by publishing innovative and high-quality research and teaching content. Today, we publish over 900 journals, including those of more than 400 learned societies, more than 800 new books per year, and a growing range of library products including archives, data, case studies, reports, and video. SAGE remains majority-owned by our founder, and after Sara's lifetime will become owned by a charitable trust that secures our continued independence.

Los Angeles | London | New Delhi | Singapore | Washington DC | Melbourne

Social Network Analysis

Methods and Examples

Song Yang

University of Arkansas
Shanghai University

Franziska B. Keller

Hong Kong University of Science and Technology

Lu Zheng

Tsinghua University

Los Angeles | London | New Delhi
Singapore | Washington DC | Melbourne

FOR INFORMATION:

SAGE Publications, Inc.
2455 Teller Road
Thousand Oaks, California 91320
E-mail: order@sagepub.com

SAGE Publications Ltd.
1 Oliver's Yard
55 City Road
London EC1Y 1SP
United Kingdom

SAGE Publications India Pvt. Ltd.
B 1/I 1 Mohan Cooperative Industrial Area
Mathura Road, New Delhi 110 044
India

SAGE Publications Asia-Pacific Pte. Ltd.
3 Church Street
#10-04 Samsung Hub
Singapore 049483

ISBN: 978-1-4833-2521-7

Acquisitions Editor: Helen Salmon
Editorial Assistant: Yvonne McDuffee
Production Editor: Kelly DeRosa
Copy Editor: Sheree Van Vreede
Typesetter: C&M Digitals (P) Ltd.
Proofreader: Jennifer Grubba
Indexer: Sheila Bodell
Cover Designer: Candice Harman
Marketing Manager: Susannah Goldes

16 17 18 19 20 10 9 8 7 6 5 4 3 2 1

• Contents •

• Preface •

With the rise of social media, social network analysis (SNA) has become increasingly popular with researchers, journalists, and the general public. Most readers will probably have come across examples of the visualizations for which SNA is known: a graph of how a corrupt politician is linked to assets overseas through shell companies, an illustration of a terrorist network, or a figure of the trade flows between different countries. Or they may have used websites to plot their own friendship network on social media platforms like Facebook or their follower network on Twitter. But SNA can do much more than such visualizations, as we will show in this book.

Unlike most introductions to basic SNA concepts and statistical tools, however, this book also covers practical applications in the social sciences. It provides the reader with a comprehensive overview of SNA research conducted in four fields: politics (Chapter 8), work and organizations (Chapter 5), emotional and physical health (Chapter 7), and crime and terrorism studies (Chapter 6). The purpose of this book is, thus, to introduce advanced undergraduate and graduate students in the social sciences to both the basic methodological tools and the extensive examples in their various fields to prepare and inspire them to conduct their own research in SNA. The nature of the book makes it particularly suitable for teaching interdisciplinary introductory courses to SNA. But the variegated examples, ranging from the management sciences, to political science, psychology and public health, to economics and sociology, mean that this book can be used in a wide range of social science departments.

Nevertheless, the book can be used outside college classrooms as well. Professionals who want to learn more about social network analysis and its applications, and scholars who are looking for an overview of what SNA has to offer and how it is applied to important substantive subjects, will find this book useful. Workshops at professional association conferences may also consider adopting the material presented here.

This unique combination of methods and application will help instructors overcome common misperceptions deterring students and laypeople from taking a course on social network analysis, namely, that SNA is a collection of mathematical methods, developed and used by technical geeks. This couldn't be farther from the truth as the four application chapters show: It is a method applied by a wide range of scholars. At the same time, the books take great care to explain concepts in plain language instead of in technical jargon without altogether sidestepping mathematical formulas and more in-depth explanation of statistical techniques. The examples in the four application chapters are also selected and discussed to illustrate how the specific SNA concepts and methods help uncover patterns and evidence that would otherwise remain hidden. Finally, to highlight the practical use of the social network approach, we include in every chapter boxes titled "Social Networks in Action," which provide concise examples of how social networks influence individuals and their social environment.

Another feature that will help both instructors and students is the extensive glossary at the end of the book. Unfortunately, many disciplines involved in social network research have developed their own terminology, and the glossary helps students keep track of the special terms employed in each field covered.

The beginning of each chapter provides the reader with a quick overview by stating its learning objectives. These help instructors structure their courses and guide students in their learning process. The students can also use them for reviews and in preparation for the exams, together with the glossary provided.

Most importantly, each chapter concludes with a series of questions and exercises. The questions test students' understanding of the material and encourage them to apply concepts learned to practical problems. The exercises ensure that they know how to apply the methods to a specific dataset.

Last, but not least, no book on social network analysis would be complete without social network visualizations. The reader will find them interspersed in each chapter, reflecting the broad range of topics covered—from terrorist networks to networks of interactions among co-workers or sexual intercourse among adolescents. Some are used to illustrate important studies, some highlight methods discussed in the text, and others are schematics explaining concepts.

This book is divided into two sections. The first section consists of four method-ological chapters. The first chapter familiarizes the reader with basic SNA concepts and terminology. The second chapter explains how network data are collected, as well as the potential pitfalls involved in that process. Chapter 3 discusses the most common descriptive statistics in SNA, and Chapter 4 highlights the most up-to-date inferential statistical tools available. As mentioned earlier, the second part of the book consists of the four applied chapters, which illustrate how social network analysis is applied in substantive areas, such as work and organizations (Chapter 5); delinquency, crime, and terrorism network studies (Chapter 6); emotional and physical health (Chapter 7); and political network analysis (Chapter 8). Depending on their interests, readers may focus on only one or two of these chapters. Scholars studying organizational sociology or labor markets will find Chapter 5 most relevant, which discusses personal network and job search, individual networks in workplaces and career advancement, and inter-firm relations such as knowledge transfers, directorate interlock, venture capital syn-dication, and entrepreneurial processes. Researchers focused on crime, delinquency, and terrorism network studies can relate to Chapter 6. This chapter starts off by inves-tigating the interdependence between selection and influence in deviance and crime network. The chapter also examines social disorganization theory at the community level, as well as the evolution and consequences of criminal networks. Finally, the chapter discusses terror networks and the effectiveness of antiterrorism measures by using social network analysis. Chapter 7 should appeal most to scholars and professionals in the public health domain as it presents social network analyses in public health, including emotional and physical health problems. Issues investigated in this chapter include happiness, loneliness, depression, alcohol use, smoking, obesity, illicit drug use, as well as social network analysis of sexually transmitted diseases, in general, and of HIV/AIDs, in particular. Students of political sciences, public policy, and government studies will benefit greatly from Chapter 8 because SNA is relatively new to this field and few comprehensive overviews exist. This chapter discusses, for instance, social network studies in international relations and American politics, such as network analysis of political campaign networks. In short, the book provides examples of interest for any reader and will help them appreciate the depth and scope of social network analysis.

The authors would like to thank the reviewers from several rounds of external reviews for SAGE:

Tim J. Anderson, Old Dominion University

Scott A. Comparato, Southern Illinois University

Emmanuel F. Koku, Drexel University

Zachary P. Neal, Michigan State University

Tracy M. Walker, Virginia State University

Weihua An, Indiana University

Renato Corbetta, University of Alabama—Birmingham

Diane Felmlee, Pennsylvania State University

Neha Gondal, Ohio State University

Dane Christian Joseph, Pacific University

Carol Ann MacGregor, Loyola University New Orleans

Min Zhou, University of Victoria

Song Yang would like to thank his doctoral degree advisors, David Knoke and Joe Galaskiewicz, who educated him in social network analysis throughout the dissertation process. He has also benefited greatly from his life-long mentor, Professor Yanjie Bian at Minnesota, a student of one of the earliest pioneers to introduce and centralize structural network perspectives into social science studies, Nan Lin. Yanjie Bian's passion for social network analysis and his insights into Chinese society have motivated Song throughout his career. Franziska Keller would like to thank her advisor, Jenn Larson, for encouragement and support while writing her dissertation on informal networks among Chinese political elites, and Lada Adamic, who initiated her to social network analysis. To those people, we owe intellectual debts. We are very grateful to our editor, Helen Salmon, for her great guidance and coordination during the writing of the book, and we are responsible for any remaining errors the book may still have.

• About the Authors •

Song Yang (PhD, University of Minnesota, 2002) is Professor at the Department of Sociology and Criminal Justice at the University of Arkansas. He also holds Qianren Professorship with the School of Sociology and Political Science at Shanghai University. His research areas are social network analysis, sociology of work, and organizational studies. He published *Social Network Analysis, Second Edition* with David Knoke (Sage, 2008), and *The Invisible Hands of Political Parties in Presidential Elections: Party Activists and Political Aggregation from 2004 to 2012* with Andrew Dowdle, Scott Limbocker, Patrick A. Stewart, and Karen Sebold (Palgrave MacMillan, 2013). He has published more than 20 articles in various peer-reviewed journals such as *Party Politics, Social Science Research, Sociological Spectrum*, and *Sociological Inquiry*.

Franziska B. Keller has received her PhD degree from New York University's Department of Politics, and is currently Assistant Professor at the Division of Social Science at the Hong Kong University of Science and Technology. Her work uses social network analysis to examine informal politics in authoritarian regimes. Her research has been supported by organizations such as the Chiang Ching-Kuo Foundation, and has received the John Sprague Award by the Political Network Section of the American Political Science Association. Her most recent publication, "Moving Beyond Factions: Using Social Network Analysis to Uncover Patronage Networks Among Chinese Elites", has appeared in the *Journal of East Asian Studies*.

Lu Zheng is Associate Professor of Sociology at Tsinghua University, China and Adjunct Professor of Sociology at Texas A&M University, USA. His research projects focus on corporate social responsibility (CSR), social governance, and China's ongoing urbanization process. His publications appear in *Social Forces, British Journal of Sociology, Social Science Research,* and *China Quarterly,* etc. His paper on listed firms in China's stock market won the Best Paper Award from the International Association of Chinese Management Research (IACMR) Biennial Conference in 2012. His most recent coauthored book is *Data You Need to Know About China: Research Report of China Household Finance Survey* (Springer, 2014).

1

Basics of Social Network Analysis

●

Learning Objectives

- Describe basic concepts in social network analysis (SNA) such as nodes, actors, and ties or relations

- Identify different types of social networks, such as directed or undirected, binary or valued, and bipartite or one-mode

- Assess research designs in social network research, and distinguish *sampling units*, relational forms and contents, and levels of analysis

- Identify network actors at different levels of analysis (e.g., individuals or aggregate units) when reading social network literature

- Describe bipartite networks, know when to use them, and what their advantages are

- Explain the three theoretical assumptions that undergird social network studies

- Discuss problems of causality in social network analysis, and suggest methods to establish causality in network studies

1.1 Introduction

The term "social network" entered everyday language with the advent of the Internet. As a result, most people will connect the term with the Internet and social media platforms, but it has in fact a much broader application, as we will see shortly. Still, pictures like Figure 1.1 are what most people will think of when they hear the word "social network": thousands of points connected to each other. In this particular case, the points represent political blogs in the United States (grey ones are Republican, and dark grey ones are Democrat), the ties indicating hyperlinks between them. The polarization between the two parties in real life is clearly reflected online as well.

SOCIAL NETWORK IN ACTION: THOSE REAL-LIFE SOCIAL NETWORKS

At the individual level, people form friendships, become enemies, and help each other by passing useful information, giving rides, fixing cars and houses, and providing emotional support; pupils play together or fight with each other; co-workers collaborate, collude, or backstab; and college students form study groups or social clubs. At the group or team level, teams compete and collaborate as well as imitate

(Continued)

(Continued)

and emulate each other. Organizations may collude or compete for scarce resources, be it tangible goods, such as bank loans, markets, or valuable material input, or intangible ones, such as reputation and legitimacy. Nation states wage war against each other, form alliances, and interact in different international organizations. All these actions involve at least two people, and we can thus envision the combined actions as a network between the actors involved.

In other cases, the points may be users of social media platforms such as Facebook (Menlo Park, CA), where the links indicate friends or "likes," or Twitter (San Francisco, CA), where the links may be "retweets" or "followers." In this chapter, we will start by describing some real-life social networks such as pre-World War I (WWI) international networks and the *Star Wars* (see Kurtz, 1977) character network. Then, we

FIGURE 1.1 • Political Blogosphere in the United States in 2004

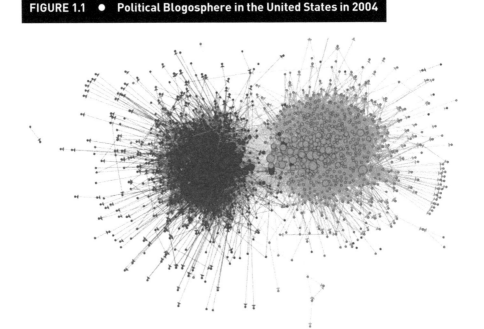

Notes: Political blogs in the United States in 2004: Democrats in dark grey, Republican in grey. Light grey links indicate hyperlinks across the aisle. Adapted from Adamic, L. A., & Glance, N. (2005). The political blogosphere and the 2004 US election: Divided they blog. In *Proceedings of the 3rd International Workshop on Link Discovery* (pp. 36–43). New York, NY: ACM.

will discuss the basic components of a network, types of social network, and levels of analysis in social network studies. We also will illustrate the theoretical aspects of social network analysis, covering such topics as the social network as institutions, the theoretical assumptions, and ***causality*** issues with social network analysis. We will conclude this chapter with a brief history of social network analysis, underscoring its multidisciplinary roots and strengths.

To start, social networks have been a defining feature of society since the early dawn of humanity—people have always interacted with each other or have made friends or enemies. These social interactions can be depicted as networks between individuals but also between smaller and larger groups of people. Figure 1.2 displays a network of the latter: the alliance networks between European countries before (top) and after (bottom) the Archduke of Austria-Hungary was assassinated by a Serbian nationalist, an event that precipitated the cataclysm of WWI.

The assassination and the subsequent war between Austria and Serbia pulled their respective allies into the fray. The bottom of Figure 1.2 shows how their declarations of war on each other resulted in some members searching and finding new allies, which then got attacked by members of the opposite side, until the war engulfed half the world. In the world of social networks, actors never act in isolation. Instead they influence and are influenced by others. Therefore, the consequences of their actions may reach well beyond their immediate environment. The goal of this book is to provide the reader with the tools to understand these interactions and interdependencies that affect both the small world of our immediate friends, online or offline, and the larger world of national blogospheres, global alliances, or trade networks.

But the analysis of social networks has even more applications, some of which may be surprising or whimsical. Take Figure 1.3 as an example, which displays a network of characters from the *Star Wars* franchise, connected by whether they share scenes in two different *Star Wars* movies.

What may at first appear only of interest to fans of the series could, in fact, convey a deeper insight into good storytelling. Or so the author of the relevant blog post, Evelina Gabasova (2016), claims. She has found that the protagonist of the more popular second three episodes, Luke Skywalker, indirectly connects many other characters through shared scenes (he is *betweenness central*—see Chapter 3), whereas the main character of the first three episodes, Anakin Skywalker, occupies a less central network position.

In short: Social network analysis has a wide variety of applications. But the term "network" has become vague exactly because of its increasingly widespread use. It is thus important that we start by defining what social network analysts mean when they talk about networks.

1.2 The Social Network and How to Represent It

A social network consists of a set of ***nodes*** (sometimes referred to as *actors* or *vertices* in graph theory) connected via some type of ***relations***, which are also called *ties*, *links*, *arcs*, or *edges*. The nodes usually represent actors, be that individuals, groups, teams,

FIGURE 1.2 ● Alliance and Enemy Networks Before and After the Death of Archduke Ferdinand

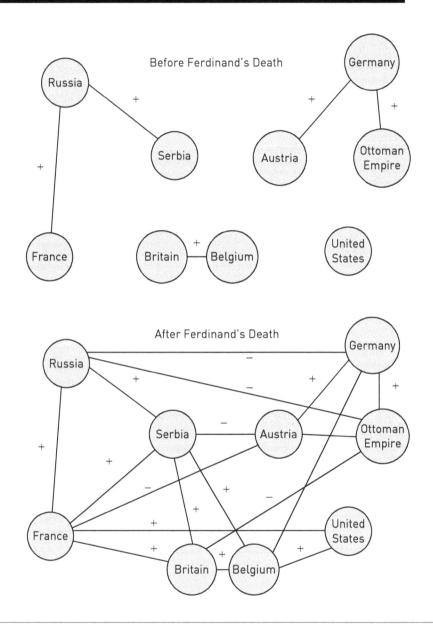

Notes: Some alliances and war declarations were left out for clarity. Adapted from Assassination of Archduke Franz Ferdinand [Course blog]. Retrieved June 7, 2016, from https://blogs.cornell.edu/info2040/2015/09/14/assassination-of-archduke-franz-ferdinand/

FIGURE 1.3 ● *Star Wars* Character Network

Episode III: Revenge of the Sith

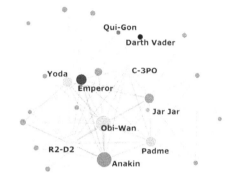

Episode V: The Empire Strikes Back

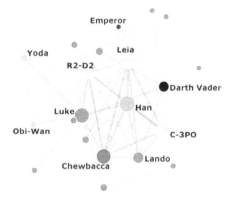

Notes: Co-appearances of *Star Wars* characters in the same scene in two *Star Wars* movies. The main character in the relatively unpopular Episode III (Anakin) is more peripheral to the network than the main character in Episode V (Luke), who directly and indirectly connects other characters. Adapted from Gabasova, E. (2016, January 25). Star Wars social networks: The Force Awakens [Blog]. Retrieved June 7, 2016, from http://evelinag.com/blog/2015/12-15-star-wars-social-network/index.html

communities, organizations, political parties, or even nation states. *Social* networks thus either have nodes that are social beings or organizations (lobbyists, voters, parties, etc.) or ties that represent some form of social interaction (voting for a candidate, re-tweeting a message, etc.). The relations between the nodes can be multidimensional and can include a whole array of different relationship types.

Unlike data used in other fields of statistical analysis, network data always consists of at least two datasets: a regular dataset—sometimes called the ***nodelist***—where the nodes are the units of observation (i.e., the rows) and a dataset that defines the relationships among those units of observation. The latter may have different shapes—the two most common ones are called ***adjacency matrix*** and ***edgelist***. In an adjacency matrix (or simply *network matrix*), the nodes constitute both the rows and the columns, and the cells specify if and what kind of relationship exists between the nodes in the row and in the column. An edgelist is a dataset in which each existing tie, with both actors involved and the nature of their relationship, is listed as one observation. Adjacency matrices can be transformed into edgelists, and vice versa.

Figure 1.4 illustrates this with an example network of 10 individuals: At the bottom right, we see the graph or network illustration; the actors or nodes are usually represented as circles, but different shapes or colors can be used to indicate different groups or types of actors. In this example, the two colors indicate the actor's genders. The relations are represented by lines between the two actors.

Although such a visual display of a network can be insightful, it is not useful for statistical analysis, for which we need the nodelist (top left) and the adjacency matrix (top right) or edgelist (bottom left). The nodelist can have all sorts of additional information about the actors. Only one thing is absolutely necessary: an unambiguous identifier for each actor. This identifier can be a name, as long as no two actors share the same name, or a number. In our case, it is the first character of the actor's name.

An unambiguous identifier is important because it links entries in the relationship database (the adjacency matrix or edgelist) with the corresponding node. In the case of the adjacency matrix, the identifier appears again as the names of the rows and columns. We therefore know that column and row A indicate A's (Andrei's) ties. In the simplest case, the ***binary*** network, we simply distinguish whether a tie does or does not exist between a pair of actors. A cell with a one indicates that the actor in the row and in the column share a tie, a zero that they do not. Another way to represent the same information is the edgelist. This dataset has as many rows as there are ties and two or more columns. In each row, the two identifiers of the nodes connected by the tie are listed.

Figure 1.4 has presented perhaps the most common example of a social network: a group of humans connected by, for instance, friendship ties. But as we've seen at the beginning, nodes need not be individuals. Many disciplines within the social sciences use social network analysis, and the node's level of aggregation may reflect the disciplinary difference. Sociologists often take the individual as the node, focusing on the formation of friendship, liking, trust, and support between different individuals. They may also study networks between aggregate units, such as communities, teams, organizations, and states. Political scientists analyze networks between political actors on both levels, such as politicians, voters, parties, or nation states. Economists and management scholars are interested in for-profit firms as actors, the process of maintaining and managing of network alliances, the evolution of network alliances, and the consequences of networks on the firms.

The ties examined also vary. In fact, there can always be multiple networks for a given set of actors as different types of relations define different types of network. In Figure 1.4, we could, for instance, imagine a second adjacency matrix or edgelist that

FIGURE 1.4 • Example (Undirected, Binary) Network Graph With Its Nodelist, Adjacency Matrix, and Edgelist

Nodelist

A	Andrei	male	Russian
B	Barbara	female	US
C	Chris	male	US
D	Denis	male	Russian
E	Erica	female	German
F	Fanny	female	British
G	Galina	female	Russian
H	Hans	male	German
I	Igor	male	Russian
J	Jenny	female	British

Adjacency matrix

	A	B	C	D	E	F	G	H	I	J
A	0	1	0	0	1	0	0	1	1	0
B	1	0	0	0	1	0	0	0	0	0
C	0	0	0	0	1	0	0	0	0	0
D	0	0	0	0	0	0	0	0	0	0
E	1	1	1	0	0	0	0	0	0	0
F	0	0	0	0	0	0	0	0	1	0
G	0	0	0	0	0	0	0	0	0	0
H	1	0	0	0	0	0	0	0	0	0
I	1	0	0	0	0	1	0	0	0	1
J	0	0	0	0	0	0	0	0	1	0

Edgelist (undirected)

A	B
A	E
A	H
A	I
E	B
E	C
I	F
I	J

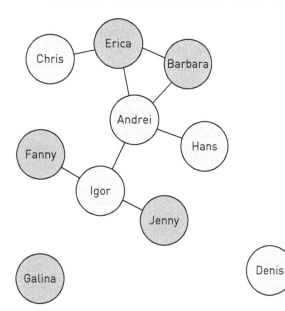

records the enmities among the 10 people, which would likely look very different. In a company, a formal hierarchical network among employees, defined by who is allowed to give orders to whom, will not always be the same as an informal network defined by who is seeking advice from whom. The official leader in the formal hierarchy may not necessarily be the most important person in the informal advice-seeking network.

1.3 Types of Networks

Depending on the nature of the relationship, ***networks*** or ***graphs*** can be ***directed*** or ***undirected***. Directed graphs consist of relations between pairs of actors, or ***dyads,*** which are not necessarily mutual. Figure 1.5 shows a directed version of the network discussed earlier: Now, friendships are not necessarily reciprocated. Although Erica considers Chris to be her friend, Chris does not share that feeling. Many other relations are directed, for instance, seeking advice from someone or passing a message to him or her. The members of a dyad connected by a directed tie cannot switch places without change of meaning: A seeking advice from B is not the same as B seeking advice from A. In the latter case, B would thus often be called the ***sender*** or *source*, whereas A is called the ***receiver*** or *target* (Knoke & Burt, 1983). Note how the edgelist in Figure 1.5 now distinguishes between a source and a target column. And although the adjacency matrix in Figure 1.4 was symmetrical (if one was in row A, column B, one was in row B, column A), this is not true for the matrix here.

A directed tie implies an asymmetric relationship. But it may still be reciprocated in some form, and this can make the label "sender" or "receiver" somewhat arbitrary: Employer–employee relations are clearly directed, but the employer could be the receiver (of the work carried out by the employee) or the sender (of the salary). It is thus particularly important to specify clearly what a tie signifies in a particular network.[1] Undirected graphs, in contrast, contain relations that do not distinguish between senders and receivers. Alliance partners, classmate or co-worker relationships, information exchanges, or marriages all fall into this category.

It is possible to combine both directed and undirected ties into one network: If John considers Aisha his friend, and Aisha shares this feeling, then John may have a directed tie to Amy (who does not consider him to be her friend) and an undirected tie to Aisha. Nevertheless, it is more common and usually less confusing to stick with one type of network and instead to create a graph in which a tie leads from John to Aisha and another one from Aisha to John. Such a configuration is called a ***reciprocated tie***. In many social networks, reciprocated relations occur much more frequently than would be expected if such relations were formed at random. In Figure 1.5, there is a reciprocated tie between Andrei and Hans, who both nominate each other as friends.

---

[1] This is of course true for all social science concepts and pertains therefore to the other terms defined in this book. Nevertheless, confusion about the definition and measurement of connections seems particularly common when discussing networks.

FIGURE 1.5 ● Example (Directed, Binary) Network Graph With Its Nodelist, Adjacency Matrix, and Edgelist

FIGURE 1.5 ● Example (Directed, Binary) Network Graph With Its Nodelist, Adjacency Matrix, and Edgelist

Nodelist

A	Andrei	male	Russian
B	Barbara	female	US
C	Chris	male	US
D	Denis	male	Russian
E	Erica	female	German
F	Fanny	female	British
G	Galina	female	Russian
H	Hans	male	German
I	Igor	male	Russian
J	Jenny	female	British

Adjacency matrix

	A	B	C	D	E	F	G	H	I	J
A	0	1	0	0	0	0	0	1	1	0
B	0	0	0	0	1	0	0	0	0	0
C	0	0	0	0	0	0	0	0	0	0
D	0	0	0	0	0	0	0	0	0	0
E	1	0	1	0	0	0	0	0	0	0
F	0	0	0	0	0	0	0	1	0	0
G	0	0	0	0	0	0	0	0	0	0
H	1	0	0	0	0	0	0	0	0	0
I	0	0	0	0	0	0	0	0	0	0
J	0	0	0	0	0	0	0	0	1	0

Edgelist (directed)

Source	Target
A	B
A	H
A	I
B	E
E	A
E	C
F	I
H	A
J	I

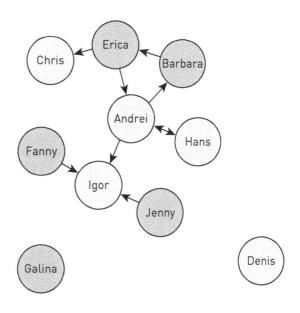

Social network data can also be distinguished by the values that are attached to the ties that link network actors. If the network data only capture presence or absence of certain relations, then the social network is called a *binary network*, in which values of 0 and 1 indicate the presence or absence, respectively, of the specified ties. In contrast, other network data reflects relational intensity between network actors on an ordinal or continuous scale, which results in a **valued network**. The choice between collecting binary or valued network data rests with the researcher. Compared with valued data, binary data are easier to collect and do not create as much of a burden to the informants. But valued data are usually more informative than are binary data. For example, a communication network among co-workers measured on a binary scale (0/1) may not be as revealing as on a valued scale (0, 1, 2, 3 . . .). Almost all co-workers communicate with each other at some point, but some of them exchange a great deal of information, whereas others have short and superficial interactions. Unlike binary data, valued network data capture those fine-grained differences.

NETWORK IN ACTION: A TYPOLOGY OF NETWORK TIES

- Transaction relations: actors exchange control over physical or symbolic objects; most economic exchanges fall in this category.
- Communication relations: almost all kinds of social networks can be used to pass messages between the actors.
- Instrumental relations: actors contact one another to obtain tangible goods, assistance, or information. Examples of instrumental relations include employers using existing employees for recruitment of talents, employees using personal networks to obtain jobs, people using friends or neighbors to attend to their houses while they are away, friends giving rides, fixing cars, repairing houses, and providing day care.
- Sentiment relations: relations that are used to express emotions, such as affection, frustration, admiration, deference, and hostility.
- Authority/power relations: most of those network relations occur in formal hierarchical organizations where social actors assume formal roles and positions; accepting responsibilities, obligations, and privileges; receiving and sending commands; and reporting or being reported to.
- Kinship and descent relations: relations between family members linked via biological ties.

Finally, relationships can be of different kinds. An almost unlimited number of relationship types exists. The box provides one possible typology suggested by David Knoke and Song Yang (2008, p. 12). There are at least two ways to deal with data on several kinds of relationships: One option is to combine them all into one **matrix** or edgelist. In this case, the matrix cell will be filled with a description of the relationship or a number corresponding to the relationship type. This approach becomes difficult if several different types of relationships exist between the same pair of nodes. In edgelist

FIGURE 1.6 • Affiliation Network of the "Southern Women Study"

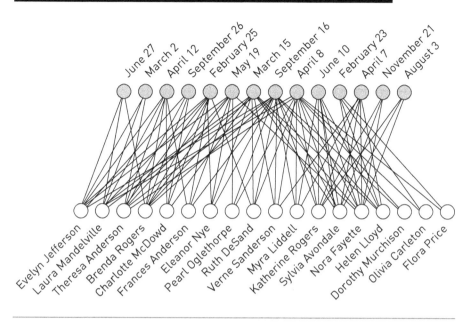

Note: Adapted from Newman, M. E. (2010). *Networks: An introduction* (p. 39). New York, NY: Oxford University Press.

form, the edgelist will contain an additional column, in which the relationship is described. An alternative approach is creating multiple matrices and edgelists among the same set of nodes: one for each type of relationship.

So far we have discussed only networks in which the nodes are on the same aggregate level: They are either all individuals or all organizations or countries, for instance. We have a special name for those types of networks: ***one-mode networks***. Bipartite networks (also called ***bipartite graphs***), on the other hand, have two sets of nodes on different levels of aggregation, and the ties indicate membership or participation by the members of one set in the other. For example, individuals (one set of nodes) have a tie with each organization (the other set of nodes) to which they belong. Such networks are often used when social scientists cannot ask actors to report their relations with other actors or directly observe their interaction. They then resort to indirect methods of inferring ties through reports or archival data of the social events in which actors participate, or the organizations to which they belong.

For example, Allison Davis, Burleigh Gardner, and Mary Gardner (1941) made use of newspaper reports to study the social network of 18 women in the American South. This famous study, often called the "Southern Women Study," contains a sample of 14 social events and a set of 18 women attending each of the 14 events. The network is depicted in Figure 1.6, where the top nodes indicate events, which were attended by the bottom nodes connected to them. So, for instance, Evelyn Jefferson, Laura Mandeville, and Brenda Rodgers took part in the event on June 27.

In Chapter 3, we will discuss how such a network can be analyzed and even turned into the more familiar one-mode or *unipartite network* presented earlier. In the case of the southern women, it turns out that such an analysis shows how they were likely split in two groups that had little contact with each other.

1.4 Network Parts and Levels of Analysis

One of the biggest advantages of social network analysis is that it helps address the multilevel phenomenon by combining individual-level (micro-level) behavior with macro-level environments. In a non-network setting, we are often forced to focus unduly either just on the individual and his or her behavior (why does a pupil skip class?) or only on the level of society (how does the high school or the government address truancy?). The network perspective makes it easier to build the connection between the individual behavior and the systemic changes or vice versa. For instance, a pupil may be the first to form a friendship with someone from another classroom. This individual act builds a connection between two gossip networks that were not previously connected. The fact that rumors now can spread between both classrooms may create changes that affect everyone involved, not just the two new friends.

Depending on one's viewpoint (the ***level of analysis***), a social network is a collection of individual actors, of dyadic pairs, of small groups (triad structures, cliques, or clusters, as we will discuss shortly), or of a wider environment or society (the entire network). We can thus easily switch from an analysis of the individual to that of the group, examining the influence and position of an actor within the group (or cluster), and the effect of the group on the actor and vice versa.

Individual actors are the lowest level of analysis, often representing the individual human being, or else collective entities such as organizations or communities. Nevertheless, unlike in the ***atomistic model*** (see Sections 1.5 and 1.6), where individual actors do not influence each other, actors in a network design are at least aware of each other's existence, and their interaction is likely what interests us most.

Dyadic pairs, pairs of two actors in a network, are the most important units of analysis in many network studies. In undirected full networks with N actors, where the direction of relation between a pair is irrelevant (because if John marries Amy, Amy also marries John), the total number of dyadic pairs is

$$\frac{N!}{2(N-2)!}$$

or simply $(N(N-1))/2$. For example, a network with 20 actors would have 190 dyadic pairs

$$\left(\frac{20!}{2(20-2)!} = \frac{19 \times 20}{2} = 190\right)$$

In a directed network with N actors, the total number of dyadic pairs is

$$\frac{N!}{(N-2)!}$$

Thus, a network with 20 actors would have 380 dyadic pairs. Note that this computation ignores the possibility of loops (ties that connect an actor to him- or herself), the occurrence of which presents great challenges to the computation of dyadic pairs (Newman, 2010, pp. 137–139).

Dyadic level network analysis is common in social network studies. In management science, strategic alliances between pairs of firms form the fundamental unit of analysis for interfirm network studies (Carpenter, Li, & Jiang, 2012; Gulati, 1995). In public health, Suzanne Wenzel et al. (2012) studied pairs of homeless youth and showed how risky sexual behavior leads to **HIV/AIDS** infection. Dyadic studies also often explore the commonality between two connected actors. In social networks, **homophily** is common—a term indicating that individuals who are similar to each other are more likely to form a tie between themselves. Do birds of a feather flock together, or do opposites attract? Those questions are often asked and addressed by network studies focusing on dyadic levels.

Triadic structures, consisting of three social actors, are a level of analysis that has particularly fascinated sociologists. They were the first to notice the phenomenon of **triadic closure** (Davis & Leinhardt, 1972) or *transitivity*. Triadic closure is the tendency of "friends of friends to be friends": If John is friends with Amy and with Yuki, then Yuki and Amy are also likely to be friends (in Figure 1.4, Erica, Barbara, and Andrei form such a triad). Such a process is common in social networks. Sometimes, the triadic process is more complex, however. The enemy of my enemy may not be an enemy but an ally, for instance. Triadic structures can be overwhelming in number—the total enumeration of triadic structure for a network with 20 actors is 1,140 or

$$\frac{20!}{17! \times 3!}$$

triads for undirected graphs and 6,840 or

$$\frac{20!}{17!}$$

for directed ones. Fortunately, high-speed computers and recent developments in social network modeling make systemic analysis with triads possible. In particular, exponential random graph/p* models, which we will discuss in Chapter 4, can help analyze such endogenous structural features.

A substructure, subgroup, or subgraph, such as a **clique**, is an important unit of analysis in social networks studies. In its most general definition, the clique is a substructure in which actors are connected with each other in a particular way. Often they are more densely connected to each other than to other members of the network.

We will discuss the many different possible substructures, including cliques, clusters, (weakly and strongly) connected components, circles, k-cores, n-cores, k-plex, and n-plex in Chapter 4.

The *full or complete network*, or graph, is the most important macro-level unit of analysis in social network studies. Networks have many different characteristics that can explain outcomes on the individual and the network level, such as *density* (the proportion of ties present; see Chapter 3) or *centralization* (the degree to which nodes have, for instance, the same number of ties; see Chapter 3). Empirically, researchers that use this level of analysis sometimes compare several networks with each other: Michael Fritsch and Martina Kauffeld-Monz (2010), for instance, have studied 16 German innovation networks, finding that strong ties and dense networks disseminate information and knowledge more successfully than sparse networks with weak ties. Other researchers are interested in knowing what formative processes have led to the shape of a particular network, or how unusual specific features (e.g., the number of *closed triangles*) in a network are. In Chapter 4, we will discuss *ERGM (exponential random graph models)/P**, a method that helps answer such questions (Lusher, Koskinen, & Robins, 2013).

The previously mentioned studies are representative of two different approaches in social network analysis: The latter treats the network as a dependent variable, trying to explain its formation. In the former, the social network is an independent variable, which affects the outcome on the aggregate level. Such a separation of the analytical focus suits the scientific study of social network well, but in reality, the two processes (the formation of the social network and its impact) are usually interdependent, creating a fascinating challenge to social scientists. One application of full network analysis is to map the instructorship in different classrooms. Figure 1.7 displays the two hypothetical types of instructorship. On the left is the traditional teaching method, in which the instructor only gives lectures to students. On the right is the innovative teaching method, in which the instructor also organizes small discussion groups. Such different network configurations can serve as dependent variables in empirical studies that endeavor to identify the causes of such disparity in instructorship. The network configurations can also be the key independent variables that produce different results to students, measured with student evaluations of the class, or the average grade. By following such an approach, one can examine an important empirical question "is student-participatory teaching more effective than the traditional method?"

Another well-known characteristic of a network is its average path length, popularized in the term "six degrees of separation." We can calculate the average path length by measuring the shortest path that connects each pair of individuals along network ties and by taking the average of all those paths. Researchers have found evidence (see box) that all individuals on this planet can reach another through on average only five intermediaries (i.e., through six intermediate ties or steps). This is also known as the *small-world phenomenon*.

FIGURE 1.7 • **Typology of Different Teaching Methods**

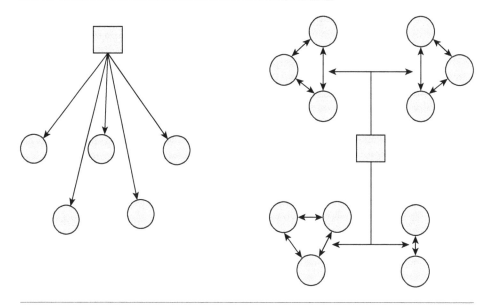

Note: Square: teacher; circle: students.

SOCIAL NETWORK IN ACTION: THE SMALL-WORLD EXPERIMENT

The "small-world" experiment was conducted by social psychologist Stanley Milgram (1967). In the experiment, he asked volunteers in two different U.S. states to relay a briefcase to a stockbroker in Boston, MA. The subjects were given a description of the target but not his address, and they were only allowed to pass the briefcase on to someone they knew on a personal basis (and who they thought would be closer to the target). Many briefcases never arrived, but those that did passed on average through the hands of five intermediaries. Hence, Milgram concluded that every U.S. citizen is connected to everybody else within the United States through no more than five intermediary steps. This finding has been the subject of both anecdotal and scientific fascination. For example, the "Bacon number" calculates the path length that connects any actor to Kevin Bacon in a network of co-appearances in the same move. With the appearance of the Internet and social media, the world seems to have become even smaller—a recent study showed that the average path length connecting any two Facebook users in the world is only 4.74 (Ugander, Karrer, Backstrom, & Marlow, 2011).

1.5 Networks as Social Structure and Institution

Social sciences often divide their research subject into two spheres: that of the individual and that of a more abstract, aggregate social context that constrains the individual's actions and which he or she is able to influence only marginally. In the case of political science, the latter is the state and its institutions, whereas economists focus on the market, and sociologists study society. In such a framework, networks hold, as hinted at in the previous section, an oddly intermediate position. Network relations, directed or undirected, are not individual attributes. Rather, they are dyadic properties connected to both actors involved. Like the social context, the network is thus in many ways external to an individual actor, who might only have limited ability to change its structure. The actor's position in that network can enable or restrict: Having a tie to an owner of a company may grant access to a job, whereas holding a peripheral position in the network makes it less likely that one hears certain news. And the network structure does not just influence the outcomes of individual nodes but also of the whole group connected through it: Diseases may travel slowly or fail to spread among a group of individuals with few connections, for instance.

But neither is the network just an externally given group-level characteristic: The network structure is the result of the combined actions of its nodes, who form friendships, send e-mails, or dissolve contracts. These combined actions are not a simple aggregation of individual attributes either: A marriage between two "nice" persons does not guarantee a lifelong relationship, and simple summation of the actor attributes of a social network does not always predict the performance or outcome of the network system—a network with the most talented physicians isolated from each other is not conducive to information sharing and mutual learning. Conversely, social network performance cannot be reduced to individual attributes. A highly successful team with many innovations and patents can be the result of great collaborations between its members who complement each other's expertise through networking but who might not be (individual) geniuses. Sociologists like Mustafa Emirbayer (1997) have thus argued that networks are a conceptual bridge between the individual and the societal level, explaining how both levels influence and mutually change each other.

1.6 Theoretical Assumptions

Social network analysis is thus not simply a set of methodological tools to detect and analyze human relationships and interaction. This point is best illustrated by Mark Granovetter's (1985) classic piece on social embeddedness and economic action and by Emirbayer's (1997) manifesto on relational sociology. Granovetter (1985) emphasized the importance of embeddedness, social relations, and social networks to overcome both the economist's undersocialized view of human behavior and the oversocialized view by sociologists. He proposed decentralized networks as a third way to govern interfirm relations, challenging transaction-cost economy's standard view that the only two options are either hierarchical integration into one entity or lateral contract between two different entities.

The network perspective stresses structural relations as its key orienting principle where social structure consists of regularities in the patterns of relations among concrete entities. The central objectives in social network analysis are to measure and represent these structural relations accurately, as well as to explain both why they occur and what their consequences are. Knoke and Yang (2008, pp. 4–6) suggested that social network analysis relies on the following three assumptions.

First, structural relations are often more important for understanding observed behaviors than attributes such as age, gender, values, race, education, and income. For example, people make decisions about their political views and actions, such as whether to vote, whom to vote for, or to support or oppose certain political bills based on their network and interpersonal ties with other people. Several studies by a group of political scientists (Fowler, Heaney, Nickerson, Padgett, & Sinclair, 2011) have shown that social networks often exert independent influences on political actions. Social network analysis rightly treats attributes and identities of social actors as more fluid than in the traditional atomistic studies, which examine individuals without taking into account their relationships with others. But in the social network approach, almost all individual-level attributes are highly contingent on specific time and place. Student–teacher relations, for instance, dissolve with the end of the class and have a different meaning inside and outside the classroom. A woman who holds a menial job requiring little initiative could become an outspoken and assertive leader in local city governance. Such drastic changes sit perfectly well with the network view that is premised on a ***structural-relational model***. One's behaviors, such as with whom one talks, how he or she talks, and what he or she talks about, are highly contextual, depending on the social context that is constructed by many other relations and ties between many other actors.

Second, social networks affect perceptions, beliefs, and actions through a variety of structural mechanisms that are socially constructed by relations among entities. In his famous study on the "strength of weak ties," Granovetter (1973) demonstrated that job seekers often obtain less useful information from their close contacts than from acquaintances because the former mainly provide redundant information already known to the job seekers. This finding may admittedly apply to the U.S. context only. Yanjie Bian (1997) found that in China, strong ties are more useful for finding a job because close contacts are more willing to influence the hiring process. Another example for how findings may depend on the context is provided in a public health study documenting two sexual contact networks in Colorado and Georgia. The former experienced decreasing network cohesion, resulting in low HIV transmission, whereas the Georgia one went through increasing cohesion, producing fast syphilis transmission (Potterat, Rothenberg, & Muth, 1999). Thus, the network cohesion, which results mostly from dyadic interactions between pairs of participants, has an impact on the transmission of sexual diseases among those network actors.

The third underlying assumption is that structural relations should be viewed as dynamic processes. Network structures are continually changing through interactions among their constituent individuals, teams, organizations, or nations. Scholars in management have long observed the evolutionary nature of interfirm relations (Gulati, 1995, 1998; Kenis & Knoke, 2002). In organization field networks, antecedent communication affects subsequent strategic alliance choices, which alter the later flow of information, providing constraints and opportunities to each firm in the network (Kenis & Knoke, 2002). Between a pair of firms, strategic alliances start with the most contractual governance forms; but over time, they are relaxed to adopt less rigorous contractual forms to reflect more mutual understanding and trust developed between the pair (Gulati, 1995).

1.7 Causality in Social Network Studies

Nevertheless, the fluidity and flexibility of networks described earlier also pose big problems to social scientists, who are often interested in uncovering the causes of social phenomena. In Chapter 5 of this book, for instance, researchers try to understand why some job seekers find a position, whereas others do not. What causes some pupils to turn to petty crime (Chapter 6)? Why do people vote (Chapter 8)? In all these cases, we find that social connections and networks influence people's behavior. But **causality ambiguity** often makes establishing *causal effects* in social settings difficult because either cause and effect cannot be clearly distinguished or we might not observe the true cause of the phenomenon. We know that individuals with a high income also have a high level of education. But did their education help them find a well-paid job? Or did their high income allow them to attend higher education? Or is the cause their parents, who financed their education and helped them find a high-income position?

One key area in social network research is the examination of social influence, also called peer pressure, relational effects, or contagion. This area denotes the phenomenon in which the behavior or attitude of actor A influences the behavior or attitude of other actors to which actor A is directly or indirectly connected through social ties (VanderWeele & An, 2013). Common examples can be found in the field of health (Chapter 7), such as smoking, drinking, obesity, or depression.

But if researchers find that smokers tend to be friends with other smokers, does this mean that smoking is "contagious?" Does it prove that Aisha's smoking habit "caused" Ben to pick up the habit as well? Not necessarily. It is also plausible that people with the same status—smoker or nonsmoker—come to form social relations with each other in a process introduced earlier called *homophily*. In other words, rather than smoking habits spreading from one person to the other through social ties, smoker/nonsmoker status may bundle people with the same habits together. These are two different causal mechanisms: In the case of peer pressure or social influence, the connection to a smoker causes smoking. In the homophily mechanism, the shared smoking habit is the cause of the tie or friendship formation.

In addition to social influence and homophily, there is a third possible mechanism: environmental confounding. Unobserved environmental factors can also play a role in determining the outcomes of interests between network peers. For example, growing up in a social environment where smoking is either stigmatized or encouraged can explain why nonsmokers or smokers tend to cluster together. Fortunately, recent social network research has developed methods to distinguish among influence, homophily, and environmental confounding, identifying a clearer pattern of causality between network variables.

One of those methods takes advantage of the conventional experimental method, changing a few features to make the method feasible for social network studies. This ***partial treatment group design*** (see Figure 1.8) assigns units with natural social boundaries, such as classrooms, clubs, or military units, to the control and experimental group. In the experimental group, researchers randomly select individuals to be subjected to the treatment or external intervention (the dark grey actors in Figure 1.8). Those who are not selected in the experimental group, along with all individuals in the control group, are left untreated. Researchers then measure the outcomes of all individuals in the control and experimental groups. The key in this process is the comparison between individuals in the experimental group who did not receive intervention (the light grey individuals in Figure 1.8) and those in the control group (white). The difference between the two group averages can be attributed to the spillover effect or peer influence from those in the experimental group who received the intervention to those who did not.

A specific example can illustrate how the partial treatment group design can establish causal effects in networks. Assume that we want to understand how a smoking prevention program helps reduce smoking. We randomly select two military units for control and experimental groups. In the experimental group, we randomly select a few

FIGURE 1.8 ● Illustration of the Partial Treatment Group Design

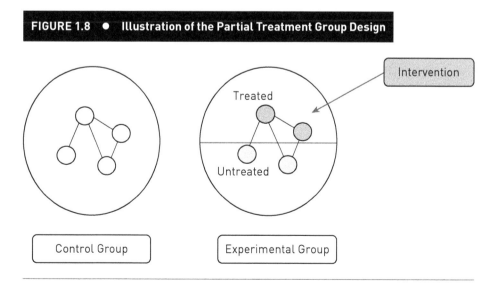

soldiers to watch a documentary on the hazards of smoking, but we leave the rest of the unit unaware of the prevention program. Afterward, we measure the prevalence of smoking in both control and experimental groups. If the prevention program works, we would expect the soldiers of the control unit to smoke more than those of the experimental unit. The difference between smoking behavior in the control unit and that of those soldiers of the experimental unit who watched the documentary tells us the direct causal effect of the prevention program. The difference between control unit and soldiers in the experimental unit who did not watch the documentary gives us the size of the spillover effect—the indirect effect of the prevention program.

Experimental designs are usually the best way to establish causal mechanisms, but it is not always possible or ethical to assign random actors to receive interventions: Clearly, we cannot force subjects to start taking intravenous drugs or to contract HIV just to measure spillover effects. In these cases, ***longitudinal data*** from social networks can help identify causality between social network actors. In longitudinal social network studies, researchers collect individuals' behaviors and traits, as well as their connections, across multiple time periods. Researchers can therefore observe the order in which ties are formed and behaviors or attitudes change. By assuming that causes happen earlier than effects, a researcher can distinguish between homophily and social influence. This distinction is imperfect, however, as humans sometimes act in anticipation of other's behavior. For instance, an individual may start smoking because he wants to be friends with a smoker. He will thus first become a smoker and only afterward form a tie to the smoker, making it look like an example of the homophily mechanism, even though he was in fact influenced by his future friend's smoking behavior. The longitudinal social network design may also not be able to exclude the possibility of environmental confounding.

1.8 A Brief History of Social Network Analysis

Nowadays, social network analysis is often associated with social media, such as Facebook and Twitter. The analysis of social media data is indeed a promising avenue to study human interaction that researchers have only started to explore (Ellison, Vitak, Gray, & Lampe, 2014; Lewis, Kaufman, Gonzalez, Wimmer, & Christakis, 2008). In looking back, however, academic fascination with social networks has a long history, beginning as early as the late 19th century, when sociologists such as Georg Simmel, Émile Durkheim, and Max Weber propagated the structural perspective in the study of human behaviors. The scholar who is credited for laying the foundation for modern social network analysis is the psychiatrist Jacob Moreno (Freeman, 2004). Moreno was interested in how an individual's psychological well-being was linked to his or her relations with other individuals. Together with Helen Jennings, Moreno developed a technique called "sociometry" to visualize individuals and their interpersonal relations with their contacts. Sociometry drew huge attention from academics and elsewhere as it can reveal the hidden structure of complex interpersonal networks through simple and straightforward visualization. Moreno and Jennings later founded a journal called *Sociometry*, devoted to publishing articles examining structural relations, networks, and their effects on human behaviors and psychological states.

But according to Linton Freeman (2004), social network analysis experienced a "dark age" shortly after Moreno's groundbreaking work, during which it ceased to be the focus of social sciences—it was not identifiable as a theoretical perspective or as an approach to data collection and analysis. Still, social network analysts continued their research at several important universities. One of those strongholds was the University of Michigan in the 1960s when Edward Laumann, a Harvard graduate under Talcott Parsons, George Homans, and Harrison White, conducted social network analysis of politics, sexual behaviors, and stratifications. Laumann has trained many doctoral students, many of whom are leaders in social network analysis today: Ronald Burt, Peter Marsden, Joseph Galaskiewicz, and David Knoke, to name a few.

The "dark ages" ended in the 1970s when Harrison White at Harvard revived the social network analysis with his path-breaking work on structural equivalence and "blockmodeling" (Freeman, 2004). In addition to this foundational research, White produced a group of doctoral students who are now distinguished scholars in social network analysis, such as Peter Bearman, Philip Bonacich, Ronald Breiger, Kathleen Carley, Bonnie Erickson, Claude Fischer, Mark Granovetter, and Barry Wellman.

Another important school that contributes to current social network analysis is the University of California at Irvine (UCI). UCI capitalizes greatly from its flexible structure that facilitates significant multidisciplinary efforts in its building of social network concentration. Thanks to the leadership of James March, then the dean of the School of Social Sciences, and his successor Linton Freeman, the school was able to develop a Ph.D. concentration in social network analysis, which drew expertise not only from social sciences but also heavily from mathematics. The school at UCI soon became a hub attracting renowned U.S. scholars, such as Ronald Burt, Patrick Doreian, and Harrison White, as well as international scholars such as Wenhong Zhang from Shanghai University, China. UCI also hosted conferences that featured many mathematicians of social network analysis, such as Martin Everett, Tom A.B. Snijders, Stanley Wasserman, Stephen Borgatti, and Philippa Pattison.

Social network analysis started off as a multidisciplinary effort, and it has benefitted greatly from its multidisciplinary traditions (Knoke & Yang, 2008; Newman, 2010). Its scope includes psychology, sociology, economics, and recently political science. It is also a branch within network analysis, which covers science majors such as computer science, mathematics, statistics, physics, biology, and food science (Yang, 2013). One of the most exciting and recent developments in network analysis is exponential random graph modeling (ERGM), which will be discussed in Chapter 4 of this book. ERGM allows for examining the wide range of mechanisms that could have given rise to the social network of interest and explores how the actors within the network decide to form ties. Two other monographs provide much fuller treatment to the methodology. One is an edited volume by Dean Lusher et al. (2013), and another is Jenine Harris's (2014) introduction monograph to ERGM, which provides a hands-on tutorial to the ERGM using *R*.

End-of-Chapter Questions

1. Imagine a network that describes which countries trade with each other. Who are the actors in this network? What are the ties?

2. Is a "marriage network" in which multiple families are tied with each other through marriages a directed or an undirected network? How about a network of friendship ties between classmates?

3. What are the differences between binary and valued social networks? Imagine a network of militarized conflict between nations. What do the ties represent in a binary network? In a valued network?

4. What is a bipartite network? Produce an example of a bipartite network. What are the main differences between a bipartite network and other types of (one-mode) networks?

5. Design a network study that can capture the informal advising network among employees in a workplace, and compare the network with the formal hierarchical structure depicting the hierarchical relations between those employees.

6. Discuss the three theoretical assumptions that undergird the social network analyses.

7. In a directed network of 50 actors/nodes, how many dyadic pairs and triadic pairs does it have?

8. Explain how you would use the partial treatment group design to determine whether a drug prevention program can curb the drug use among a group of students living in the same university dorm.

2

Data Collection

●

Learning Objectives

- Describe the six sampling methods when conducting a full network study

- Explain the differences between realist and nominalist strategies when specifying network boundaries

- Compare and contrast the positional, relational, and event-based approaches when defining network boundaries

- Design the name generator, positional generator, and resource generator when collecting data for the egocentric network

- Discuss the major differences between full network analysis and egocentric network studies

- Explain the informant bias and the issues of reliability and validity when evaluating social network data

- Examine various archival methods when collecting and preparing data for social network analysis

This chapter discusses issues related to collecting data for social network analysis. We will start by distinguishing between *egocentric network studies* and *full or complete network studies* but later also discuss approaches like snowball sampling, which in some ways blurs the line between the two. Full or complete network studies ideally examine all specific ties between the full population of interest (e.g., the students in a class or the members of a work team), whereas egocentric network studies often follow the standards of conventional representative sample surveys and examine the immediate network neighborhood of a random sample of the population, usually by asking respondents to identify individuals to whom they have specific ties. We then discuss a series of problems pertaining to either or both forms of studies. Section 2.1 discusses boundary specifications, that is, the question of which actors to include in the examination. Section 2.2 discusses problems that can occur in the data collection process. Section 2.3 discusses informant bias and other questions regarding the reliability of sources for network data, and Section 2.4 reviews issues of collecting archival data.

The examples given in the previous chapter were mainly from full network studies—examinations of all pairs of actors among the relevant population. This approach may be appropriate if we want to study the friendship network in a school class, but it becomes infeasible when studying the friendship network of a whole country's population. For such a question, researchers often study egocentric networks instead. These networks consist of one actor (the *ego*) and its contacts (the *alters*) with whom the ego has direct relations, as well as sometimes the relations between those alters. An egocentric network design uses conventional sample surveys, relying on their sampling methods to select a representative set of focal actors, the egos (Marsden, 2011). Egocentric network studies bear great similarities with other non-network studies, except that they pose the respondents (the egos) some relational questions to elicit their contacts (alters). Notable examples of egocentric network design and implementation are the two rounds of the General Social Survey (GSS) in 1985 and 2004, where interviewers asked respondents to name individuals with whom they discuss important matters. There are different ways in which such questions about the respondent's ego-network can be phrased, and they can lead to very different results. The most common instruments are **name generators**, but sometimes researchers use **positional generators** (Lin & Dumin, 1985) or **resource generators** (Gaag & Snijders, 2004). We will discuss those instruments in more detail in Section 2.2. For more information on egocentric network studies and an excellent discussion of their design and implementation, we defer readers to Peter Marsden (2011, pp. 370–388).

2.1 Boundary Specification

At the beginning of every research study, one has to define the target population. In network studies, the issue of which actors and ties to measure is called the **boundary specification problem** (Laumann, Marsden, & Prensky, 1989) because in full or complete network studies, it is equivalent to the question of where to draw the boundary of the network: Should the friendship network include only the students of one particular class, or should it also include their friends in the rest of the high school or even outside of school? Egocentric network studies, as mentioned earlier, often use a standard survey design. The problem thus at first might seem to be simply that of ensuring that the sampling frame chosen will yield a representative (ideally, random) sample of the target population (Babbie, 2009). But the questions asked about the ego's alters raise a more subtle, **second boundary determination issue** (Marsden, 2011): Which alters is the ego allowed to name or select? For instance, in a nationally representative survey, can the respondent name friends from abroad or only citizens or residents of the country? We discuss the details of this issue in Section 2.2 of Chapter 3.

In full network studies, boundaries often seem self-evident, such as when employees in one workplace, members in a social club, or churchgoers in the same church are being studied. But sometimes the target population is less clearly delineated—for instance, in the case of studying of "beachgoers" (Freeman & Webster, 1994), in which beachgoers were recorded and those regulars who appeared in the observation for three or more days were included in the network study. In general, Edward Laumann et al. (1989) proposed two generic strategies—**realist** or **nominalist**—for determining the boundary and the type of relations to be analyzed for network actors. They also

TABLE 2.1 ● Cross-Tabulation of Topology of Social Network Samplings		
Approach	Realistic Strategy	Nominalistic Strategy
Positional approach	Research informants identify additional informants by using social positions or organizational affiliation as threshold for inclusion.	Researchers identify informants by using social positions or organizational affiliation as threshold for inclusion. Examples are Morimoto and Yang's (2013) classroom friendship network study and Knoke's (2001) GIS network analysis.
Reputational approach	Research informants identify additional informants by using reputation as threshold for inclusion. Example of such approach is Knoke and Laumann's (1982) network analysis of U.S. energy and national health policy domain.	Researchers identify informants by using reputation as threshold for inclusion.
Event-based approach	Research informants identify additional informants by using participations in certain events as threshold for inclusion.	Researchers identify informants by using participations in certain events as threshold for inclusion. Example includes Freeman and Webster's (1994) beachgoer study.

described three approaches, ***positional, reputational,*** or ***event-based,*** which are commonly used to define network boundaries. Because those strategies and approaches can be confusing at times, we present Table 2.1 to describe the six sampling methods in general by cross-tabulating the two strategies with the three approaches. Please note that even though each cell of the table represents a unique sampling method, the six sampling methods in the table are not mutually exclusive in practice. Researchers can use combinations of methods in their research designs.

2.1.1 Realist Strategy

In the realist strategy, the network analyst adopts the presumed subjective perceptions of system actors themselves, defining boundaries as the limits that are consciously experienced by all or most actors in the entity. Actors and their relations are included or excluded to the extent that the other actors judge them to be part of the network.

David Knoke and Edward Laumann (1982) used this principle to select the core organizations of the U.S. energy and national health policy domain. They excluded any organizations that domain informants did not perceive as influential in energy and health policy making. One problem with such treatment lies in the subjectivity of the informants. "Influential actors in national energy policy with which your organization cooperates," for instance, may mean different things to different informants, depending on their conceptions of the meaning "influential" (and, of course, the tie definition of "cooperate"). Some may be stringent, whereas others may adopt more loose criteria. The realist strategy makes the boundary specification of network studies vulnerable to informants' subjective minds, resulting in inconsistencies if two actors disagree about whether a third actor belongs to the relevant network. Subjectivity can be reduced by providing a definition of key words in the nomination process, such as the meaning of "influential" (Scott, 2012, p. 43), but it cannot be completely eliminated. A similar problem occurs with respondents' tie definitions (see the discussion in the next strategy). The subjectivity issue has become the topic of some methodology studies. Liz Spencer and Ray Pahl (2006), for instance, ask informants to map their various friends on a chart of concentric circles representing their subjective closeness.

2.1.2 Nominalist Strategy

When using the nominalist strategy, researchers impose an *a priori* conceptual framework that delineates the boundary of the network, such as students in one classroom, lawyers in a bar association, or presidential candidates in a presidential election cycle. Sometimes, such boundaries exist as abstract concepts, such as when Marxists identify all employees having a common relation to a mode of production as belonging to the working class. Much like the realist strategy, the nominalist strategy is subject to the criticism that by imposing boundaries, investigators may miss some important activities and social phenomena. For instance, the friendship formation in the classroom may not be as relevant as students forming important relations beyond the classroom settings. Nevertheless, the main strength of the nominalist strategy is that the boundaries result from a theoretically informed decision about what is significant in the situation under investigation (Scott, 2012, p. 44). Friendship formation in college may not be as significant for the informants as friends from childhood; yet, network scholars arbitrarily imposing the boundary of classroom to study friendship formation are interested in the process and dynamics of friendship in college life, which in and of themselves are socially significant. It would obviously be desirable to contextualize further the social network under investigation by also measuring the relationships beyond the network, but clearly any study needs limits.

The previous sections discussed two general strategies that researchers can use to identify the relevant social network actors—one relying on the actor's own and the other on the researcher's assessment. The following three sections introduce three specific rules that actors or researchers can use to guide their assessment. In the *positional approach*, actors are identified based on their position—membership in certain organizations, for instance. To implement the *reputational approach*, the researcher will ask experts or reputable players in the field to compile a list of the relevant actors. The *event-based approach* identifies actors based on their participation in certain events. The subsequent three sections discuss those approaches in detail.

2.1.3 Positional Approach

In the positional approach, researchers sample from among the occupants of a formally defined position—the criteria are thus some form of formal membership. Examples of the positional approach include students in one classroom (Morimoto & Yang, 2013), employees of an organization (Krackhardt & Killduff, 1999), a corporate board of directors (Useem, 1979), members of a hometown association in an African village (Feldman-Savelsberg, Ndonko, & Yang, 2005), or corporations in information technology in the joint list of Fortune 1000 and Global 500 (Knoke, 2001).

One of the main tasks facing researchers using the positional approach is consequently to provide explicit theoretical or empirical justifications for their rules of inclusion or exclusion. In practice, researchers are often accused of setting the boundaries arbitrarily as, in reality, there is rarely a natural division to draw. For example, a study of interlocking boards of directors may focus on the connections among the top 50 companies (in revenue or in employment size) in the Fortune 1000 list. But in reality, the difference between the 50th and the 51st company may be trivial, providing weak justification as to why the cut-off point must be drawn there. Perhaps the most commonly cited reasons for delimiting the boundaries are time and budget constraints, which although certainly relevant, almost never provide a good reason for a specific cut-off.

In particular, the positional approach can produce results that are sensitive to where the boundary is drawn: The network structure among the top 25 companies can be drastically different from the top 50 or 100 companies in the Fortune 1000 ranking. Likewise, the interpersonal network among chief executive officers (CEOs) is very different from the network among middle managers and the rank-and-file, and so on. Missingness is another issue that can significantly distort the network structure even if boundary specification issues have been solved in a satisfactory manner. For example, a friendship network of a class in which some pupils could not be interviewed may look very different from the network of the whole class.

Sometimes, researchers will notice that their positional definition of the network is not congruent with the subjective experience of the actors. For example, students may have difficulties naming their friends within a classroom if many of them form friendships outside of their school (Morimoto & Yang, 2013). Feldman-Savelsberg et al.'s (2005) African women belonging to the same hometown association did often not know each other. In such cases, the resulting social networks may have low density.

2.1.4 Reputational Approach

The reputational approach can be applied as part of either a more nominalist or a more realist strategy. In the former case, researchers ask a set of experts to nominate important actors to be included in the study, and then they sample from that list (or study all of the nominated actors). In the more often applied realist strategy, the researchers will start by asking some actors for other important actors; for example, a study of a physician network will start with a few prominent physicians in a city, asking each of them to nominate other well-known physicians in that city, who then may be asked to nominate others as well. Those nominations are used to compile the list of physicians to be studied.

The reputational method requires that the researchers can identify informants knowledgeable about other social actors important to the network relations under study. Such a task is formidable, but more problematic is the fact that it is almost impossible to assess the representativeness of actors identified through any such relational approach. The actors any given informant can name are clearly not selected at random, but they depend again on a network—the ego-network of the informant. The researchers should thus always interview multiple informants, trying to cast the net as wide as possible. Scott (2012, p. 46) also advocated that network researchers rely on theoretical and empirical reasons for the choice of informants, which are, as far as is possible, independent of the particular social relations being investigated. The latter is important because one could imagine a situation in which several communities exist without knowing of one another. If the informant the researcher contacts only knows of one community, then even a researcher who interviews all other members of said community asking for further members (see subsequent discussion on snowball sampling) would never find out about the actors in the disconnected communities. A further worry is that informants have biases, or they may have no interest in disclosing all actors to the researcher: Physicians in the previous example may not know practitioners of alternative or traditional medicine, may not consider them relevant actors in the physician network, or may not want the researchers to waste their time with "those quacks."

Nevertheless, reputational approaches are often the only option when a complete list of the actors is lacking, when relevant positions are unclear, or when the knowledge of key informants is crucial in determining the boundary of the network being studied. The reputational approach includes a few more specific strategies, which we will discuss here.

Snowball sampling starts with one or several informants (often called "seeds"), asking each one of them to nominate additional actors based on a specific relationship. Such a nomination process can continue until no new actors can be identified. The rules of the nomination process can vary, requiring the informant to specify only a certain number of contacts, for instance, or only a certain type. The snowball sampling of each seed will produce a network in which all actors are at least indirectly connected (i.e., a connected component—see Chapter 4). Figure 2.1 illustrates a snowball sampling, in which researchers start with only four informants, asking them to identify additional subjects for inclusion in the study. For simplicity, the hypothetical situation presumes that each subject identifies four additional informants; each of the additional informants identifies four additional informants. The figure shows that with only three rounds of nomination, the total number of informants using such snowballing is 84 (4 + 4 × 4 + 4 × 4 × 4 = 84). Snowball sampling is therefore a powerful method for producing many actors in a network even if the researcher knows only a handful of actors at the beginning.

Snowball sampling is especially useful for uncovering **hidden populations** (individuals with rare, potentially stigmatizing characteristics), such as drug dealers, sex workers, HIV-positive people, illegal immigrants, terrorists, or gang and mafia members. Snowball sampling can start with a few interesting parties from certain locales, such as clinics, street corners frequented by drug dealers, or congregation sites of militia or mafia members. In anti-terrorism combat, the seeds may be known from long-term investigation (Krebs, 2002), whose arrest and interrogation may lead to the identification of additional targets.

But snowball sampling, in particular when applied to hidden populations, can also raise serious ethical concerns: Maintaining anonymity and confidentiality is obviously

FIGURE 2.1 ● Hypothetical Situation of a Snowball Sampling

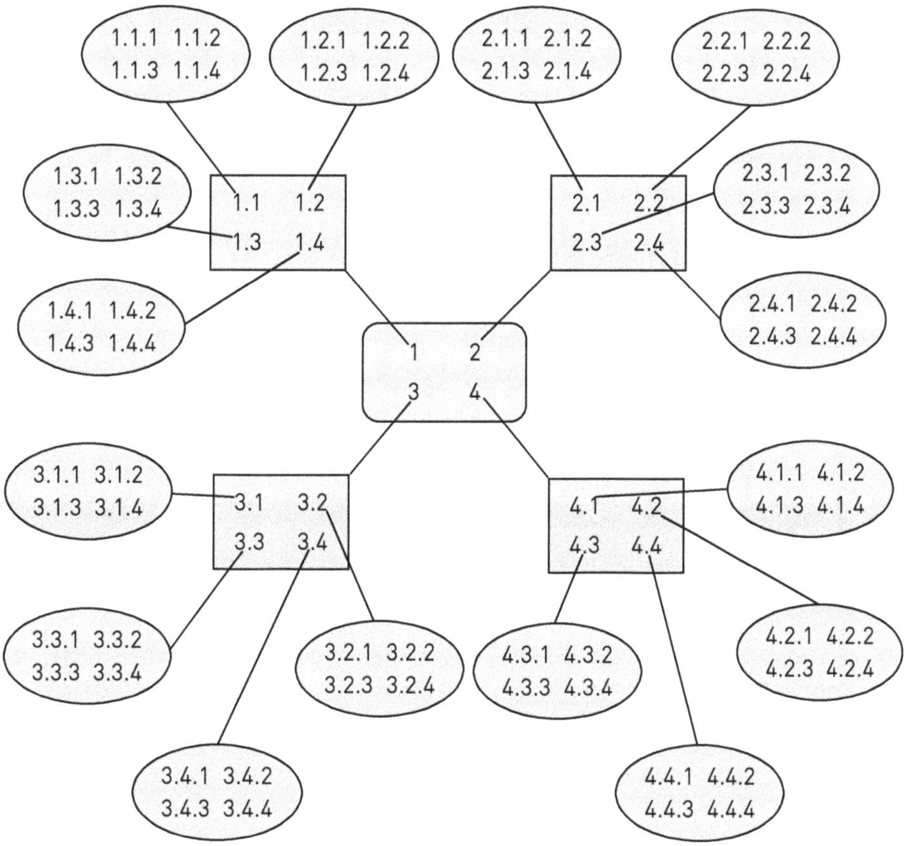

very important when handling such potentially stigmatizing personal data. A specific concern in snowball sampling approaches is the issue of informed consent: A drug user whose habit is revealed to researchers by one of his or her acquaintances has not given prior consent for that sensitive information to be revealed. Researchers, thus, increasingly resort to "respondent-driven sampling" (RDS; Heckathorn, 1997), a method in which the informant informs his alters about the researcher's study, who then contact the researcher(s) out of their own volition.

Snowball sampling is an extreme case of the realist method: Every informant is also an actor in the network, and when the researchers start their network study, they may know no other network actor but the seeds. At the other end of the spectrum is a nominalist approach in which researchers create a list of relevant actors based on information provided by experts (who may or may not be actors on that list). In what is called *fixed list selection*, they then ask respondents to identify actors with whom they share a specific tie (e.g., friendship) from that list.

The network thus derived can vary drastically from snowball sampling's *expanding selection*, where respondents are asked to name any actor with whom they share the specific tie, as a comparative study conducted by Patrick Doreian and Katherine Woodard (1992) showed. They found that their standard fixed list selection produced only 50% of the actors and 40% of the dyadic ties found using the expanding selection method. Furthermore, the "missing" actors are not missing at random: Fixed list selection is more likely to ignore the more peripheral actors. The authors therefore conclude that fixed list selection, despite its low administrative cost, cannot be used to replace expanding selection.

2.1.5 Event-based Approach

The event-based approach uses actors' participation in certain events to establish the inclusion in the network. Participation in specific social events is recorded and tallied, and those who reach a certain threshold are included in the sample for further network studies.

SOCIAL NETWORK IN ACTION: USING AN EVENT-BASED STRATEGY TO IDENTIFY ACTIVE PARTICIPANTS

In his study on political power in New Haven, Connecticut, Robert Alan Dahl (1961) used participation in the making of key decisions as the basis of selection – a selection criteria neither dependent on people's formal affiliation or position with an organization nor on their perception by other actors. Such a strategy ensures that those included are active participants of the organization and excludes those who, despite their affiliation with the organization, do not actively engage in the decision-making process.

Selection of key events is crucial in an event-based strategy (Scott, 2012, p. 46). A departmental meeting to discuss routine business may attract whoever has time to attend, and those staying away may do so for idiosyncratic reasons. In contrast, a board meeting to advocate an important new program may attract only those who are behind the initiative—those not present may be boycotting the new plan and stay away knowing that they will be outvoted in any case. In the latter case, there will be systemic bias, and a network study that attempts to uncover the divisiveness of the decision will base its conclusion solely on the seemingly cohesive group of individuals who supported the program. Methods to counteract such biases are to record multiple events, to identify the patterns and associations of regular attendees, and to triangulate findings with information collected from other sources. For example, Linton Freeman and Cynthia Webster (1994) recorded the behavioral data of regular beachgoers who appeared at least three times in their 31-day observation period. They then compared this behavioral data with self-reported data collected at a later stage.

The famous study of the South Women Affiliation (Davis, Gardner, & Gardner, 1941) that was discussed in Chapter 1 illustrates the application of event-based sampling. The chief purpose of using event-based sampling in social network analysis is to identify sets of social actors who are affiliated with each other through co-participation of some events. Figure 2.2 uses an artificial example to display how such a proposal can be achieved through matrix rearrangement. The original matrix reflects a dataset collected based on participations in eight events by eight individuals—an event-based sampling. The rearranged matrix in the bottom shows a clear cleavage among the eight actors participating in two different sets of events.

2.2. Data Collection Process

Once researchers have identified a set of network actors, they need to decide on how to collect network data, that is, data on the ties. One major source of network data is self-reported and collected through surveys with actors. Starting with the next paragraph, we will discuss different survey instruments used especially for egocentric social network studies, in particular, a wide range of name generators. Another source is observational data collected from newspaper or archival sources recording interactions by or affiliations of different actors. Finally, we will also discuss data collected from the Internet and other electronic means of communication. Note that because of page restriction, we do not cover some important topics for network scholars; readers can consult alternative sources for those topics, such as cognitive social structures (see Knoke & Yang, 2008, pp. 32–34), existing network data (Robins, 2015), and research ethics issues in data collection, in particular, the issue of secondary participants (Lee, 2011, pp. 590–593).

2.2.1 Name Generators

Name generators are used in social surveys to capture data on a respondent's immediate network neighborhood. Individual respondents, also called "egos" or "focal

---

FIGURE 2.2 ● Artificial Example Illustrative of Rearranging of an Actor-Event Matrix

---

(i) Original Matrix

		Events							
		1	2	3	4	5	6	7	8
	Ann	X		X		X		X	
	Beth		X		X		X		X
People	Chris	X		X		X		X	
	Don		X		X		X		X
	Ed	X		X		X		X	
	Flo		X		X		X		X
	Gill	X		X		X		X	
	Hal		X		X		X		X

(ii) Re-Arranged Matrix

		Events							
		1	2	3	4	5	6	7	8
	Ann	X	X	X	X				
	Beth	X	X	X	X				
People	Chris	X	X	X	X				
	Don	X	X	X	X				
	Ed					X	X	X	X
	Flo					X	X	X	X
	Gill					X	X	X	X
	Hal					X	X	X	X

Note: Adapted from p. 27 of Scott, J. G. (2012). *Social network analysis* (3rd ed.). London, England: Sage Ltd.

---

actors," are asked questions to elicit a roster of alters with whom they have a specific relation. The egocentric studies rely solely on the egos to enumerate their network contacts, without pursuing those alters for further corroboration. If the researchers are also interested in the relationships between the alters, they will ask the ego to specify those relations as well.

The most well-known name generator is *the important matter discussion generator*, implemented in the 1985 and 2004 General Social Surveys (GSS). The name generator prompt is as follows: "From time to time, most people discuss important matters with other people. Looking back over the last six months, who are the people with whom you discussed matters important to you? Just tell me their first names or initials." Such a name generator item is often followed by name interpreter questions to probe information about race, age, and education for each named **alter**, and the relationship between each alter and the ego, and between alters. The questionnaire items may look like the example from Marsden (2011, p. 376) found in the box.

SOCIAL NETWORK IN ACTION: COLLECTING ALTERS' INFORMATION IN EGOCENTRIC NETWORK STUDIES

Questions about the alter's characteristics:

Is (NAME) Asian, Black, Hispanic, White, or something else?

ASK FOR EACH NAME

How old is (NAME)?

ASK FOR EACH NAME

Questions about ego-alter ties:

How close do you feel to this person? Please describe how close you feel on a scale from 1 to 5—1 means not close, 5 means very close.

Questions about the alter relational structures:

Please think about the relations between the people you just mentioned. Some of them may be total strangers, in that they would not recognize one another if they bumped into each other on the street. Others may be especially close, as close to each other as they are to you.

First, think about (NAME 1) and (NAME 2),

A: Are they total strangers?

IF YES, PROCEED TO NEXT PAIR

B: Are they especially close?

REPEAT FOR EACH PAIR OF NAMES

The two waves of the GSS, conducted almost 20 years apart, found quite different results for the same questions. The 1985 GSS important matter name generator elicited, on average, 2.94 persons with whom egos discuss important matters, a number that had dropped by almost one person to 2.08 in 2004 (McPherson, Smith-Lovin, & Brashears, 2006). In 1985, approximately 55% of the core discussion group members were kin (Marsden, 1987), even more in 2004. Most alters in an ego's network knew one another and tended to be more similar to the ego with regard to age and education than a random member of the overall population. Although the ego-networks tended to be very balanced in their gender composition (heterophily), they often included only members from one racial group (homophily). Marsden (1987) attributed the great gender mixing and low racial mixing to the high number of kinship ties in the network.

More recent scholars have challenged the finding of substantial changes between the two waves of the survey and have instead blamed so-called ***interviewer effects***, claiming that some of the 2004 interviewers were unskilled or untrained and intentionally avoided collecting egocentric network data (Paik & Sanchagrin, 2013). Another study attributed the larger numbers of social isolates to the increase in the use of virtual space and computer-supported social networks, and it noted that respondents may have not have mentioned those online contacts to the interviewers (Morimoto & Yang, 2013).

Other researchers were interested in less close relationships than those measured by the GSS name generator. Claude Fischer (1982) developed a measuring instrument for different definitions of friendship through ***multiple name generators***, which included questions about taking care of someone's house, asking him or her for a loan, socializing, and discussing jobs and hobbies. His northern California respondents elicited anywhere from 2 to 65 alters, with an average of 18.5 per respondent—much larger ego-networks than the ones found in the GSS.

But if different questions result in such large differences even just in the size of the ego-networks, how reliable are such studies? To examine this question, Tina Kogovšek and Anuška Ferligoj (2005) interviewed 1,033 residents of the Slovenian capital Ljubljana on five name generators, inquiring about alters that provide the respondents with information, emotional support, financial support, material support, and social companionship, respectively. They found that the first three name generators (informational, emotional, and financial support) generate more reliable and valid data than the last two items. They speculated that respondents reported more distant acquaintances in the latter two items, which may lead to many reporting errors.

Scholars also examined whether name generators are transferable across cultures or whether they would produce different networks in different countries. Danching Ruan, Linton Freeman, Xinyuan Dai, Yunkang Pan, and Wenhong Zhang (1997) surveyed respondents of the Chinese city Tianjin with the GSS single name generator in 1986 and 1993. Both Tianjin surveys generated larger ego-networks (4.58 in 1986 and 3.30 in 1993) than were generated in the United States. Tianjin respondents were also less likely to nominate kin. Ruan et al. noted that respondents named far fewer co-workers in 1993 than in 1986, and they argued that this reflects China's institutional transformation from planned economy of lifelong employment to market-based contractual employment. As the reform progressed, people acquired more contacts outside their workplace. Ruan (1998) also implemented multiple name generators and found that Tianjin respondents tended to name the same set of alters when answering the GSS core discussion name generator and when asked about persons whom they visit or with whom they go out for dinner or go shopping with. "Instrumental" name generators (asking for alters who help with house repair, child care, or lend money) produced a set of alters least likely to overlap with the GSS important matter generator. This finding resonates to some degree with Stefanie Bailey and Peter Marsden's (1999) findings, according to which U.S. respondents interpreted the alters from the GSS important matter name generator as chatting confidants with whom they discuss familial or interpersonal problems. These studies have raised important questions about the measurement of social networks. After all, the researcher rarely cares about who repairs someone else's bicycle. More likely she wants to study the nature and effect of an actor's social support network, but she suspects that respondents will have difficulty understanding the concept of "social support" or may interpret it very differently. Choosing more specific questions can help, but it places a higher burden on the researcher to pick questions that measure the underlying concept of interest in the specific social context.

Name generators and ***name interpreters*** impose a great burden on the respondents (the egos), especially if they also need to describe the relationships among their alters. The number of answers needed increases exponentially with the number of alters: For undirected ties, an ego with two alters reports one relation, egos with three alters three relations, egos with four alters six relations, and so on. Mathematically, the number of relations an ego with *N* alters needs to report is:

$$C_N^2 = \frac{N!}{2 \times (N-2)!}$$

Few methods exist to alleviate this burden. Visual interfaces have been proposed as assistance (Kahn & Antonucci, 1980; McCarty & Govindaramanujam, 2005), for example, by asking respondents to place alters in concentric circles surrounding them or to produce a sketch placing alters in relation to one another. Such visual assistances are of course only possible for some modes of interviewing, such as face-to-face interviews or mailed surveys. To complicate matters even more, switching to a mode suitable for using such visual interfaces, such as from telephone to face-to-face interviews, can itself affect ego's responses (Gerich & Lehner, 2006).

To ease the respondent's burden, researchers often place further constraints on name generators, in effect specifying *secondary boundaries* on the network measured. Common constraints are the role or content constraint discussed earlier: geographic constraints ("name your best friends *in this neighborhood*"), temporal constraints ("name individuals with whom you discussed political issues *during the past three months*") and numerical constraint (name *five* individuals with whom you discuss important matters"). Karen Campbell and Barrett Lee (1991) discussed these common constraints and argued that the difference in the size of ego-networks between the GSS and Fischer's (1982) survey of northern Californians mentioned earlier is a result of the former imposing more restrictions.

Imposing such constraints of course also has an effect on the statistical properties of the ego-networks measured: If respondents are asked to name five friends, then the ego networks will usually at most have size 6 (ego and 5 friends).

2.2.2 Positional Generators

Positional generators are a way to measure the social resources an ego can draw on through her contacts to facilitate her actions (Lin & Dumin, 1986; Marsden & Lin, 1982). In the box is an example of a positional generator used by Nan Lin, Yang-chih Fu, and Ray-May Hsung (2001, p. 77).

SOCIAL NETWORK IN ACTION: USING POSITIONAL GENERATOR IN EGO-CENTRIC NETWORK STUDIES

Among your relatives, friends, or acquaintances, are there people who have the following jobs?

a. High school teacher

b. Electrician

c. Owner of small factory

d. Nurse

For each job for which the respondent answers "yes," ask what is his or her relationship to you?

1. Relative

2. Friend

3. Acquaintance

The underlying assumption for studies involving positional generators is often that individuals can use the resources available to their contacts through the latter's formal position. But positional generators have also been used to gauge a respondent's overall ego-network size if the number of holders of specific positions in the overall population is known (McCormick, Salganik, & Zheng, 2010), or to estimate the prevalence of certain positions in the population if it is not (Calvo & Murillo, 2013).

Unlike the name generator that emphasizes the social contacts of a specific relationship type, the positional generator stresses the social positions of the ego's contact, which serve as proxies of social resources. Researchers using such generators are often sociologists concerned with social stratification and status. They are interested in knowing whether respondents have access to higher strata, as measured through contacts in professions associated with high social status, and how social stratification is maintained. Nan Lin and Mary Dumin (1986) used the top 20 most frequently mentioned job titles from the 1970 U.S. Census Classified Index of Occupations in their positional generator. They found that respondents with high-status origins—measured through their father's occupation—tend to have both relatives or friends (i.e., strong ties) and acquaintances (i.e., weak ties) in prestigious positions. Respondents of lower origins only have access to such positions through weak ties, however.

But this is not the only way social networks can perpetuate inequality: Lin et al. (2001), for instance, found that the social capital, which is defined as the capital captured through social relations, helps men obtain prestigious positions and a higher income in Taiwanese society, whereas women achieve such goals mainly through accumulation of human capital (i.e., obtaining educational degrees). In Canada, Bonnie Erickson (2004) found that men are more likely to know people in female-dominated jobs than females are to know someone in male-dominated jobs. She argued that this is a result of men strategically positioning themselves in different social spheres to further their career.

An ego-network measured through positional generators can have three status-related properties: *Extensity* measures the number of different positions generated by the respondents. *Upper reachability* measures the highest occupation status reported. *Range* denotes the distance between the most prestigious position and the least prestigious position.

2.2.3 Resource Generators

A resource generator captures an ego's social resources more directly by asking for contacts who can provide certain forms of facilitation. The box provides an example of a resource generator from a survey conducted in the Netherlands (Gaag & Snijders, 2004).

SOCIAL NETWORK IN ACTION: USING RESOURCE GENERATORS TO COLLECT EGO-CENTRIC NETWORK DATA

Do you know anyone who . . . .

A: can repair a car, bike, etc.?

B: can visit socially?

C: repairs household equipment?

D: knows a lot about government regulations?

E: can give a good reference when you are applying for a job?

(Continued)

(Continued)

For each item to which the respondent answers "yes":

What is his/her relationship to you?

A: family members

B: friend

C: acquaintance

Martin van der Gaag and Tom A.B. Snijders (2004) then formed four distinctive resource subgroups from some of their 35 resource generators by examining which of them produced similar responses. One of those subgroups, which they called "access to prestigious occupations," correlated strongly with Lin and Dumin's (1986) positional generator. Two other subgroups—access to information and access to instrumental support (e.g., providing help when moving)—correlated weakly with the positional generator, indicating that the resource generators in those subgroups capture other dimensions of social capital.

2.3 Informant Bias and Issue of Reliability

Informant bias is well documented in social science literature, dating back to Richard LaPierre's (1934) famous study of the differences in his and a Chinese couple's restaurant experiences. David Kronenfeld and Jennie Kronenfeld (1972) also reported that respondents created a false scene of the restaurant they had just patronized, in which waiters and waitresses dressed up and the restaurant played specific kinds of music; in reality, the restaurant did not have any waiters and did not play music.

Informant bias refers to the discrepancy between self-reported and actual behavioral data. Regarding informant bias in social network analysis, H. Russell Bernard and his associates (Bernard & Killworth, 1977; Bernard, Killworth, & Sailer, 1981; Bernard, Kilworth, Sailer, & Kronenfeld, 1984) conducted a series of experiments to examine the extent to which self-reported data reflect a network actor's behavioral data. They constructed and compared seven sets of paired communication network datasets, based on data from a machine-monitoring system or "objective" observer records and on the participant's recollection of the communication. For the latter, they asked participants with whom they've had contact, and with whom they've communicated for how often and how long. By comparing the self-reported data with the behavioral records, Bernard and his associates found that approximately half of the self-reports were erroneous in some ways, and they concluded, "people do not know, with any acceptable accuracy, to whom they talk over any given period of time." They continued: "We are now convinced that cognitive data about communication cannot be used as proxy for the equivalent behavioral data" (Bernard et al., 1981, p. 17). Their pessimistic view did not go unchallenged. David Knoke and James Kuklinski (1982), for instance, questioned the accuracy and unobtrusiveness of the objective observers, leading Bernard et al. (1984) to adjust their original statement.

Multiple sources of informant bias exist. Most often, the large quantity of information overwhelms informants, so that they cannot recall their behavior accurately (Bernard et al., 1984). Other common sources of bias are caused by informants cognitively imposing a categorical form on noncategorical affiliation patterns (Freeman, 1992) and by informants correcting their perceptions to maintain a balanced network among their close friends and remote contacts (Krackhardt & Kilduff, 1999). For example, individuals tend to perceive themselves to be surrounded by their friends who are also friends with each other, so that they avoid the emotional stress of enduring an unbalanced network. More cogently, such perception may or may not reflect the factual structure of their friendship networks.

Informant bias varies between informants and topics: Familiarity with the interview topic increases the informant's ability to recall events (Romney, Weller, & Batchelder, 1986). Those very familiar with the topic forget little, but they falsely tend to recall nonexistent members (i.e., remember individuals being present at an event that weren't actually there; Freeman, Romney, & Freeman, 1987). Often informants portray themselves as more central than reported by other network participants. Thus, network data aggregated at the group level is more accurate in describing network positioning than individual-level reports (Kumbasar, Romney, & Batchelder, 1994). Informant bias can be substantive in ego-centric network studies. Kevin White and Susan Watkins (2000), for instance, reported sizable disparities between respondents' reports of their alters' contraceptive behavior and self-report data from those alters.

Reliability refers to the extent to which the same survey instruments, when applied to the same set of informants in multiple time periods, yield identical results. This "test–retest" is a general approach used to measure reliability, which can also be applied to social network data. Test–retest measures the extent to which the respondents produce the same results at the test and at a later retest. Respondents enumerating the same sets of alters in the test and the retest for a given survey item would result in a score of 100% reliability, whereas 0% reliability is equivalent to the respondents naming completely different sets of alters. Nevertheless, reliability scores of a survey item also vary with the interval time between the two tests, and sometimes the differences simply reflect the genuine changes that have occurred in the network. Too long a time span between test and retest is therefore not desirable, but too short is not good either, because respondents will just restate in the retest the answer that they remember from the original test.

One commonly used test–retest reliability measure is ***Jaccard's coefficient***, which is calculated as the number of persons nominated ("checked") by an informant in both tests divided by the total number of unique nominations for both tests (Brewer, 2000). Table 2.2 provides an example of how to calculate the Jaccard coefficient.

TABLE 2.2 ● Artificial Example of Computing Jaccard Coefficient		
	Second Interview	
First Interview	**Names Checked**	**Not Checked**
Names Checked	A = 25	C = 12
Not Checked	B = 18	D = 20

A given respondent named 43 (25 + 18 = 43) contacts in the first interview and 37 (25 + 12 = 37) contacts in the second interview. The Jaccard coefficient is A / (A + B + C) as the A reflects the number of contacts named at both test and retest and A + B + C is the total of unique nominations. For this particular example, the Jaccard coefficient is 25 / 55 = 45.45%. Thus, the Jaccard coefficient ranges from 0% to 100%, with the coefficient close to 100% indicating great reliability. The Jaccard coefficient is a variable associated with individual respondents. At the level of the entire sample, mean, median, variance, and standard deviation can be used to describe this measure.

A reliable measure is not necessarily valid, however. A consistent liar may name Napoleon Bonaparte, Richard Nixon, and Vladimir Putin as his closest friends in test and every retest, but a Jaccard coefficient of 1 doesn't make those answers true. One approach to validation specific to social network analysis, thus, uses reciprocation as a form of ***external validity***, reasoning that a conceptually undirected relationship should be reported by both actors involved in it. But reciprocation rates often depend on the types of relations. College students reporting on whom they spend time with achieved only a reciprocation rate of 58% in Scott Feld and William Carter's (2002) study, for instance. Jimi Adams and James Moody (2007), on the other hand, found high rates of reciprocation—85% for sexual relationships, 72% for drug sharing, and 79% for social ties—among their examined high-risk population (sex workers and drug users). In using the same logic, respondents with high levels of consensus between them are usually considered to be sources of valid responses, whereas respondents with divergent answers to a given survey instrument are regarded with more skepticism.

Kimball Romney and Susan Weller (1984) have applied these criteria of reliability and validity to reanalyze Bernard et al.'s (Bernard & Killworth, 1977; Bernard, Killworth, & Sailer, 1981; Bernard, Kilworth, Sailer, & Kronenfeld, 1984) dataset to distinguish between good and bad informants. They have suggested that researchers should weigh informants by their "quality"—the answers of more reliable informants should be taken more seriously than those from less reliable informants.

Researchers have experimented with providing informants with checklists, such as cues and prompts, to enhance the validity and reliability of the social network data. One study attempted two rounds of interviews with informants (Jones & Fischer, 1978). The first interview asked the respondents about specific network relations such as "borrowing money" and "discussing work-related matters" without any assists. The second interview repeated the same question but with a checklist to aid the respondents. Compared with the first interview, the second interview elicited 34% more names. A total of 27% of the names mentioned in the first interview did not appear in the second interview. By following a similar procedure, another study interviewed students living at a university resident hall (Brewer & Webster, 1999). The first round of interviews asked students to name their friends living in the same building. In the second round, the students were provided with a roster of the students living in the resident hall. The second round produced 20% more names than did the first round. Those who were forgotten in the first round tended to have a more distant relationship with the ego.

Variances in reliability and validity can thus also stem from the specific types of relations being reported. The multitrait–multimethod (MTMM) approach is developed to measure several relationships using different methods, therefore, identifying different sources of variation in reliability. By using MTMM, one study showed that emotional and social support relations tend to be reported with higher reliability than informational support and companionship relations (Ferligoj & Hlebec, 1999). Another study using MTMM examined the reliability of advice, collaboration, information exchange, and socializing relationships and found that collaboration had the highest and socializing the lowest reliability (Coromina & Coenders, 2006). Finally, Valentina Hlebec and Anuška Ferligoj (2002) found that a binary scale—that is, a tie either exists or it doesn't—is less reliable than an ordinal scale—that is, a tie may have different levels of strength—in social network data.

2.4 Archival Data

A quite different approach to constructing a social network relies on unearthing unobtrusive observational data from already existing information sources without posing questions to the actors themselves. **Archival data** inventories come in several forms and need not necessarily be traditional (paper-based) archives: Researchers can code traditional means of communications found in such archives, for example, personal letters, but they can also create citation networks from the bibliographies in published books and articles or references in patents. Other sources of network data exist electronically in data repositories such as Lexis/Nexis, Free Adgar, SDC Platinum, or the electronic files in the Federal Election Commission (FEC). Especially for such electronic databases, a trained programmer can mine massive amounts of electronic files to extract large amounts of data in a relatively short period of time. A particular advantage is also that data may be available over many time periods in a similar format, allowing the researcher to examine network changes over time without much additional cost. Informant bias—i.e. actors falsifying answers to make them appear in a better light—is less of an issue with observational data, but misreporting and mismeasurement can of course occur in other forms. The sections below discuss different applications of collecting observational network data.

2.4.1 Historical Networks Derived From Archival Data

First, the clear advantage of a longitudinal data structure is evidenced in historians' studies of ancient societies, in which interviewing informants is impossible. The well-known study of marriage networks among 15 ruling families in 15th century Florence illustrates the use of archival data to examine the historical network (Padgett & Ansell, 1993). The intermarriage network, shown in Figure 2.3, reveals the central family "Medici Family," which tied with six other families via intermarriage. The authors speculated that such a discerning maneuver by the Medici Family contributes to their eventual rise to power in the Florentine society.

In particular, John Padgett and Christopher Ansell (1993) made use of the detailed accounts of the Medici party and of the looser alliance system of their opponents that were provided by Dale Kent (1978) in his book *The Rise of the Medici*. Other historians also turned to archival sources for some rich historical data to construct social networks for ancient societies. Michael Alexander and James Danowski (1990) investigated the social structure of ancient Rome through the letters of Cicero, the renowned orator and

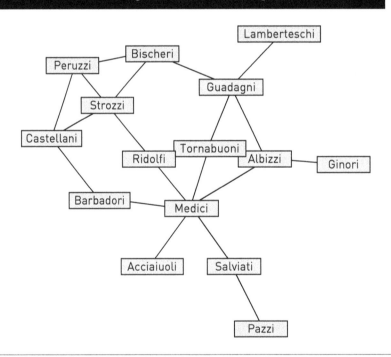

FIGURE 2.3 ● Intermarriage Network of the Ruling Families of Florence

Notes: The nodes represent the 15th century Florentine families, and the ties represent marital relations among those families. Adapted from p. 48 of Newman, M. E. (2010). *Networks: An introduction.* New York, NY: Oxford University Press.

influential politician who straddled two elite social classes: the "knight class" and the "senatorial class" of officeholders. They analyzed data from a corpus of ancient texts, reviewing 280 letters between Cicero and his acquaintances, friends, and relatives spanning 18 years. They recorded 1,914 relations among 524 individuals. Their major finding was that although senators and knights opposed one another on particular issues, they appeared to make up a single, well-integrated, and interlocked social class.

2.4.2 Collaboration and Citation Networks

Intellectual products are often "coalitions in the mind," involving multiple authors in one or more publications (White, 2011). By examining the patterns of co-authorship, social network analysts can reveal the structures of knowledge formation and diffusion within one or across diverse disciplines. One such study by James Moody (2004) investigated the issue of specialty integration of sociology by looking at the co-author pattern of published manuscripts. By using articles indexed in *Sociological Abstract*, Moody constructed an author collaboration network to reveal the loosely overlapping specialty structure in sociology. Figure 2.4 illustrates the process of Moody's conversion from individual publications to author collaboration network. The upper portion of the graph shows the four hypothetical situations of co-authorship: Situation 1 is solo-author publication (A, B, C, and D), situation 2 is the single co-author between two scholars (E and F, and G and H), situation 3 is the co-authorship involving two and three scholars (I, J, and K), and situation 4 is a cluster of scholars involved in multiple publications between them (L, M, N, O, P, Q, R, S, T, U, and V). The bottom portion of the graph depicts how this bipartite network is turned into a one-mode network of collaborations among the authors.

Citation networks—networks in which either texts or their authors are linked through a directed tie indicating whether they have been cited by other texts or their authors—have become common in a variety of fields. Researchers, unsurprisingly, want to know who is the most influential member of their research community. But outside the different field's navel-gazing, studies have also tried to find influential inventors (from citations in patents) or influential Supreme Court judges and rulings (citations of legal texts; Fowler & Jeon, 2008).

In all those fields, texts cite other manuscripts previously published, providing important clues about who or what has influenced their content. Researchers have, for instance, compared citation patterns in different disciplines. Lowell Hargens (2000), for example, compared how fields cite other works for the following purposes: to criticize and correct others' research procedures, to identify with large theoretical strands, to disagree with previous discussions, to point out information useful to the reader, or to give credit to prior work. Hargens found that in the physical sciences, the main purpose of a citation is to reject or correct specific experimental methods. Social science articles cite other publications mainly to identify with or to challenge fundamental assumptions of the discipline. Critiques and disagreements are more common in the field of literature than in the physical or social sciences.

FIGURE 2.4 ● Moody's Construction of Collaboration Networks

a) Individual Publications

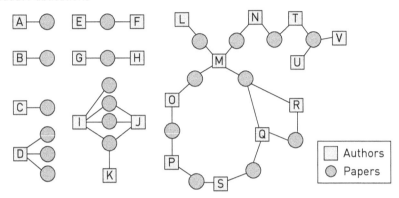

b) Collaboration Network

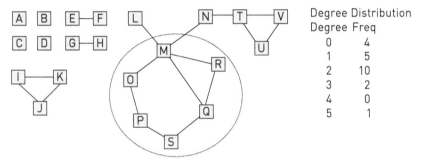

Degree Distribution	
Degree	Freq
0	4
1	5
2	10
3	2
4	0
5	1

Note: Adapted from p. 220 of Moody, J. (2004). The structure of a social science collaboration network: Disciplinary cohesion from 1963 to 1999. *American Sociological Review, 69,* 213–238.

It is worth noting that journal citation networks are acyclical. Acyclical refers to a situation in directed graphs or networks in which the direction of network ties can only go one way. Table 2.3 presents a hypothetical example in which five papers in a given subject were published from 1975 to 2015, 10 years apart from each other. The paper published in 2015 cited all papers in the table that were published before it, and so did the papers in 2005, in 1995, and in 1985. However, the reverse is impossible—the paper published in 1975 could not cite papers published after it. Figure 2.5 presents a graph illustrative of the situation depicted in Table 2.3, in which an arrow points from a paper that is being cited to the paper that is the citer.

Howard White (2011) made use of citations among 14 of the most cited network papers to create a genealogy of the "small-world problem." Figure 2.6 shows that on

Citer \ Citee	P1975	P1985	P1995	P2005	P2015
P1975	—	—	—	—	—
P1985	X	—	—	—	—
P1995	X	X	—	—	—
P2005	X	X	X	—	—
P2015	X	X	X	X	—

TABLE 2.3 ● **Artificial Example of Citation Network Among Five Papers**

Note: X: cites, –: N/A.

the top of the genealogical tree is the original piece of "Six Degree of Separation" by Stanley Milgram (1967). After a gap of more than 30 years, the paper was cited by Duncan Watts (1998), which was followed by an explosion of interest in the small-world phenomenon.

Similar acyclical citation networks can be constructed between patents to understand the flow of technology from one patent to the other. Patents temporarily grant ownership for inventions and give their holders the right to take legal action against others who attempt to profit from the protected invention without permission by the inventor. Although journal citations may have many purposes (as discussed), patents are usually cited for two simple reasons: (1) to acknowledge the contribution of previous

FIGURE 2.5 ● **Graph of Citation Network of Five Papers**

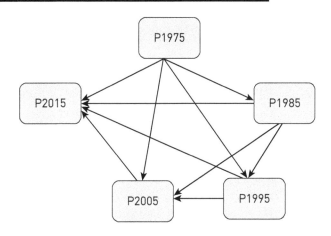

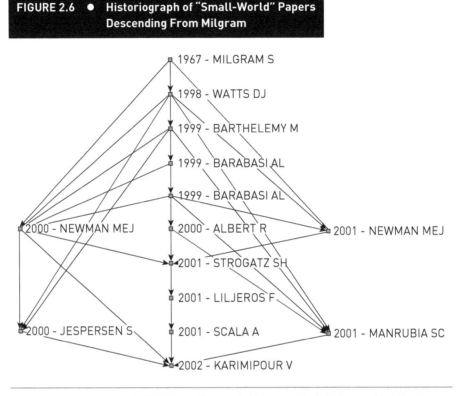

FIGURE 2.6 • **Historiograph of "Small-World" Papers Descending From Milgram**

1967 - MILGRAM S
1998 - WATTS DJ
1999 - BARTHELEMY M
1999 - BARABASI AL
1999 - BARABASI AL
2000 - NEWMAN MEJ
2000 - ALBERT R
2001 - NEWMAN MEJ
2001 - STROGATZ SH
2001 - LILJEROS F
2000 - JESPERSEN S
2001 - SCALA A
2001 - MANRUBIA SC
2002 - KARIMIPOUR V

Note: Adapted from White, H. D. (2011). Scientific and scholarly networks. In (J. Scott and P. J. Carrington, Eds.), *The SAGE handbook of social network analysis* (pp. 271–286). London, England: Sage Ltd.

patents or (2) to present arguments as to why the new technology is significantly different from previous ones. Therefore, they merit a separate patent. In most countries, patents are stored in electronic databases, from which citation networks can be mined (Podolny & Stuart, 1995).

Another form of citation networks is a co-citation network: In such a network, nodes represent papers, and ties represent the fact that both papers were cited together once or several times by a third paper (Ding, 2011; Guardo & Harrigan, 2012). Thus, the co-citation network is a valued and undirected network in which the strength of the tie indicates the number of such co-citations. A co-citation is an indication for papers dealing with related topics, the analysis of such a network yields insights into the structure of knowledge in a given field. A very similar analysis is that of bibliographic coupling, which denotes a pair of papers that cite the same article(s). The bibliographic coupling network also measures how different topics relate to each other in a given field (Yan & Ding, 2012; Youtie, Kay, & Melkers, 2013).

With the advent of e-government and the demands of activists for more transparency, more and more electronic data sources usable for social network analysis are made available by governments. For example, Song Yang, Scott Limbocker, Andrew Dowdle, Patrick Stewart, and Karen Sebold (2015) extracted large amounts of information on donations to presidential candidates to construct a network between the candidates in the three election cycles of 2004, 2008, and 2012. Analyzing this network of shared donors yields insights into the ideology and party cleavage in the American political arena.

2.4.3 Social Media and Other
Forms of Electronic Communication

Recent years have witnessed the widespread use of social media platforms and other forms of electronic communication. These sources are a treasure trove of network data for those with access to them (Rice, 1994; Rice, Borgman, Bednarski, & Hart, 1989). E-mail logs provide rich data on the senders, receivers, and contents of a giant number of e-mail exchanges. In an e-mail communication network, the nodes are the owners of the specific e-mail account, and the e-mails the (usually directed) ties that link them. The intensity of e-mail exchanges is also often used as a proxy for the strength of interaction. As an alternative, the user's address book can also be used to construct network contacts and, hence, the network.

Researchers often complain about not having enough data, but online interaction is one case where an overabundance of data can cause problems—either because researchers lack the computing resources to handle such large datasets or because it is just difficult to grasp conceptually a large and messy dataset. Finally, any e-mail communication network is unlikely to be self-contained, and therefore, the researchers will have to decide on where to draw the boundary. Researchers thus place restrictions when extracting e-mail message data. Those restrictions can be role based (e.g., only e-mails sent among managers), time based (e.g., only e-mail exchanges during the last two weeks), or content based, in which researchers, for instance, scan the subject line to determine whether it is relevant for the research topic or search for specific terms in the body of the message.

Jana Diesner, Terrill Frantz, and Kathleen Carley (2005) made use of such an e-mail corpus to analyze organizational behavior during crisis in the case of the energy company Enron. Enron's sudden collapse triggered a massive public outcry and political pressure for independent investigations by the U.S. Securities and Exchange Commission (SEC) and the Federal Energy Regulatory Commission (FERC). In an unprecedented move, FERC released a corpus of actual e-mails from 158 Enron employees, which included those from its CEOs, Kenneth Lay and Jeffrey Skilling. Diesner et al. started with 151 employees in the original FERC release, expanding to 557 Enron employees through data enhancement. The researchers were able to construct directed and valued matrices across multiple time periods, including nodes representing employees, values indicating the frequency of e-mail exchanges, and direction distinguishing senders from receivers.

Compared with self-reported survey data, such data are immune to certain measurement errors, such as inaccurate recall, biased responses, and forgetting. But of course e-mail communication only captures parts of the social interaction occurring between the actors of the network and may therefore reflect the underlying social dynamic incompletely. Simple counts of e-mails exchanged may fail to capture the true nature of the networked conversation. Some e-mails may seem to be routine and insignificant, but one or two sentences embedded in them may be highly consequential. Without rich contextual information, researchers may not be able to distinguish between routine contents and critical sentences, which is a limitation scholars should be aware of.

With the popularization of Facebook, Twitter, or Instagram, people have come to associate the term "social network" with such social media platforms because all of them have a relationship component built into them: Facebook users can be "friends" with other users and "like" or repost their content, Twitter users can "follow" other users, and so on. At the same time, the companies running such platforms have collected an enormous amount of information on their users. Social scientists who would like to use such data often face two limitations: first, their capacity to deal with such massive amounts of data, be it the technology to identify relevant actors, extract their communications, or manage and store the data. This problem often can be solved by working with programmers or acquiring the necessary programming skills (Boyd & Ellison, 2007). Second, the data stored on those commercial servers are proprietary assets of the companies. Thus, researchers often have to form collaborations or propose specific research projects that are also of interest to the company to gain access. Another problem occurs when the researcher would like to publish results based on such data in journals that demand that the replication data be made public; the social media companies may not be willing to share the data more broadly, or it might not be possible to anonymize the data to a degree that would prohibit the identification of individual users.

Nevertheless, social media data can form the basis of intriguing studies: Petter Holme, Christofer Edling, and Fredrik Liljeros (2004), for instance, investigated records of interactions between members of a Swedish dating website and reconstructed from them the network of interactions between its members. The network is unique in that the interactions between members are timestamped, enabling researchers to construct a longitudinal timeline to document the timing and duration of the relationships. Lada Adamic and Eytan Adar (2003) developed tools to extract information of personal webpages hosted on two university servers (Stanford and MIT), and they concluded that MIT students tend to get acquainted mainly through fraternities and sororities. In contrast, Stanford University students get to know each other in much more diverse social settings, such as research teams, religious groups, ethnicity-based associations, and sororities and fraternities. Other sources of data that are publicly available are online message-boards and forums. Christopher Lueg and Danyel Fisher (2003), for instance, constructed a network of posters connected through responses to each other's posts on one such message-board, *usenet*.

A good online source for researchers of citation networks is Google Scholar. In addition to its powerful search algorithm that allows it to list not just published articles, but also working papers, researchers also increasingly use it as their "calling card." They will thus clean the automated collection of their research manually, combining different versions of the same working paper and weeding out articles written by different scholars with the same name.

Readers wishing to get in-depth information on network data collected from the Internet and the specific design issues associated with it may want to consult Robert Ackland's (2013) excellent book on this topic.

End-of-Chapter Questions

1. A team of researchers is interested in how social networking lends support to victims of sexual assaults. They plan to start with a sampling of victims. If you are the consultant assisting with the sampling, describe the sampling design using the realist strategy. What is the sampling design if they are to use the nominalist strategy?

2. Compare and contrast the three main sampling approaches in social network design: the positional approach, the relational approach, and the event-based approach.

3. In implementing the relational approach, researchers commonly use two methods: expending selection and fixed list selection. Doreian and Woodard (1992, 1994) found that the two selection methods produce drastically different samples. Describe these two methods, and discuss why they produce samples that are so different from one another.

4. A scholar is interested in studying friendships formed among first-year students in a university dormitory. Can you help him to draw a network sample using the event-based approach?

5. Compare and contrast the three types of generators in ego-centric network studies: name generator, positional generator, and resource generator. Could you produce examples in questionnaire surveys that are illustrative of the three generators?

6. When asked "with whom do you play a sport?" one respondent produced 20 names in the first interview and 22 names in the second interview. Fifteen names mentioned in the first interview appeared in the second interview. What is the Jaccard coefficient for this respondent?

7. Imagine a situation in which you are the researcher who is interested in "study group" in a class of 50 students. You survey the students twice with the following question: "Who do you study with in this class?" The first time you ask the students to answer the question without any assistance, and the second time you provide them with the class roster. Based on the information in this chapter, are students likely to produce different sets of names between the two interviews? If so, what are the differences?

3

Descriptive Methods in Social Network Analysis

●

Learning Objectives

- Describe the relations between social network graphs and matrices

- Calculate the density measure for the entire network, and interpret the results

- Calculate and interpret centrality, centralization, and prestige for nodes and entire networks

- Examine various methods to measure cliques and subgroups in networks

- Demonstrate different visualization methods in social network analysis, such as multidimensional scaling and dendograms and their applications when analyzing structures of networks and positions of actors within it

- Calculate structural equivalence when examining relations between pairs of actors

- Examine bipartite matrices as a way to analyze social networks with heterogeneous nodes

The previous chapter discussed research designs to collect social network data. But it can be hard to understand what is going on in even a small network without statistical tools because of the sheer number of possible ties and configurations. In this chapter, we will introduce such tools. We will examine ways to visualize networks or identify different positions that nodes can occupy within a network by using centrality measures and the concept of structural equivalence. We will also discuss how clusters and cliques help define subgroups of individuals within a network, as well as how different networks can be distinguished using measures of density or centralization. We will also introduce visualization methods such as multidimensional scaling for entire graphs, as well as an agglomerate clustering method to partition actors based on their network positions. Finally, we will analyze two-mode or bipartite networks and explain the necessary matrix manipulation and interpretation of those results. Topics in this chapter cover descriptive methods, whereas the next chapter discusses inferential network statistics.

3.1 Graph and Matrix— Social Network Representation

3.1.1 Graphs

A *graph* is a visual illustration of a network. A graph consists of a set of nodes and the ties connecting those nodes. In *binary graphs*, ties are either present or absent between pairs of nodes. In *valued graphs*, the ties that are present have values attached to them, indicating their strength. If actors can have different kinds of relationships (e.g., friendship and marriage ties), multiple graphs are needed, each of which represents one particular type of relation.

3.1.2 Matrices

An *(adjacency) matrix* is another way to represent social network data. In this square matrix, the actors appear once and in the same order in both the row and the column margins; in directed networks, the tie senders are listed in the rows and the receivers in the columns. The entries of the matrix cells represent the values of the relations between pairs of nodes in the respective column and row (*i* and *j*) or, in the case of binary networks, whether a relationship does (1) or does not (0) exist. Several features of the matrix demand further explanation. In many cases, diagonal values in the matrix do not denote anything—their values are null or 0 by default; as for many kinds of ties, it would not make sense to connect the actors with themselves. There are, however, exceptions: Individuals may nominate themselves as experts, or they may cite their own articles, for instance. Second, not all possible values in the off-diagonal cells may be allowed: In binary networks, for instance, only 0 and 1 appear. In a valued graph, they can take on almost any value. Third, if the network data are undirected (e.g., a marriage network), then the values in the upper triangle cells (i.e., above the diagonal leading from the top left to the bottom right cell) in a given network equal the values in their corresponding cells of the lower triangle ($X_{i,j} = X_{j,i}$). This is not the case in a directed network, such as a network of who reports to whom at work ($X_{i,j} \neq X_{j,i}$).

Although it is possible to have binary undirected, binary directed, valued undirected, and valued directed networks, a large part of social network analytical methods can only be applied to binary undirected networks. Some more can also be applied to binary directed networks. Nevertheless, when it comes to analyzing valued graphs, especially directed valued networks, available analytical methods are limited. Readers who want to analyze such networks should, therefore, consult the manual of their social network analysis software to understand how and if a given method can be used for their network datasets. Stephen Borgatti, Martin Everett, and Jeffrey Johnson (2013), for instance, provided such a guide for the software UCINET.

Graphs are powerful tools to illustrate network connections and node positions, but they do not allow for computer simulation and processing. In contrast, an adjacency matrix does not present an ideal visualization of the network, but it facilitates computer processing of the network. To illustrate the use of a graph and a matrix to represent social network data, we present an artificial friendship network among seven individuals in Figure 3.1. Note that this is an undirected binary graph.

Table 3.1 shows the corresponding adjacency matrix. A friendship between two actors is indicated by a "1" in the respective cell or a tie between the two nodes,

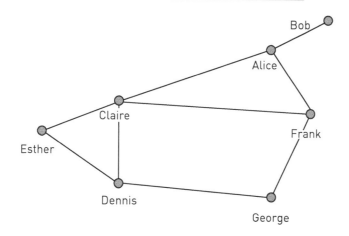

FIGURE 3.1 ● Friendship Network Among Seven Individuals

TABLE 3.1 ● Adjacency Matrix of Friendship Network Among the Seven Individuals

	Bob	Alice	Frank	George	Dennis	Claire	Esther	RM
Bob	0	1	0	0	0	0	0	1
Alice	1	0	1	0	0	1	0	3
Frank	0	1	0	1	0	1	0	3
George	0	0	1	0	1	0	0	2
Dennis	0	0	0	1	0	1	1	3
Claire	0	1	1	0	1	0	1	4
Esther	0	0	0	0	1	1	0	2
CM	1	3	3	2	3	4	2	—

Notes: RM: row margin—aggregating cell values within a given row across columns. CM: column margin—aggregating cell values within a given column across rows.

whereas the absence of a tie is represented by a "0". For example, Claire and Frank are friends, and so they share a tie in the graph. Bob and Esther are not friends; therefore, no line connects them directly. In the matrix, the entry between Claire and Frank is "1", whereas the entry between Bob and Esther is "0". The adjacency matrix does not reflect indirect ties. For example, in Figure 3.1, all actors are connected via shortest paths that are no longer than three steps. It is possible to develop algorithms and write computer programs to trace such indirect two-step or three-step connections via the shortest paths between the pairs—they always use the more convenient matrix network representation for that purpose.

In the network discussed earlier, all nodes belong to a similar class: people. The network is therefore a *one-mode network*. Social network analysts sometimes deal with heterogeneous sets of actors and organize them in one network/graph, which is called a *two-mode network* or *bipartite graph*. In Section 3.7 of this chapter, we will discuss the details of matrices manipulations and interpretations of bipartite graphs.

3.2 Density

3.2.1 Density in Full Networks

Density is the most basic measure at the network level. It reflects the extent to which the nodes in a network are connected with each other. Density is calculated as the total number of dyadic ties that are present in a network, divided by the maximum number of dyadic ties possible in the network. In a binary graph, the formula for density is

$$D = \frac{\sum\sum X_{i,j}}{P_N^2} \qquad i \neq j \tag{3.1}$$

Formula 3.1 shows that the numerator is the arithmetic aggregation of all the dyadic ties that are present in the graph and the denominator is the maximum possible dyadic ties that exist for a network with N nodes. Note that the denominator is

$P_N^2 = \dfrac{N!}{(N-2)!} = N \times (N-1)$. Thus, Formula 3.1 is simplified as follows:

$$D = \frac{\sum\sum X_{i,j}}{N \times (N-1)} \tag{3.2}$$

Formula 3.2 is the computational formula for density, which appears in many textbooks of social network analysis. Note that this formula presumes matrix representation of the network: The numerator is simply the sum of all cells in a row added together for all rows, whereas the denominator is the maximal number of ties possible. For binary undirected graphs, this formula counts each tie present in the graph twice, thus, inflating the numerator. This is not a problem as the denominator of the maximum possible of dyadic ties is inflated by the same factor. By using this formula, it is easy to calculate the density for the graph in Figure 3.1: It is 42.86% (18 / 42 = 9 / 21 = 42.86%).

This formula can be used in binary directed graphs as well, in which the maximum number of dyadic ties is indeed $N \times (N - 1)$. Figure 3.2 provides an example for a directed binary graph, with the corresponding adjacency matrix in Table 3.2. A total of

FIGURE 3.2 • Binary-Directed Graph of Friendship Among Seven Nodes

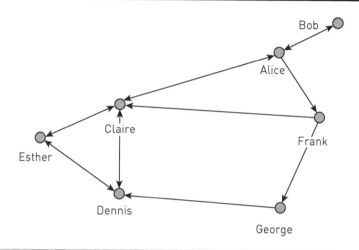

TABLE 3.2 • Binary-Directed Matrix of Friendship Among Seven Individuals

	Bob	Alice	Frank	George	Dennis	Claire	Esther	RM
Bob	0	0	0	0	0	0	0	0
Alice	1	0	1	0	0	1	0	3
Frank	0	0	0	1	0	1	0	2
George	0	0	0	0	1	0	0	1
Dennis	0	0	0	0	0	1	0	1
Claire	0	1	0	0	1	0	1	3
Esther	0	0	0	0	1	1	0	2
CM	1	1	1	1	3	4	1	—

Notes: RM: row margin—aggregating cell values within a given row across columns. CM: column margin—aggregating cell values within a given column across rows.

13 directed dyadic ties are present in the graph, and the maximum dyadic tie for the directed graph with 7 nodes is 42 (7 × 6 = 42). By applying Formula 3.2, we find that the density of the graph is 30.95% (13 / 42 = 30.95%).

3.2.2 Density in Egocentric Network Data

The density in egocentric network data can be calculated in a similar fashion. Nevertheless, including the ego will inflate the density because ego, by definition, would have ties with all alters it elicits. Thus, egocentric network density should be computed with the following formula:

$$D_{ego_i} = \frac{\Sigma\Sigma a_{j,k}}{c_n^2 = \dfrac{n!}{2! \times (n-2)!}} \tag{3.3}$$

The numerator tallies the number of dyadic pairs that are present for the ego i; the denominator is the total maximum possible dyadic pairs for the ego i with N alters (thus, N does not include the ego i). For example, Figure 3.3 shows an example egocentric network, in which an ego nominates six alters, among which there are three ties. The maximum possible dyadic ties among six alters is 15. Thus, the density for such an ego would be 3 / 15 = 20%. The density of the network a survey respondent (the ego)

FIGURE 3.3 ● Density in Egocentric Network

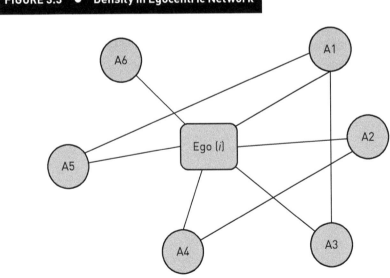

is embedded in can be an important independent or dependent variable, as shown in the examples provided in the previous chapter.

3.3 Centrality, Centralization, and Prestige

Centrality measures are one of the most commonly used indicators for the importance of an actor in a given network. There is a multitude of them, but the most commonly used are *degree centrality, betweenness centrality,* and *closeness centrality*. Centrality is a measure at the node level; the distribution of this measure among the different actors in the network, however, is captured in *centralization measures*, which is a network-level characteristic. The greater the centralization of a network, the larger the disparity between the nodes' individual centrality measures. *Prestige* also measures the prominence of individual nodes in a network, but it distinguishes between senders and receivers of a given relationship (Knoke & Burt, 1983). In this section, we discuss how to compute these different measurements.

3.3.1 Degree Centrality

The first and simplest centrality measure is degree centrality (Freeman, 1979), which simply counts the number of connections an actor or node has. Those with a high degree centrality are active players in a given network: They have many friends, report to many superiors, gossip a lot, and so on. The degree centrality of actors in undirected graphs is simply the tallying of the lines incidental to the nodes or—in matrix form—the adding up the number of "1s" in the actor's row:

$$C_D(N_i) = \sum_{j=1}^{g} x_{i,j} \ (i \neq j) \tag{3.4}$$

Applying Formula 3.4 to Table 3.1 produces a degree centrality for each node in the graph, listed in the row margins (RMs) or column margins (CMs). The most central player is Claire with four friends, whereas the most marginal player is Bob with only one friend.

Degree centrality as measured through Formula 3.4 is not easily comparable across the network, however. A small number might mark a node that is well connected in a small network or a node that is sparsely connected in a large network. To eliminate the effect of network size on degree centrality of individual nodes, Stanley Wasserman and Katherine Faust (1994) have suggested the following normalization:

$$C'_D(N_i) = \frac{C_D(N_i)}{g-1} \tag{3.5}$$

$C'_D(N_i)$ stands for the normalized degree centrality, which divides an actor's degree centrality by the total number of connections he or she could have in a network with *g* actors. Thus, a node with six connections in a seven-node network would have a normalized degree centrality of 1 or 100% (6 / (7 − 1) = 100%), whereas a node with six connections in a 50-node network would have 0.1224, or 12.24%, in its normalized degree centrality (6 / (50 − 1) = 12.24%). Like others, normalized degree centrality ranges from 0 to 1, with values closer to 1 indicating great connectivity or degree centrality for the node. Note that it is not necessary to normalize degree centrality when comparing nodes within one network only.

The distribution of degree centrality among the nodes of a network often helps us to understand how equal network actors are. One useful way to summarize this (in) equality is degree centralization:

$$C_D = \frac{\sum_{i=1}^{N}\left(C_D\left(N^*\right) - C_D\left(N_i\right)\right)}{(N-1)(N-2)} \tag{3.6}$$

In the numerator, we sum up the difference between the highest degree actor and each other actor and divide this (in the denominator) by the number of possible ties that could exist in the network. The centralization measure is a network or graph level indicator, with "0" suggesting complete equality in degree centrality among nodes, whereas "1" indicates complete inequality in degree centrality. Readers can understand this better by looking at the artificial examples of the "star graph" and the "circle graph," which have 1 and 0 in their respective degree centralization in Wasserman and Faust (1994, p. 171). Figure 3.4 shows the two types of graph.

3.3.2 Betweenness Centrality

In his famous thesis on "structural holes," Ronald Burt (1992) proposed that individuals who connect otherwise disconnected nodes or parts of the network stand to gain from their position through "brokerage." In the case of a trade network, they can extract a premium for being the middleman. In a gossip network, they may be able to withhold or manipulate the information that reaches either side of their network. An actor can be highly betweenness central without having a high degree centrality: A node that connects two otherwise separate networks may have a degree centrality of only 2, but it may be highly influential because it sits on the only path through which the nodes of the two networks could reach each other.

In Figure 3.1, for instance, Alice has such a position: Without her, Bob would be completely disconnected from the remaining network (i.e., Alice plugs a "structural hole"), which may give her considerable power over Bob or anyone in the remaining network who wants to gain access to Bob. Claire is also quite betweenness central. This may be less obvious because the network would not fall into two parts if she was removed, but it would become a straight line, with Esther and Bob forming the end points. Claire is on the shortest path if Esther or Dennis wants to reach Frank and Alice. One way to measure betweenness centrality is thus to count the number of times an actor lies on the shortest (*geodesic*) path between pairs of actors in a network. Betweenness centrality captures an actor's potential to control the information and

FIGURE 3.4 • Star and Circle Graph

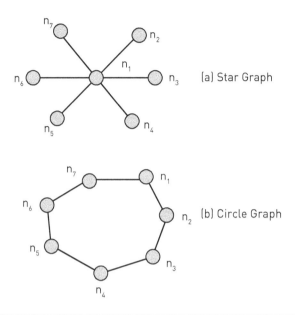

(a) Star Graph

(b) Circle Graph

Note: Adapted from p. 171 of Wasserman, S., & Faust, K. (1994). *Social network analysis: Methods and applications.* New York, NY: Cambridge University Press.

resources exchanged between other pairs. Supposing actors j and k must go through actor i to exchange information or resources, actor i would have great leverage over the timing and the contents of the information or the resources exchanged between j and k. Thus, the shorter the paths an actor lies on, the more such exchanges and interactions he or she can influence within that network.

In many cases, there might be several geodesic paths between two individuals: If Dennis wants to reach Frank in Figure 3.1, he could either go through George or Claire, for instance. Freeman (1977) thus proposed the following computing method to measure the betweenness centrality: Supposing $g_{j,k}$ is the number of geodesic paths between a given pair j and k, $g_{j,k}(N_i)$ is the number of geodesic pairs between j and k that contains i, dividing $g_{j,k}(N_i)$ by $g_{j,k}$ reflects the extent to which node i lies on the geodesic of the pair j and k. Tallying the number of times node i sits on the geodesic paths of all other pairs in a network produces the measure for node i's betweenness centrality.

$$C_B(N_i) = \sum_{j<k} \frac{g_{j,k}(N_i)}{g_{j,k}} \tag{3.7}$$

For a given node *i*, the index of betweenness centrality has a minimum value of 0, meaning that the node *i* sits on no geodesic distances between other pairs in a network, and a maximum value of $\frac{(g-1)(g-2)}{2}$, suggesting that node *i* lies on the shortest path between all other pairs of the network (this assumes that each pair has only one geodesic path between them, and the network is undirected). The undirected graphs would have maximum $\frac{(g-1)(g-2)}{2}$ geodesic paths for the $g-1$ nodes as $C_{g-1}^2 = \frac{(g-1)!}{2 \times (g-1-2)!} = \frac{(g-1)(g-2)}{2}$. For directed graphs, the maximum value of betweenness centrality measure for a given node *i* would be $(g-1)(g-2)$ as $P_{g-1}^2 = \frac{(g-1)!}{(g-1-2)!} = (g-1)(g-2)$. To illustrate the maximum betweenness centrality in directed and undirected graphs, we use two artificial star-shape networks in Figures 3.5 and 3.6, respectively. In Figure 3.5, actor *i* lies on all geodesic paths among actors A, B, C, and D, reaching its maximum value of 6. Those paths are *A-i-B*, *A-i-C*, *A-i-D*, *B-i-C*, *B-i-D*, and *C-i-D*. In Figure 3.6, actor *i* sits on all geodesic paths among actors A, B, C, and D, reaching its maximum value of 12.

Much like degree centrality, betweenness centrality is sensitive to the size of the network: An actor with 6 in betweenness centrality in a network of 5 actors is likely in a very different situation than an actor with the same betweenness centrality in a network of 10. We can use the maximum value mentioned to standardize betweenness centrality (Wasserman & Stanley, 1994):

$$C_B'(N_i) = \frac{C_B N_i \times 2}{(g-1)(g-2)} \tag{3.8}$$

$$C_B'(N_i) = \frac{C_B N_i}{(g-1)(g-2)} \tag{3.9}$$

Formula 3.8 applies to undirected graphs. Formula 3.9 applies to directed graphs, where every possible shortest path from actor A to actor B could also have a reverse path back. For example, the previously mentioned actor with betweenness 6 would only have a standardized betweenness centrality of 8.33% (6 / 72 = 0.0833) in the network of 10 actors. Standardized betweenness centrality ranges from 0 to 1 and is particularly useful for comparing actors across networks of different sizes.

As with degree centrality and centralization, we can also calculate betweenness centralization. For undirected graphs, the formula is as follows:

$$C_B = \frac{\sum_{i=1}^g \left[C_B(N^*) - C_B(N_i) \right]}{\left((g-1)^2 (g-2) \right)/2} \tag{3.10}$$

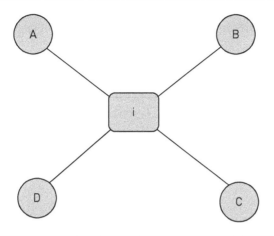

FIGURE 3.5 • **Betweenness Centrality in an Undirected Graph**

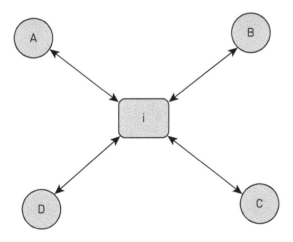

FIGURE 3.6 • **Betweenness Centrality in a Directed Graph**

In the numerator, $C_B(N^*)$ denotes the node with the highest betweenness centrality, whereas $C_B(N_i)$ represents the other nodes. The Σ sign requires the highest betweenness centrality minus the betweenness centrality of other nodes, and the differences summed up. The denominator represents the theoretical maximum value of the differences in the betweenness centrality of the nodes in a given network. In particular, the greatest betweenness centrality value in a network with g actors is $\dfrac{(g-1)(g-2)}{2}$.

The theoretical maximum value in the betweenness centralization would be obtained when only one actor reaches the maximum betweenness centrality and other actors have betweenness centrality of 0. Then, the greatest betweenness centrality is minus 0 for $(g - 1)$ times, producing a theoretical maximum value in betweenness centralization in a given graph of $\frac{(g-1)^2 (g-2)}{2}$.

The betweenness centralization ranges from 0 to 1, with 0 indicating the most egalitarian network in which each node has the same betweenness centrality, and 1 suggesting the most hierarchical network in which one node has the highest centrality, and others have 0 in their betweenness centrality. Figure 3.5 demonstrates such a hierarchical structure with 5 nodes and node i having the highest betweenness centrality of 6, and others having 0. This graph would have betweenness centralization of 1, deduced as $\frac{(6-0)(g-1)}{((g-1)^2(g-2))/2} = \frac{6 \times 4}{(4^2 \times 3)/2} = 1$.

Computation of betweenness centralization for directed graphs is very similar to what it is for the undirected graphs, except for a small change in the denominator as $((g - 1)^2 (g - 2))$. This is because the maximum value in betweenness centrality in directed graphs is $(g - 1) (g - 2)$. The denominator represents the most hierarchical (unequal) structure in betweenness centrality for a network, in which one node has the greatest centrality score of $(g - 1) (g - 2)$ and other nodes have the centrality of 0. Therefore, the theoretical maximum value of the denominator is $((g - 1)^2 (g - 2))$.

3.3.3 Closeness Centrality

Closeness centrality measures how fast a given node i in a network can reach other nodes. It is calculated by taking the inverse of a given node i's geodesic (shortest path length) with all other nodes in a given network (Sabidussi, 1966):

$$C_C(N_i) = \frac{1}{\left[\sum_{j=1}^{g} d\left(N_i, N_j\right)\right]} \quad (i \neq j) \tag{3.11}$$

Closeness centrality has three features: (1) The shorter the geodesic distance between a given node i and all other nodes in a network, the larger node i's closeness centrality. Thus, the closeness centrality is inversely related to its geodesic distances with other nodes. (2) As the denominator is the summation of node i's geodesic distances with other nodes, it cannot be 0. Thus, closeness centrality does not apply to isolated nodes in a network, that is, nodes that are neither directly nor indirectly connected to other nodes in a network. (3) Closeness centrality is very sensitive to the size of a network. A node with direct connections (geodesic distance of 1) to all other nodes in a small network would have a higher value in its closeness centrality than a node with direct connection with other nodes in a large network. A standardized closeness centrality (Beauchamp, 1965) makes comparison across networks of different sizes possible by controlling for the size of networks:

$$C_C'(N_i) = (g-1)(C_C(N_i)) = \frac{g-1}{\left[\sum_{j=1}^{g} d(N_i, N_j)\right]}$$ (3.12)

The standardized closeness centrality can be infinitely close to 0, but it cannot be 0. It reaches its maximum value of 1 when a node i has direct connection with all other nodes in a network. Figure 3.7 illustrates how closeness centrality is calculated. Applying Formula 3.11 to node i in Figures 3.5 and 3.7, respectively, would produce identical closeness centrality of 0.25 for the node. Such computation fails to distinguish between the nodes in their closeness with other nodes in that the node appears to be more directly connected with other nodes in Figure 3.5 than it does in Figure 3.7. Applying the standardized Formula 3.12 distinguishes between the two scenarios, producing $1\left((5-1)\frac{1}{4}=1\right)$ for Figure 3.5 and $0.75\left((4-1)\frac{1}{4}=0.75\right)$ for Figure 3.7, with the larger number indicating the great closeness centrality (short distance to other nodes) for the node i in Figure 3.5 than in Figure 3.7.

The closeness centrality measure can be applied to directed graphs. Nevertheless, as the edges between nodes have directions, closeness centrality for a given node has both in-degree closeness centrality and out-degree closeness centrality. One can apply Formula 3.11 to directed graphs to compute the in- and out-degree closeness centrality for each node. The same three features apply, which means that the same node may have a large in-degree closeness centrality (short geodesic distance to other nodes) but undefined out-degree closeness centrality, or vice versa. For example, in Figure 3.8, node i has out-degree closeness centrality 0.25, but its in-degree closeness centrality is undefined as node i does not have any in-degree edge (i only reaches out, no one can reach i).

Applying Formula 3.12 to directed graphs poses some difficulties in interpreting the results. For instance, in Figure 3.8, node A has a standardized in-degree and out-degree closeness centrality of 3[3 × (1) = 3]. Thus, the high values, in many cases values greater than 1, can result from a graph having many nodes. We suggest that (g – 1)

FIGURE 3.7 ● Closeness Centrality in a Graph With Four Nodes

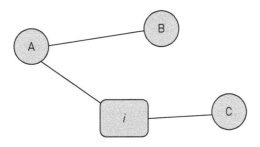

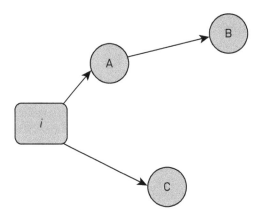

FIGURE 3.8 ● Closeness Centrality in a Directed Graph With Four Nodes

in Formula 3.12 be replaced with the number of nodes reachable (either in-degree or out-degree) by the node i, denoted as R_i, shown as follows:

$$C_C'\left(N_{i,\,directed}\right) = R_i\left(C_C\left(N_i\right)\right) = \frac{R_i}{\left[\sum_{j=1}^{g}d\left(N_i,N_j\right)\right]} \qquad (3.13)$$

Applying Formula 3.13 to the directed graph in Figure 3.8 standardizes the results for node A, which are now both 1 for in-degree and out-degree centrality. Node's out-degree standardized closeness centrality is 0.75 $\left((3\times\frac{3}{4})=0.75\right)$, whereas its in-degree standardized closeness centrality is undefined, much like its closeness centrality. Therefore, the out-degree closeness centrality for node i is lower than that for node A.

3.3.4 Prestige

Many social relations involve distinction between senders and receivers or between initiators and objects. In this case, directed networks best capture the features of interest to the researcher. For example, in a reporting network, low echelon workers routinely report their work activities and merits to their supervisors, who in turn report to their managers. Conversely, high-ranking employees rarely or never report to their subordinates. In those networks, the direction indicates the power flow. Those who receive the reports or serve as objects of the reporting have greater administrative power than do those who initialize or send those reports. Another example for a power structure network, an advising network, consists of a group of people seeking advice from each other. Those who are sought after in those advice-seeking networks can influence others' behavior to a greater extent, thus, exerting power over others. Unlike the reporting network in which the power is exercised through administrative fiats, power in advice-seeking networks is exercised in soft, noncoercive ways, which can sometimes be more effective in changing behavior than administrative sanctions and commands.

Measuring a node's prestige in a directed network is straightforward. The column margin of a node in a matrix shows the number of times the node receives or serves as a target of a relationship, such as reporting, or advice-seeking. So the measure for a node's prestige is the same as the measure for its in-degree in a directed network.

$$P_D(N_i) = \sum_{j=1}^{g} X_{j,i} \qquad (3.14)$$

Note that nodes or actors in a network also have out-degree measures, which are simply their row margins in a matrix. Much like in-degrees, interpretations of out-degrees depend on the substantive meaning of the tie. For example, in a friendship network, the out-degree (the row margins) of the actors suggests the extent to which actors nominate others as their friends, whereas the in-degree (the column margins) indicates the extent to which others are nominating actors as friends.

Much like computation of in-degree centrality in directed graphs, Formula 3.14 is sensitive to the size of the network. An actor with an in-degree centrality of 6 in a directed network of 7 employees stands to be very different from one with an in-degree of 6 in a network of 100 employees. As a node can have at most an in-degree centrality of $(g-1)$ in a directed network, a standardized measure for a node's prestige would control for the size of the network by dividing Formula 3.14 by $(g-1)$, as shown as follows:

$$P'_D(N_i) = \frac{\sum_{j=1}^{g} X_{j,i}}{g-1} \qquad (3.15)$$

Analogous to standardized degree centrality, the quantity calculated in Formula 3.15 ranges from 0 (no one sends a relation to the node) to 1 (everybody else sends a relation to the node). Thus, the closer the index is to 1, the greater the node's prestige. Conversely, the closer the index is to 0, the lower the node's prestige.

3.3.5 Centrality in Egocentric Network

Most measures of centrality have been developed for complete network data. But Peter Marsden (2002) has applied some of them also to ego-networks, illustrating that *centrality in the egocentric network* can reliably replace those measures for a complete network when the latter are hard to come by.

By the nature of its design, ego i will have a direct tie with all alters (g). Therefore, each ego in a sample would have the same standardized degree centrality of $g/g = 1$. The only variation for ego i in a sample is the size of its network (g), which is also its (nonstandardized) degree centrality. For example, the 2004 General Social Survey found that U.S. respondents named, on average, 2.08 alters when asked with whom they have an "important matter discussion" (McPherson, Smith-Lovin, & Cook, 2006), which was a decline from 2.94 in 1985 (Marsden, 1987). The authors consider this to be evidence for increasing social isolation in American society.

Standardized closeness centrality is not of much use in ego-centric networks, however, because the ego i is by definition as close as possible to all alters in the network, and non-standardized closeness centrality simply reflects the size of the ego-network. Betweenness centrality, however, can be revealing and informative for egocentric network analysis at least if the egos were also questioned about their alters' relationships. An ego's standardized betweenness centrality ranges from 0 to 1, where 0 means that all pairs of alters are directly connected with each other (and, thus, no pair has a geodesic path that passes through the ego). On the contrary, 1 means that the ego sits at the center of a star network and its alters are only connected through the ego. Therefore, the closer the ego's betweenness centrality is to 0, the denser the egocentric network surrounding the ego. Conversely, the closer the betweenness of the ego is to 1, the sparser the egocentric network of the ego. In other words, the ego i's betweenness centrality is inversely correlated with its ego-networks density. Another term for betweenness centrality that is often used in the context of ego-networks is *constraint*. A dense ego-network implies that the ego may be constrained in his or her action—high betweenness centrality, thus, equals low constraint, and vice versa. Marsden's (2002) research suggested that ego-network betweenness centrality is a reasonable proxy for the ego's betweenness centrality in the wider network.

3.4 Cliques

Social network analysts are often interested in social cohesion and in identifying cohesive groups in the wider network. A cohesive subgroup normally consists of a group of people connected by direct, strong, and reciprocated ties with each other. Such cohesive groups can exist in workplaces where a team of colleagues forms a small group to nurture collegiality and camaraderie, in neighborhoods where a group of neighbors frequently socialize, in sports teams where players form strong friendships to foster mutual support, or in terrorism cells where terrorists concoct plots. Social network analysts characterize such cohesive groups as cliques. Cliques are defined as groups of nodes that are more closely and intensely connected with each other than they are with nodes outside of the cliques (Luce & Perry, 1949). The smallest cliques have three nodes, which are called triads in social network analysis.

Cliques are often formed based on shared characteristics, such as race, sex, age, academic aptitudes, educational attainment, social economic factors, geographic proximity, religious belief, and ideology. Once formed, cliques also exert an important influence on their members' behavior (Borgatti, Mehra, Brass, & Labianca, 2009). The term "clique" is often used interchangeably with other concepts such as cluster, gang, or faction. Wasserman and Faust (1994), therefore, named four essential features that define cliques: (1) mutuality of ties, (2) reachability of subgroups, (3) frequency of ties among members, and (4) frequency of ties among members as opposed to ties with outsiders. Those four features lay the foundation to operationalize a definition of cliques.

3.4.1 Definition of Clique

The most rigid definition of a *clique* is a maximal complete subgraph of three or more nodes, all of which are directly connected to one another, with no other node in the network having direct ties to every member of the clique. An example may illuminate this terse definition. Figure 3.1 has two cliques: the "Claire, Frank, and Alice" clique and the "Esther, Dennis, Claire" clique. Both cliques have (a) at least three nodes, (b) the nodes within each clique are directly tied with each other, and (c) no other node in the network has direct ties with all the nodes in the cliques. Conversely, the subgraph of Claire, Frank, George, and Dennis does not form a clique because of the absence of direct ties between Frank and Dennis and between Claire and George.

Under such a rigid definition, large cliques are rare in many social networks (Wasserman & Faust, 1994). An absence of one link prevents a cohesive group from being a clique. Moreover, the rigid separation between in-clique and out-clique also tends to overlook the finer gradation of the relations between network nodes. To capture those finer distinctions between nodes in their cohesive groups, researchers have developed alternative measures and definitions, such as **N-clique**, *k-plex*, *components*, and *factions*. In the following sections, we discuss the most commonly used *N-clique* and *K-core* techniques. Readers who are interested in the other measures may consult Robert Hanneman and Mark Riddle (2005) for more information.

3.4.2 N-clique

N-clique is defined as a subgroup with at least three members, all of whom are connected with each other with no more than N steps in their geodesic distances, and with no other nodes in the network being connected with the all members of the clique with N steps. Thus, rather than requesting direct connection for all pairs of nodes in a subgroup, N-clique gives researchers the opportunity to define the cliques with their own variable thresholds of N. The clique definition given earlier corresponds to a one-clique, the most restrictive N-clique. Generally, the value of N is positively correlated with the inclusiveness of the clique but negatively correlated with the cohesiveness of the clique. An N-clique with a large N is inclusive but not very cohesive, whereas the opposite is true for a small N. The researcher can thus experiment with different thresholds. When cohesive subgroups are scarce, imposing a small value of N produces few if any cohesive cliques. Conversely, when a network is full of strongly connected, highly cohesive subgroups, using a large N may result in too many N-cliques to be useful. By changing the N value, researchers can exercise and determine the best N value to present a network configuration with a balanced view of the cohesive cliques and division between those cliques.

In Figure 3.1, a two-clique analysis would produce two cliques—the clique of "Alice, Frank, George, Dennis, Claire, and Esther" and the clique of "Bob, Alice, Frank, and Claire." For each clique, a given pair of actors would be able to reach each other with a shortest path of no more than two steps. Compared with the one-clique result, this is more inclusive—everybody in the graph, including Bob and George, can find a clique to which they belong. Meanwhile, as the inclusiveness increases, the cohesiveness decreases. Many pairs of nodes in the two-cliques are not directly connected but have to go through an intermediary to reach each other.

3.4.3 Cliques in Directed Graphs

In directed graphs, standard clique definitions are even more rigid because not all ties in the network may be reciprocal. In addition to the conditions for cliques in undirected graphs that must be satisfied, cliques in directed graphs require nodes to have mutual or reciprocated ties between each pair. In Figure 3.3, we therefore only have one clique (Claire, Esther, and Dennis) because only there is each pair directly connected via reciprocated ties. Claire, Alice, and Frank, who were still a one-clique in the undirected network (see Figure 3.1), are no longer a clique because of the unreciprocated ties between Claire and Frank and between Alice and Frank.

The N-clique technique can also be applied to directed graphs by adding the requirement of mutuality or reciprocity of ties. For example, if we apply two-clique to analyze the directed graph in Figure 3.2, we will have one clique consisting of Esther, Dennis, Claire, and Alice. Alice is added to the original one-clique (Esther, Dennis, and Claire) as Alice has a mutual tie with Claire, who in turn has mutual ties with Esther and Dennis. Therefore, Alice is reachable within two steps via mutual ties with Esther and Dennis and directly connected with Claire. Much like the N-clique in undirected graphs, increasing the N value in the directed graphs raises its inclusiveness (the clique becomes bigger) but reduces its cohesiveness (the ties are more distant). Some alternative methods further relax the clique definition (see Knoke & Yang, 2008).

3.4.4 K-core

The original clique definition demanded that the members are *all directly* connected to each other. The N-clique definition relaxes this condition and allows the members to be *indirectly* connected. An alternative method to identify subgroups is the *K-core method* developed by Stephen Seidman (1983). A subset of actors is *K-core* if each actor in the subset is connected with at least K other actors in the group. This method thus relaxes the condition that *all* members need to be connected. The value of K is positively related to the restrictiveness of the subset; a high K value results in a highly restricted subgroup, whereas a low K value produces a less restrictive subgroup. Patrick Doreian and Katherine Woodard (1994) have combined K-core with expanding selection sampling to illustrate how the network sampling boundaries can vary based on the K value. In practice, this means that one includes an individual in the study only if he or she has been nominated by at least K others already sampled. By varying the K, researchers have a choice of producing a large and sparsely connected network (low K value) or a smaller and more connected network (high K value).

Doreian and Woodard (1994) recommended that researchers should apply low K value at the beginning to obtain much more inclusive network data. Once the initial network data are collected, more restricted network data can be obtained by successively applying high values of K. However, a trade-off exists between obtaining inclusive network data and logistic costs in data collection. The number of social actors needed for inclusion increases exponentially, not linearly, with lowering the K value. And interviewing a large number of respondents in each round of nomination is a costly and error-prone process.

Two notes of caution are in order regarding clique measurements: The previous clique definitions do not directly transfer to bipartite networks, making the ordinary algorithm to search cliques for those affiliation networks useless. Furthermore, computing software for clique analysis in directed graphs may adopt a variety of different algorithms, and the reader should therefore consult the manual beforehand.

3.5 Multidimensional Scaling (MDS) and Dendogram

3.5.1 MDS

Multidimensional scaling (MDS) is a visualization tool to map the distance between nodes in a network (Knoke & Yang, 2008; Kruskal & Wish, 1978; Wasserman & Stanley, 1994). The input data structure of multidimensional scaling is commonly a squared matrix, with entries indicating the distance/proximity between their corresponding nodes. The output of MDS is a spatial presentation, consisting of a geometric configuration of points. Normally the larger the similarities (or the smaller the dissimilarities) between nodes, the smaller the distance of them in the configuration map.

The building block of MDS is its simplest form: the two-dimensional (2D) scaling. If the data come with the form of a 2D plane, researchers need to first convert that into a squared matrix with the value suggesting proximity between the conjoint nodes. Assuming that we have five nodes, and their coordinates are displayed in a 2D plane, we would first produce the symmetric valued matrix using the following formula:

For a given pair of nodes between i and j, their Euclidean distance on a 2D plane is

$$d_{i,j} = \sqrt{\left(x_i - x_j\right)^2 + \left(y_i - y_j\right)^2} \tag{3.16}$$

Formula 3.16 can be used repeatedly for all the pairs that exist among the five nodes, which totals 10 dyadic pairs $\left(C_5^2 = \frac{5!}{2! \times 3!} = 10\right)$. Thus, we would have a matrix with the entries indicating the distances between the nodes

$$\begin{bmatrix} d_{1,1} & d_{1,2} & d_{1,3} & d_{1,4} & d_{1,5} \\ d_{2,1} & d_{2,2} & d_{2,3} & d_{2,4} & d_{2,5} \\ d_{3,1} & d_{3,2} & d_{3,3} & d_{3,4} & d_{3,5} \\ d_{4,1} & d_{4,2} & _{4,3} & d_{4,4} & d_{4,5} \\ d_{5,1} & d_{5,2} & d_{5,3} & d_{5,4} & d_{5,5} \end{bmatrix}$$

This matrix is a valued symmetric matrix with the diagonal values equal to 0:

$$d_{i,j} = d_{j,i}$$

$$d_{i,i} = 0$$

When this matrix is input into SNA software (such as UCINET) for MDS graphing, it will generate a map to show the proximities between the nodes. In addition to the mapping, the MDS function also produces a **stress indicator** (Knoke & Yang, 2008; Krustal & Wish, 1978). The stress indicator computes the discrepancies across all pairs between the observed matrix and the computed matrix:

$$\text{stress} = \sqrt{\frac{\Sigma\Sigma\left(f(x_{i,j}) - d_{i,j}\right)^2}{\text{scale}}} \qquad (3.17)$$

$f(x_{i,j})$ is the computed distance between a given pair, whereas $d_{i,j}$ is the observed Euclidean distance between the pair. The denominator of scale is a constraining factor to ensure the stress indicator is between 0 and 1. As the best-case scenario, the reproduced map perfectly replicates the original distance $f(x_{i,j}) = d_{i,j}$ for all pairs; the stress indicator would be 0. Conversely, when the reproduced distances between the pairs have sizable differences from their original Euclidean distances for all pairs, the stress indicator reaches 1. For this reason, the stress indicator is dubbed a "badness of fit" indicator, with the larger the value, the worse the replicated map in representing the original distances. Scholars (Kruskal & Wish, 1978) recommend the following guidelines in interpreting the stress indicator:

$0 \leq$ stress indicator ≤ 0.1	Excellent fit
$0.1 \leq$ stress indicator ≤ 0.2	Adequate fit
$0.2 \leq$ stress indicator ≤ 1	Poor fit

Many empirical studies have fruitfully applied MDS to uncover the patterns of association between social actors. Adam Slez and John Martin (2007) used MDS to map the states with regard to their voting similarity over time. Michael White, Ann Kim, and Jennifer Glick (2005) illustrated the social-spatial positions of 50 ethnic groups in Toronto, Canada. The biggest advantage of using MDS is that MDS allows the studies to map out all ethnicity groups simultaneously, as opposed to other conventional methods that isolate and analyze one group versus all other groups.

3.5.2 Dendogram: Method of Agglomerative Hierarchical Clustering

A **dendogram** is one type of visual presentation of applying the agglomerative hierarchical clustering to a social network dataset. Hierarchical clustering is an agglomerative method in which we start with individual nodes of a network and join them to form groups. The basic idea behind the hierarchical clustering is to define a measure of similarity or connection strength between nodes and then to join the closest or most similar nodes to form groups. One issue of using hierarchical clustering is how to define similarity; in practice, one common choice is using correlation coefficients, and another one is Euclidean distance. Once the similarity measure is chosen, we need to compute the measures for all pairs of nodes in a network and start the clustering processes. Some technical details further differentiate the hierarchical clustering into three types: single-, complete-, and average-linkage clustering. Dendograms visually depict the outcome of such agglomerative hierarchical clustering, in which nodes in a network are completely disconnected from each other at the beginning. Then pairs of nodes with the greatest similarities are joined to form groups; such grouping continues until the last stage in which all nodes are joined into one group, which terminates the process.

MDS and dendograms are often used in combination to show the overall network structure and the clustering or subgrouping in the network. In MDS, there is no differentiation of groups or cliques; dendograms thus complement MDS by identifying or isolating different cliques. One approach of such combined use of both is to draw a line at the dendogram that shows the snapshot of the clustering between the nodes, reflecting such clustering patterns in the MDS. The benefit of such an approach is that it provides a clear snapshot of the grouping in the network, whereas the drawback is that it is only a static picture, ignoring the dynamic processing of the agglomerative clustering. The second approach requires researchers to use some animation or simulation feature of some presentation software (such as customized animation in Microsoft PowerPoint®) to illustrate the agglomerative hierarchical clustering. Such an approach can show the dynamic process of clustering.

3.6 Structural Equivalence

3.6.1 Structural Equivalency

Structural equivalence is a social network method to analyze competitive relations between dyads, or pairs of nodes, in a given network. Two features are unique for structural equivalence analysis: (1) It is a method to measure and reflect competitive rather than cohesive relations between social actors, and (2) it operates at the level of pairs or dyads, rather than with individual actors, groups, or entire networks. Many social actors occupy social positions that are directly competitive with each other, such as two students advised by the same academic advisor, two vendors furnishing the same goods to the same retailer, or two farmers selling the same vegetable at the farmer's market. Actors in those positions are structurally equivalent with each other and are thus substitutes for each other. Suppose two card-making companies produce greeting cards for a big retailer (e.g., Wal-Mart): When one company withdraws from the supply, another company can pick up the slack, causing minimum disruption to the overall supply. The fact that they are substitutes is the primary reason behind the often-fierce competition observed between structurally equivalent dyads (Burt, 1992). From another perspective, Wal-Mart, connected to the disjoint card-making companies, occupies a structural hole (Burt, 1992), leveraging structural benefits by playing one social actor off another. If Wal-Mart is the only buyer of cards, the company can negotiate with all of its suppliers to strike the best deal from them, extracting high profits.

A pair of actors will be structurally equivalent if they have identical patterns of ties sent to and received from all the other network actors. More precisely, actors i and j are structurally equivalent if, for all actors k in the network, actor i sends a tie to actor k, if and only if actor j also sends a tie to k, and actor i receives a tie from actor k, if and only if actor j also receives a tie from actor k. Structural equivalence is determined by a pair of actors' relation with the rest of the actors in the network, independent of the presence or absence of a tie between the pair.

Nevertheless, the larger the network, the more pairs that need to be identical for two nodes to be structurally equivalent. Burt (1978) has therefore proposed to use Euclidean distance between the actors in a given pair and the remaining actors in a network to compute a continuous measure of how structurally similar a pair of actors is

$$D_{ij} = \sqrt{\sum_{k=1}^{g}\left[\left(X_{ik} - X_{jk}\right)^2 + \left(X_{ki} - X_{kj}\right)^2\right]} \quad i \neq j \neq k \qquad (3.18)$$

Formula 3.18 applies to binary directed graphs, producing an Euclidean distance between i and j that is larger or equal to 0 ($D_{ij} \geq 0$). When $D_{ij} = 0$, actors i and j are structurally equivalent because the patterns of connections between i and the other actors in the network, and between j and other actors in the network, are identical. When $D_{ij} \geq 0$, the pair of actors i and j are not structurally equivalent, and the greater the value, the greater the discrepancy between the patterns of the connection between i and the other actors in the network, and between j and the other actors in the network.

Applying Formula 3.18 to Figure 3.2, we find that the structural similarity score for the pair Bob and Alice is $\sqrt{3} = 1.73$. The ties of the two differ in three respects: Alice sends a tie to Frank and a tie to Claire (Bob does neither) and receives one from Claire (Bob again doesn't). This adds up to three (differences), from which the square root is taken:

$$\sqrt{\begin{aligned}&(X_{B,F} - X_{A,F})^2 + (X_{F,B} - X_{F,A})^2 + (X_{B,G} - X_{A,G})^2 + (X_{G,B} - X_{G,A})^2 + \\ &\quad (X_{B,D} - X_{A,D})^2 + (X_{D,B} - X_{D,A})^2 + (X_{B,C} - X_{A,C})^2 + \\ &\quad (X_{C,B} - X_{C,A})^2 + (X_{B,E} - X_{A,E})^2 + (X_{E,B} - X_{E,A})^2\end{aligned}}$$

This equation produces a result of 1.73 for the structural equivalence between Bob and Alice in Figure 3.2. Interested readers can compute the structural equivalence score for other pairs (e.g., between Alice and Dennis the score is 2.45). The social network software UCINET computes the structural equivalence for the entire network. One of its routines (Roles & Positions/Structural/Profile) produces a valued symmetric matrix to display the structural similarity between all pairs of a network. For example, Figure 3.3 has 7 actors, which has 21 pairs $\left(C_7^2 = \frac{7!}{2!5!} = 21 \right)$, each of which has a structural equivalence score. This matrix is symmetric because the structural equivalence is undirected (e.g., the structural similarity between Bob and Alice is the same as the structural similarity between Alice and Bob). The network in Figure 3.3 does not have a pair that is perfectly structural equivalent (no structural equivalence score equals 0). Nevertheless, there is gradation in structural equivalence between all the pairs in the network from low to high. The lowest scores are between Bob and Frank (1.41), and between Dennis and Esther (1.41), whereas the highest scores are between Alice and George, between Alice and Dennis, between Alice and Claire, and between Claire and George, all of which are 2.45. As structural similarity is inversely related to the competition between a pair, we would speculate that the competition between Bob and Frank and between Esther and Dennis is the highest, whereas the competition of those high-score pairs is the lowest.

Computing structural equivalence in undirected graphs is simpler than it is in directed graphs as the computation does not distinguish the direction. For a given pair of actors, examining the presence or absence of ties between each actor of the pair and the rest of the actors in a network would suffice for computing the structural equivalence between the pair:

$$D_{ij} = \sqrt{\Sigma_{k=1}^g \left[\left(X_{ik} - X_{jk} \right)^2 \right]} \quad i \neq j \neq k \tag{3.19}$$

Applying Formula 3.19 to Figure 3.1 produces the matrix of structural similarities for all pairs in the network. The lowest structural similarity score, hence, the highest level of competition, exists between Esther and Dennis (1.41), whereas the highest score, hence, the lowest competition, is present between Alice and Dennis (2.83) and between Bob and Dennis (2.83). It should be noted that although structural similarity or equivalence may indeed cause or indicate competition between the two actors, this is not a universal rule. The interpretation and consequences of structural equivalency depend very much on the nature of the network and its ties.

3.6.2 Regular Equivalency

Another way of relaxing the stringent requirements of structural equivalency has been proposed in Stephen Borgatti and Martin Everett (1992) and in Stephen Borgatti, Martin Everett, and Linton Freeman (2002). One of those alternatives is *regular equivalence*.

Actors are regularly equivalent if they have the same kinds of relations with actors that are also regularly equivalent. All mothers with children are regularly equivalent regardless of their numbers of offspring. In a hospital, the doctors are regularly equivalent in relation to their patients and nurses even though the numbers of patients and nurses per doctor differ. The generality of regular equivalence makes it one of the most important measures for sociologists attempting to capture social roles and positions.

To illustrate the difference between structural equivalence and regular equivalence, we borrow an artificial example from David Knoke and Song Yang (2008, p. 95)—an organizational hierarchical network shown in Figure 3.9. In this hierarchical structure, arrows suggest supervisory relations. For example, the CEO supervises three executives, who in turn supervise four middle managers, and so on. In this network, B and C are structurally equivalent as they supervise the same set of middle managers (F and G). But A is not structurally equivalent with B or C because A supervises different sets of middle managers (D and E). Nevertheless, the three executives (A, B, and C) are regularly equivalent as they all supervise middle managers. Along the same logic,

FIGURE 3.9 ● Artificial Hierarchy of an Organizational Formal Network

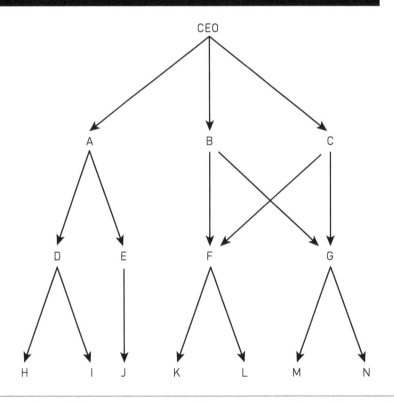

Note: Adapted from p. 95 of Knoke, D., & Yang, S. (2008). *Social network analysis* (2nd ed.). Thousand Oaks, CA: Sage.

middle managers D, E, F, and G are also regularly equivalent because they all supervise rank and file employees even though the numbers of their supervisees differ.

3.7 Two-Mode Networks and Bipartite Matrix

Two-mode networks are also called *bipartite graphs* or *bipartite networks*. In bipartite networks, nodes represent two distinctive sets of units. In addition to Galaskiewicz's (1985) bipartite network study of 26 CEOs and the 15 social clubs that they represent, substantive applications of bipartite networks are also exemplified in Linton Freeman, Kimball Romney, and Sue Freeman's (1987) study of nine faculty, student, and research colloquiums at a university campus, or the observation of regular beachgoers over 31 days to reveal the subgroups. The classic study of bipartite networks goes back to 1941 when Allison Davis and associates collected data on 18 southern women participating in 14 social events and discovered that the women clearly split into two camps (Davis, Gardner, & Gardner, 1941). Bipartite network studies are particularly useful for studying situations in which respondents cannot be interviewed or would be unlikely to report truthfully. In some cultures, respondents may feel compelled to report, e.g., friendship with everybody else in the same class or the same workplaces. In such a situation, observing actual behavior and co-attendance of events can help reveal the social structure of a group of classmates or co-workers.

A bipartite network can be converted to two different one-mode networks through matrix multiplication. The bipartite network of CEOs and social clubs in Galaskiewicz's (1985) study, for example, can be transformed into a one-mode network of 26 by 26 CEOs (linked through shared membership in a specific club) and into a one-mode network of 15 by 15 social clubs (linked by the fact that they have common members). Figure 3.10 shows a simple example for a bipartite graph, in which five individuals participated in three separate events. Joe joins the trip; Jane participates in all three events, the trip, the dinner, and the class; Joann and James only attend the class; and John only the trip.

The corresponding matrix of this bipartite graph is shown in Table 3.3. Participation of the individuals (in rows) at certain events (in columns) is indicated by "1," and non-participation is indicated by "0." For example, Jane participated in all three events, indicated by three "1s" in the matrix in her column. Joe joins the trip only, which is indicated by "1" in his column with "trip" and "0"s in his column with "dinner" and "class."

A **bipartite matrix**, representing a bipartite network, consists of g actors and h events, expressed as $g \times h$ matrix. If actor i attends event j, the entry at (i, j) would be 1; otherwise, the entry equals 0:

$$X_{i,j} = \begin{cases} 1 : \text{if actor } i \text{ attends event } j \\ 0 : \text{actor } i \text{ does not attend event } j \end{cases}$$

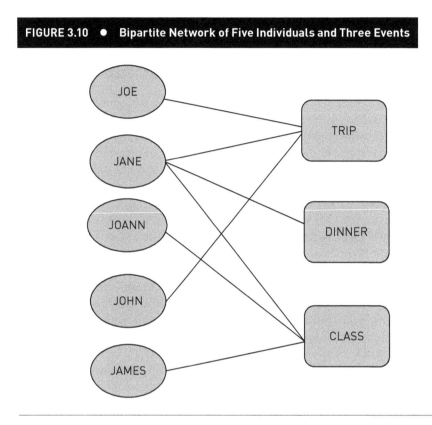

FIGURE 3.10 ● Bipartite Network of Five Individuals and Three Events

A bipartite matrix can be turned into a one-mode matrix to reveal the network structure between social actors or similarities between social events. Let's assume the matrix in Table 3.3 to be A, and A' is the transpose of the matrix A, which is shown in Table 3.4. Multiplying A with A' results in an adjacency matrix of the social network among the five actors (see also Table 3.5):

$$X^A = AA' = \begin{pmatrix} 100 \\ 111 \\ 001 \\ 100 \\ 001 \end{pmatrix} \begin{pmatrix} 11010 \\ 01000 \\ 01101 \end{pmatrix} = \begin{pmatrix} 11010 \\ 13111 \\ 01101 \\ 11010 \\ 01101 \end{pmatrix}$$

Note that the diagonal value of each actor in Table 3.5 equals the row margin of the actor in Table 3.3, in other words, the total number of events attended by

TABLE 3.3 ● Two-Mode Matrix of Five Actors and Three Events				
	Trip	**Dinner**	**Class**	**RM**
Joe	1	0	0	1
Jane	1	1	1	3
Joann	0	0	1	1
John	1	0	0	1
James	0	0	1	1
CM	3	1	3	7

Notes: RM: row margin—aggregating cell values within a given row across columns. CM: column margin—aggregating cell values within a given column across rows.

TABLE 3.4 ● Event-by-Actor Matrix (Transposed Matrix of Table 3.3)						
	Joe	**Jane**	**Joann**	**John**	**James**	**RM**
Trip	1	1	0	1	0	3
Dinner	0	1	0	0	0	1
Class	0	1	1	0	1	3
CM	1	3	1	1	1	7

Notes: RM: row margin—aggregating cell values within a given row across columns. CM: column margin—aggregating cell values within a given column across rows.

TABLE 3.5 ● Actor-by-Actor Matrix (Conversion From Two-Mode to One-Mode)					
	Joe	**Jane**	**Joann**	**John**	**James**
Joe	1	1	0	1	0
Jane	1	3	1	1	1
Joann	0	1	1	0	1
John	1	1	0	1	0
James	0	1	1	0	1

that actor. For example, Jane's diagonal value is 3 because she attends three events. The off-diagonal cells indicate the total number of events attended by both the row actor and the column actor. For example, Joe and Jane, and Joe and John, co-participate in one event. In this particular case, the off-diagonal values happen to be all 1, whereas in many empirical examples, the values do not have to be restricted between 1 and 0.

Multiplying A'A produces another matrix that reveals the network structure between the events, which is also shown in Table 3.6:

$$
X^E = A'A = \begin{pmatrix} 11010 \\ 01000 \\ 01101 \end{pmatrix} \begin{pmatrix} 100 \\ 111 \\ 001 \\ 100 \\ 001 \end{pmatrix} = \begin{pmatrix} 311 \\ 111 \\ 113 \end{pmatrix}
$$

X^E represents the event-by-event matrix, in which the off-diagonal values indicate the number of actors shared by the two events, and the diagonal values the total number of actors in that event. For example, three individuals (Joe, Jane, and John) join the trip, only one (Jane) participates in the dinner, and the class is attended by three (Jane, Joann, and James). The events "trip" and "dinner," "trip" and "class," and "dinner" and "class" each share one participant (Jane). The cells in this matrix can thus range from 0 to ∞ or however many individuals can participate in one event.

Some interesting statistics can be readily applied to the two computed matrices to yield additional information about the structures. Taking the mean of the diagonal values of the actor matrix would produce the average number of events attended by each actor $\left(\overline{X^A} = \frac{\Sigma_{i=1}^{g} x_{i,i}}{g} \right)$. Similarly, the mean of the diagonal values of the event matrix produces the average number of actors drawn to each event $\left(\overline{X^E} = \frac{\Sigma_{i=1}^{E} x_{i,i}}{E} \right)$. The two numbers for our example above are 7 / 5 = 1.4 and 7 / 3 = 2.33, respectively, suggesting that on average, each actor attends 1.4 events and each event draws 2.33 actors.

After converting the bipartite network into one-mode network, those one-mode networks (shown in Tables 3.5 and 3.6) can be subject to analyses with the measures discussed earlier, such as density, centrality, centralization, and cliques. One issue worth mentioning is that the one-mode matrix after converting from the two-mode/bipartite matrix is always undirected or symmetric as the event sharing or actor sharing does not distinguish between who is the sender and who is the receiver. Here, for simplicity, we presume that the resulting matrix is binary in applying the network measures.

Applying Formula 3.1 to the actor matrix in Table 3.5 and the event matrix in Table 3.6 produces 60% and 100%, respectively. For the actor matrix, it means that 60% of actor pairs co-participate in some events; for the event matrix, the density suggests 100% of pairs between events share participants. Other network measures can

TABLE 3.6 ● Event-by-Event Matrix (Conversion From Two-Mode to One-Mode)			
	Trip	**Dinner**	**Class**
Trip	3	1	1
Dinner	1	1	1
Class	1	1	3

be applied to analyze the bipartite matrices in the same way they are used for other one-mode networks, except that the bipartite two-mode network needs to be converted into the one-mode network before those methods can be applied (for details, see Faust, 1997).

Two-mode networks can be visualized in the same way as one-mode networks, for instance by using the routines provided by UCINET. By applying such routines (Visualize/ Netdrew, under Netdrew: File/Open/Ucinet dataset/2-mode network), we produce the diagram shown in Figure 3.11, the light grey square indicating the events, and the dark grey round indicating actors. It vividly depicts that the five actors are polarized into two camps: John and Joe in one camp (both attending the trip), and James and Joann in another camp (both attending the class). Jane is the most central actor for being the only one attending all three events and for being the bridge person between the two camps.

FIGURE 3.11 ● UCINET Visualization of Two-Mode Network in Figure 3.10

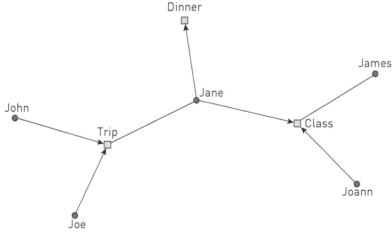

End-of-Chapter Questions

The following questions pertain to the graph (binary directed) shown in Figure 3.12.

FIGURE 3.12   ●   Artificial Communication Network Among Eight Individuals

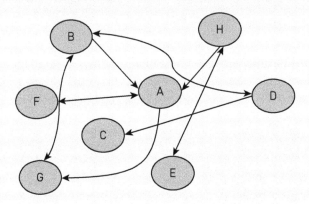

1. Present the graph/network in adjacency matrix format.

2. Compute the density for the graph.

3. Compute centrality (in-degree and out-degree) for all nodes and centralization (in-degree and out-degree) for the entire network.

4. Could you identify any one-clique and two-clique from the graph?

5. Could you use UCINET to produce the MDS for the graph?

6. Compute the structural equivalence for all pairs in the network.

The following question pertains to the graph (bipartite) shown in Figure 3.13.

1. Figure 3.13 displays a bipartite graph in which six actors participate in two separate events (parties). Convert the graph into an actor-based matrix (X^A) as well as into an event-based matrix (X^E). If co-participation between actors suggests friendship, could you detect who are friends?

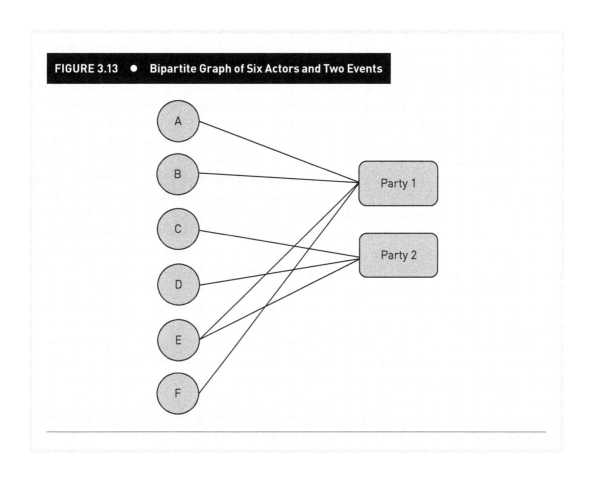

FIGURE 3.13 ● Bipartite Graph of Six Actors and Two Events

4

Inferential Methods in Social Network Analysis

●

Learning Objectives

- Explain how permutation is used for inferential statistics in social network analysis

- Discuss the underlying process of QAP correlation when examining the relations between two matrices/graphs

- Demonstrate the QAP regression when using UCINET to predict one outcome matrix with multiple explanatory matrices

- Examine the theoretical assumptions, the history, and development for ERGM

- Explain the three aspects that ERGM looks at when explaining network ties in a full network

- Construct the ERGM statistical modeling when using ERGM to investigate a given network with the three exogenous aspects

- Interpret the coefficients, standard errors, and model statistics in ERGM outputs generated by SIENA 3.0

The previous chapter discussed descriptive methods in social network analysis. But often we would like to know whether a feature in the network (e.g., a high level of centralization) is indeed as unusual as we first may think. We would thus like to conduct a test of statistical significance. This chapter presents two methods to conduct such tests: quadratic assignment procedure (QAP) and exponential random graph modeling (ERGM).

4.1 Permutation and QAP (Quadratic Assignment Procedure) Correlation

The descriptive statistics of social network analysis provide us with measures that describe the particular network that is being studied. But often we would also like to understand what that particular network tells us about other, similar networks that we have not measured. One major branch in classical statistics, inferential statistics, deals with such questions.

To assess a descriptive statistical measure, we often want to know whether a specific feature could also have come about by pure chance. Four tests for statistical significance are commonly used in such a situation: chi-square test, z test, t test, and F ratio test. Each test follows a very similar logic, computing the probability (p) that the null hypothesis (= 0) is true. When the probability that the null hypothesis is true is very low (a commonly chosen threshold is $p < .05$), we reject the null hypothesis in favor of our research hypothesis that the relation between variables under investigation is significant. Applying such significant tests to social network analysis is problematic, however (Borgatti, Everett, & Johnson, 2013, chap. 8). Most significance tests presume that the units of analysis are independent of each other, which is exactly contrary to the assumption of interdependence between cases in social network data. In network data, each node's action not only affects its relations with other nodes in the network, but also it exerts ripple effects to other nodes in the same network. This interdependence, thus, runs counter to the independence assumption in conventional statistics. Another problem pertains to the sampling process—in conventional social surveys, samples are drawn randomly from a given population in an effort to represent the population to the greatest accuracy. For any variable drawn from a sample, normal distribution is assumed, although a deviation from such assumption does not necessarily cause significant estimation bias (Allison, 1999). In social networks, however, data are rarely randomly sampled. Either they represent the entire population or the sampling distribution is unknown. Under those constraints, some novel methods are needed to produce the sampling distribution for social network data and to infer from them the significance level of test statistics. One proposed solution is the randomization or permutation test.

4.1.1 Permutation

Permutation is a nonparametric approach, which does not rely on the assumption that the data are drawn from a given probability distribution. In mathematics, permutation is a complete rearrangement of a set of numbers. For example, permutation of three numbers (3, 6, 9) produces a total of 3! = 6 distinctive sets of numbers.

$$(3, 6, 9)$$
$$(3, 9, 6)$$
$$(6, 3, 9)$$
$$(6, 9, 3)$$
$$(9, 3, 6)$$
$$(9, 6, 3)$$

A permutation of N numbers produces $N!$ distinctive sets of numbers. For social network data, permutation involves rearranging nodes within a given network structure. Permutation of social network data does not change the structure of the network; rather, it permutes the row and column of nodes in the network. Figure 4.1 shows a permuted graph from the original graph shown in Figure 3.1. Note that the network structure between the two graphs stays the same, but the positions of the nodes are changed.

The general logic of permutation is to compare the actual network data, or observed graph, against a distribution of randomly produced permuted graphs. The permutation test essentially calculates all randomly permuted graphs and counts the proportion of random assignments yielding the same network statistic as the observed

FIGURE 4.1 • Permuted Graph of Figure 3.1

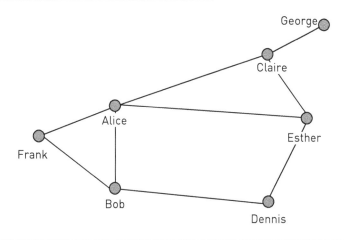

graphs. This is the "*p* value" or the significance of the test. Therefore, the higher the *p*, the more likely the observed statistic occurs because of random chance. Conversely, the lower the *p*, the higher our confidence that the observed statistic is not due to random chance. Thus, the interpretation of the *p* under permutation is similar to that of *p* in other inferential significance tests, although the underlying logic is different. The conventional threshold of significance (i.e., $p < .05$) is therefore also often applied, which suggests that the probability that the observed statistic occurs by chance is lower than 5%.

4.1.2 Quadratic Assignment Procedure (QAP)

Quadratic Assignment Procedure (QAP) was developed by Krackhardt (1987), and its logic draws from that of the permutation test. The following (non-network) example may illustrate the logic: Suppose a researcher is interested in the correlation between a number of times a student visits a professor's office and the student's grade in the class. And based on the data, he finds the correlation coefficient between the two variables to be .68. To test whether his finding is statistically significant, the researcher designs a method to set the two variables apart, independent of each other. He may have a box with many pieces of paper on which class grades are written. He then asks students to pick up pieces of paper with different grades. Thus, the office-hour visits and the grade attainments are totally independent of each other. He may repeat the processes many times; each time he calculates the correlation between the office-hour visits and the grades picked from the box. Eventually, he would have a distribution of those correlations, some of which are higher than .68, some lower, and some the same. The relevant question to test whether the correlation of .68 is significant is as follows:

What proportion of all the correlations from the random experiments are the same or higher than the one observed (.68)? If the proportion is high, say, $p = 40\%$, he would conclude that the correlation between office-hour visits and the total grades received is probably by chance, which means it is not statistically significant. Conversely, if the proportion is low, e.g., smaller than 5%, he would conclude that the probability of observing such a large correlation coefficient from the experiments is low and that the correlation between the two variables is statistically significant.

Now let's assume that we instead observe two networks among the same actors—a formal network of who reports to whom and an informal network of who seeks advice from whom. Are individuals who report to a specific superior also more likely to seek his or her advice? QAP tests this hypothesis in a very similar manner as the researcher in the example above. First, the QAP calculates the Pearson's correlation coefficient (r) between the two original matrices, treating the computed coefficient as the observed coefficient. Second, the QAP procedure permutes one of the matrices by rearranging both its rows and columns. Note that at this step, the permutation does not change the network structure of the matrix B; it changes the position of each node in the network through rearranging. So the network structural properties are preserved as the structure stays unchanged. Third, the permuted matrix from B is correlated with the original matrix of matrix A, producing a new Pearson's correlation coefficient (r) between the two matrices. Fourth, step two and step three are repeated at least a thousand times—or more if the researcher wants to be sure of the outcome. Last, the observed correlation coefficient from the first step is compared with the distribution of the coefficients generated from step 4 to determine the proportion among the coefficients from the permuted matrices that are equivalent or higher than the observed coefficient. If the proportion is high, the observed correlation between the two network matrices, that is, between reporting to a person and seeking his or her advice, is probably due to chance. In contrast, if the proportion is below conventional threshold levels (e.g., $p < .05$, .01, or .001), the observed correlation coefficient is considered to be statistically significant.

To illustrate, we created another matrix shown in Table 4.1 of the gender matching between dyads that were shown in Table 3.1. We speculate based on the first names that Bob, Frank, George, and Dennis are men, whereas Alice, Claire, and Esther are women. So, in the cells connecting the row and column, if the cell person and the column person have the same gender, the entry would be 1. Otherwise, the entry is 0. By using the UCINET QAP correlation (Tools/Testing Hypotheses/Dyadic (QAP)/ QAP Correlation), we obtain the QAP correlation coefficient between the two matrices (Table 3.1 and Table 4.1) that is .03, at a significance level of .5665. The default permutation is 5,000 times; we increase that to 50,000 times and obtain a very similar result (QAP correlation = 2.78%, $p = .5734$). Both rounds produce results that are weak and insignificant, suggesting that gender is not a significant factor affecting the formation of relations between the pairs. Such an insignificant result is probably due to the small network size under investigation.

TABLE 4.1 ● Gender Matching of the Matrix From Table 3.1							
	Bob	**Alice**	**Frank**	**George**	**Dennis**	**Claire**	**Esther**
Bob	0	0	1	1	1	0	0
Alice	0	0	0	0	0	1	1
Frank	1	0	0	1	1	0	0
George	1	0	1	0	1	0	0
Dennis	1	0	1	1	0	0	0
Claire	0	1	0	0	0	0	1
Esther	0	1	0	0	0	1	0

4.1.3 QAP Regression

The difference between **QAP regression** and **QAP correlation** is similar to that between linear OLS regression and correlation. In QAP regression, researchers must conceptually and operationally distinguish between a dependent matrix and independent matrices. As in a regular multiple regression scenario, the independent matrices are held constant of each other while examining each matrix's net effect on the dependent variable matrix.

To illustrate, we use empirical network data from surveys on friendship formation among graduate students (see Morimoto & Yang, 2013, for details on the study). We only present a small sample of 11 graduates in Figure 4.2.

The nodes, which represent the students, are distinguished by their shape (square = men, circle = women) and sizes (big = domestic, small = international). At first glance, gender does not seem to influence tie formation: The three male students are scattered and mingled with the eight female students. Nevertheless, the domestic/international status of the students seems to be dividing the students. The two international students occupy marginal positions, especially the international male student, who is in a peripheral location at the far right. The international female student is a bit more integrated but still in a relatively marginal position. But a mere visualization is not sufficient to examine rigorously the effects and the significance of each independent variable on the dependent variable. For that purpose, we use QAP regression. We regress the friendship formation matrix on the matrices of gender (1: same gender, 0: different gender) and domestic/international status (same = 1, different = 0). Gender does not affect the friendship formation: its t statistic is .346, which is larger than our threshold ($p > .05$). Domestic/international status seems to be a significant factor ($t = 1.968$, $p < .05$). The odds for nominating a friend

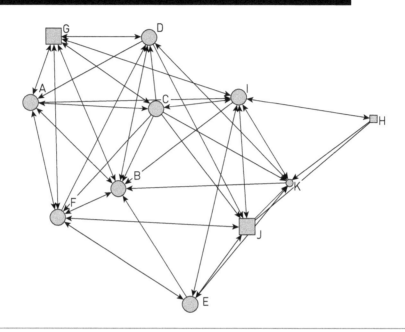

FIGURE 4.2 • Friendship Network Among 11 Graduate Students

with the same status is 228% (exponential of (1.19) = 3.28) higher than it is for the opposite status. Such a result correlates with the visual inspection of the separation between domestic and international students, in which international students are connected to each other, but only to a few domestic students, who in turn are highly interconnected.

Two interesting features of QAP are worth mentioning here. One is that QAP regression has a variety of different models. Researchers can use QAP to explain or to predict one type of tie with predictors of other types of ties or nodal attributes, or both, although in our example we only use nodal attributes (gender and international status) to explain friendship formation. By resorting to QAP regression, Borgatti et al. (2013) used Krackhardt's (1987) network data between managers to predict the advice-seeking network with predictors such as friendship and reporting network. Perhaps the QAP regression with both types of independent variables, the dyadic relations and nodal attributes, is the most commonly used model. Another feature with QAP is that its randomization significant test does not create generalizability in the common statistical sense. In our example, domestic/international status is a significant factor explaining friendship ties, which suggests that the two variables are probably not independent of each other. Nevertheless, it does not "correct" the fact that the sample does not result from random selection of students of all classrooms.

4.2 P* or Exponential Random Graph Model (ERGM)

The exponential random graph model (ERGM)/P* attempts to explain how and why social network ties arise. The main goal of ERGMs is to understand a given observed network, that is, the empirical network measured by researchers, and to obtain insight into the underlying process that creates and sustains its ties. ERGMs represent a network (graph G) through various network statistics or characteristics that make specific formations or ties more likely, such as mutuality, or transitivity. An ERGM assigns probability to graphs according to the following statistics (Lusher, Koskinen, & Robins, 2012, p. 9):

$$P_\theta(G) = ce^{\theta_1 Z_1(G) + \theta_2 Z_2(G) + \dots + \theta_p Z_p(G)} \tag{4.1}$$

Formula 4.1 stipulates that the probability of observing the specific network G is given by the sum of network statistics (the Zs in the expression, which are similar to the variables in conventional multiple regression), weighted by the parameters (the s) in the exponential function, in which c is a normalizing constant. Those network statistics exemplify a set of network configurations, which are small local subgraphs in the network. The parameter attached to each configuration informs us of the importance of the configuration.

Exponential random graph modeling results from several dedicated studies on this issue, accumulated over the last 20 years (Lusher et al., 2012). In the following sections, we discuss the ERGM theory, ERGM history, its explanatory framework, details in statistical modeling, ERGM data structure, and an application of ERGM using a dataset on friendship formation in multiple classrooms.

4.2.1 ERGM Theory

ERGM premises are a set of theoretical assumptions regarding the emergent social network among social actors (Lusher et al., 2012, p. 10):

1. Social networks are locally emergent.

2. Network ties are influenced by endogenous factors such as self-organization, as well as by exogenous factors such as actor attributes, and other covariates.

3. The patterns within networks are evidence for ongoing structural processes.

4. Multiple processes can operate simultaneously.

5. Social networks are structured and stochastic.

Stating that social networks are locally emergent amounts to asserting that the common social network phenomena like reciprocity, transitivity, and homophily influence the tie formation process. More specifically, it assumes ties are formed as a result of actors' decisions, and that the network structure is thus a result of individual choices. In ERGM, those assumptions are explicitly modeled to explain the formation of the entire network. Endogenous factors refer to "lower level" configurations such as reciprocity and transitivity, in other words, the concept that the presence of one tie influences the formation of other ties. The interdependence of network ties and their roles in network formation are well understood in sociological literature (White, Boorman, & Breiger, 1976), but they have in practice been largely ignored by many other forms of statistical analysis.

ERGM includes those interdependencies of network ties, represented in various network configurations that explain the overall network structures, and measures their respective importance in the network formation process. In addition, ERGM can also account for actor attributes, representing them as exogenous factors in the models. Such combined examination of multiple processes operating simultaneously in explaining the overall network structure is a distinctive advantage of ERGM. For example, when it comes to friendship formation in a classroom, multiple processes can occur: Endogenous factors such as reciprocity, transitivity (friends of my friends are my friends), popularity (the more popular an actor is, the more likely he or she is going to attract even more friends), as well as exogenous factors such as actor-level attributes (age, sex, race, etc.). ERGM can even control for other covariate networks when explaining the dependent network structural ties, providing a comprehensive explanatory model.

4.2.2 ERGM History

Statistical analysis of networks was conducted as early as the 1930s with Jacob Moreno and Helen Jennings comparing the observed social network data with the one expected under the null hypothesis, an approach that is analogous to conventional inferential statistics, such as chi-square or t test. Such an approach was imitated by many other studies, later called biased network theory (Rapoport, 1953, 1957), models for randomness (Erdos & Renyi, 1959), and Bernoulli graph distribution (Frank, 1981).

Research that is directly related to the ERGM traces back to Paul Holland and Samuel Leinhardt's (1981) statistical model of dyadic independence, which was dubbed the p_1 model. The p_1 model can be implemented in the standard log-linear fashion: Its units of observation are all the possible dyads in a network, and the dependent variable is the presence or value of the tie between the pair. Nevertheless, the independence assumption inherent in the log-linear model is problematic: Without further modification, the model, for instance, assumes that the presence of a tie in dyad A-B does not influence the chance of a tie being present in dyad B-C. But as node B is part of both pairs, it seems possible that B's decision to form, establish, or maintain a tie with A affects the tie formation with C as well. To take account of such interdependence, Ove Frank and David Strauss (1986) proposed to apply spatial statistical models to the social network domain. Yet, this Markov random graph model remained a theoretical discussion until Stanley Wasserman and Philippa Pattison (1996) demonstrated the applications of the model on various social network data structures.

The recent decade witnessed further developments in implementing the ERGM theories in actual network research. Those new developments in ERGM were implemented in several programs, in particular, PNet, RSiena, and a series of other R packages such as statnet.

4.2.3 Explanatory Framework

When explaining network ties in the full network, ERGM looks at three aspects: (1) the network self-organization, (2) the actor's attributes, and (3) the covariate variable(s) that need to be controlled for. Network self-organization refers to the dependency of ties within the network analyzed, and for that reason is also called the endogenous effect or, purely, the structural effect. Network self-organization can be degree based, such as popularity, an effect in which high-degree actors are likely to form even more ties. Such an effect is called preferential attachment or the Matthew effect in social science literature (Barabási & Albert, 1999). In directed networks, the same self-organization effect is called the "activity effect"—actors who are very active in a network and tend to send out even more ties. The corresponding effect for incoming ties is also called "popularity." Self-organization can also materialize in network closure or transitivity, a tendency of two actors connected to the same third actor to form a tie between them as well. In directed networks, triadic closure takes on different forms, depending on the direction of the ties. An illustration of those network self-organizational configurations is shown in Figure 4.3.

Individual attributes operate to affect the tie formation in the overall social network via two mechanisms. First, the human propensity to select others similar to oneself is well documented in social network literature (McPherson, Smith-Lovin, & Cook, 2001). This phenomenon of "birds of a feather flock together" is dubbed homophily in social science and occurs in online social networks (Barbera, 2014). Homophily can be based on many dimensions, such as age, race, gender, religion, and national origins, and it materializes in many different social settings. Second, individual attributes matter in the overall activity in tie formation. For example, women tend to be more active in friendship and social life than men. Such predispositional differences in network tie formation need to be controlled for to examine the effects of other factors. ERGM accounts for those individual attributes, treating them as exogenous.

The third aspect of variation that ERGM can account for are covariate matrices that may interfere with the relation between the key independent variables and the dependent social network graph. For example, a friendship formation in a classroom may co-vary with the previous friendship networks formed in kindergarten, in addition to effects from individual attributes and endogenous self-organizational processes. A statistical model that does not account for all variables that may co-vary with the dependent variable runs the risk of producing biased estimates for the importance of variables included in the equation. The ERGM's ability to include a comprehensive set of covariates when examining the underlying patterns of network tie formations, thus, presents a distinct advantage.

FIGURE 4.3 ● Configurations of Self-Organization

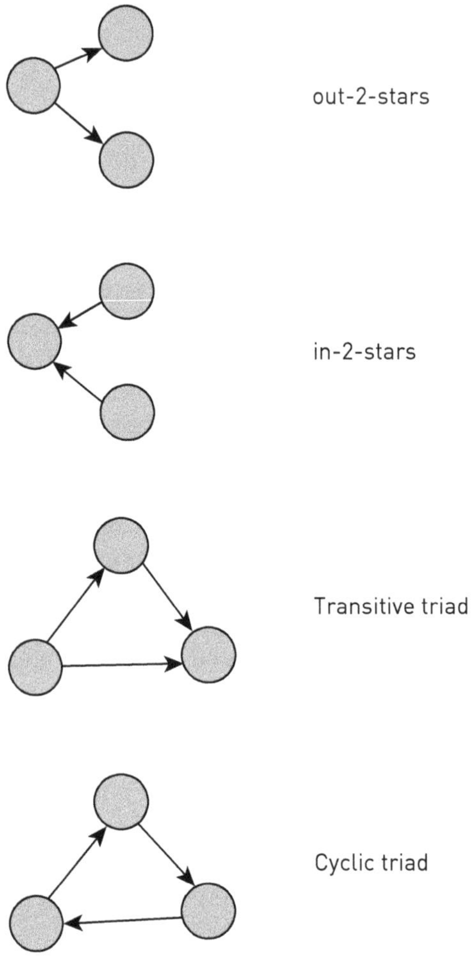

out-2-stars

in-2-stars

Transitive triad

Cyclic triad

4.2.4 Statistical Modeling with Exponential Random Graphs

ERGM investigates the observed network and tests whether particular network structures are significantly more common than would be expected by chance. A nonparametric statistical technique to address this question is to simulate a large number of random graphs and compare the count of those network structures in simulated random graphs with that in the actual observed network. The distribution of the counts in the simulated random networks is called *sampling distribution*, which is analogous to the conventional sampling distribution in parametric statistics. The count in the observed network structure is then compared with that of the sampling distribution, which in turn produces statistics, such as confidence intervals and significance levels of the observed network structures.

Let's take as an example a network with 38 nodes and 146 connections (found in Lusher et al., 2012, p. 31). Of those 146 connections, 44 are reciprocated ties, but in the sampling distribution of 1,000 simulated random graphs, the average number of the reciprocated ties is 6. The observed number of 44 thus lies in the far extreme of the sampling distribution, and it is extremely unlikely to have come about by chance. We would thus conclude that the observed graph contains a significantly higher number of reciprocated ties than would occur at random. The analogous procedure can be implemented for a wide array of network configurations. One problem with this particular simulation approach is that it can only assess each configuration separately from one other. In reality, those lower level configurations often contribute to the formations of high-level configurations. For example, increased reciprocity or homophily in a network may result in increased transitivity, which in turn produces more clique structures.

The ERGM sampling process runs in a fashion exactly opposite to that in the process discussed earlier in that instead of looking for the extreme cases for the observed graph, it tries to find a distribution of graphs in which the observed graph is the center of the distribution. Basically the ERGM program will fit the model by estimating parameters. For a finite set of nodes, a sampling distribution of ties between the nodes can be very large. In particular, for a network with size N, the total possible arrangement for possible network states is as follows: Let's start with the simplest network with only 2 nodes, which would have $2^{2(1)} = 4$ network states, which are shown in

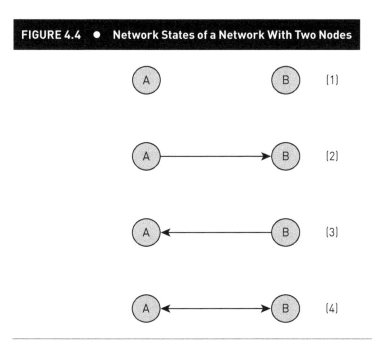

FIGURE 4.4 • Network States of a Network With Two Nodes

Figure 4.4. A network with 3 nodes would have 64 different states ($2^{3(2)} = 64$). The number becomes extremely large with a very slight increase in the size of the network—a network with merely 5 nodes would have $2^{20} = 1,048,576$ states. Simulating all possible states of a large network thus requires powerful computers and fast algorithms. For the distribution of the graphs, ERGM assigns a probability to each realization of the random graphs, so that the observed graph is in the center, not the periphery, of this distribution of random graphs.

Although an ERGM is not a logistic regression, drawing such an analogy may help the reader interpret its results. Much like logistic regression, ERGM has statistics, parameters, and standard errors for the parameters. Statistics are predictors of the presence/absence of ties in the dependent graph. In ERGM, those predictors are (a) network self-organizational configurations that are treated as endogenous explanatory factors, (b) actors' attributes that are exogenous factors, and (c) covariate network factor(s). Parameters in the ERGM indicate the importance of each explanatory variable in the model, much like their counterparts in conventional regression analysis. Standard errors delimit the confident intervals of the parameters, informing us of the significance level of each explanatory factor.

4.2.5 ERGM Data Structure and Application: Classroom Friendship Formation

Most ERGM functions found in the *R* packages pertain to full network data in a binary adjacency matrix format. Although some packages deal with weighted or valued networks or networks in which multiple ties exist between the same dyad, the most common features are available only for directed and undirected binary graphs. ERGMs have been mostly applied to cross-sectional data, although analyses of longitudinal (Snijders & Koskinen, 2012), bipartite (Wang, 2013), or even multilevel data (Lubbers & Snijders, 2007) are becoming increasingly common. Actor attributes in ERGM can be nominal, ordinal, or interval/ratio variables.

To illustrate the application of ERGM, we use the same dataset as the one used in the QAP regression earlier. The 11 MA students have a diverse background. Eight of them are female students; and three are male. Two are from India, whereas the rest are Caucasian. Four of the 11 students are in their early 20s, directly from their undergraduate training; 5 of them are in their 30s, coming back to school after a few years of work experiences; and 2 of them are older than 40 years old. The age variable is thus ordinal (1: 20s; 2: 30s, and 3: older than 40), and race and sex variables are nominal.

The overall density for the graph is 51.80%. The centralization for both in-degree and out-degree is 34.44%, suggesting moderate variability in the distribution of in-degree and out-degree friendship formations. At each level, we have in-degree (popularity) and out-degree (expansionism) measures, which are shown in Table 4.2. Student B, a White woman in her 30s, seems to be most popular among her peers, and receives the most nominations (8). Students C and I, both White women in their 40s and 50s, are most likely to nominate others as their friends, and thus have the highest score of 8. At the other end in both cases is the Indian male student, with in-degree 1 and out-degree 3.

TABLE 4.2 ● Statistics of the 11 Students in the Friendship Network

Student	Gender/Race/Age	In-degree	Out-degree	Net in-degree
A	White woman 30s	6	5	1
B	White woman 30s	8	4	4
C	White woman 50s	3	8	−5
D	White woman 20s	5	4	1
E	White woman 30s	4	5	−1
F	White woman 20s	6	6	0
G	White man 20s	6	6	0
H	Asian man 30s	1	3	−2
I	White woman 40s	7	8	−1
J	White man 20s	7	3	4
K	Asian woman 30s	4	5	−1

TABLE 4.3 ● ERGM of Friendship Formation of a Class With SIENA 3.0

Explanatory Variables	Purely Structural Effect (Endogenous Model)	Actor Attribute Effect (Exogenous Model)	Complete Model
Reciprocity	**1.86* (0.63)**	—	**1.88* (0.64)**
Transitive triplets	0.04 (0.08)	—	0.01 (0.09)
In-2-stars	0.69 (0.60)	—	0.63 (0.59)
In-3-stars	−0.15 (0.16)	—	−0.13 (0.16)
Gender	—	0.03 (0.41)	−0.02 (0.33)
Race	—	**1.14* (0.43)**	0.61 (0.40)
Age	—	−0.03 (0.41)	0.01 (0.38)

Note: Bold fonts indicate statistical significant factors, * P < .05.

Table 4.3 shows the ERGM of the class friendship formation with SIENA 3.0. We run three models separately from each other to see each aspect's (e.g., self-organization and individual attributes) effect on the observed graph. In the purely structural model, reciprocity is a significant factor influencing the formation of friendship. In particular, the odds for reciprocity to occur is 542% ($\exp^{(1.86)} - 1 = 542$) greater than what would be expected at random after taking into account the influence of the other three structural configurations. Note that, as in any regression, if the value of the coefficient is greater than roughly twice the value of standard error, the effect is significant (Lusher et al., 2012, p. 43).

The second model is the actor attribute model, regressing the formation of ties on actor attribute similarities on gender, race, and age. "Race" seems to be a significant factor for friendship formation, which coincides with our findings from the QAP regression on the same dataset. But because the only two non-White students are international students from India, the homophily could also occur along the division of international versus domestic students or cultural and linguistic differences. The first time we ran this model, we received an error message telling us that the model did not converge. Such an error message means that the estimations are too far from the maximum likelihood estimate (MLE) to be appropriate, and repeating the estimation procedure is warranted (Lusher et al., 2012, p. 154). The second attempt (shown in Table 4.3) converged.

The last model includes both the self-organizational process of pure structural effects and actor attribute effects. Only one factor is significant: reciprocity. The significant effect from race/international/cultural/linguistic division disappears, suggesting that the inclusion of the structural effects explains away the effects from racial disparity. In other words, once we take into account the propensity of individuals to reciprocate, actors don't seem to be more likely to form ties with actors with the same background. Thus, our conclusion is somewhat different from that of the QAP regression earlier. This is not an unusual occurrence: Models like QAP regression that do not account for more complex structural processes often overestimate the effect of actor attributes. The capability to account simultaneously for the structural effects, the actor effects, and covariate effects is a unique feature that makes ERGM a superior method to explain and detect underlying patterns in social networks.

End-of-Chapter Questions

1. Display the full permutation of the four numbers (2, 4, 6, 8).

2. Explain in general how such permutation can be used for inferential statistics in social network analysis.

3. Assuming we have data on friendship between a group of students, and their co-adviser (two or more students share one adviser), describe how we can use QAP correlation offered through UCINET to examine the correlation between the two matrices.

4. Continuing from the previous example, assume we have two more matrices depicting relations between the group of students. One matrix is racial similarity, and the other is gender similarity. Describe how we can use QAP regression offered through UCINET to explain the friendship network with the three explanatory matrices: gender, racial, and advisor matrices.

5. Explain what ERGM is, and why we need it. What are the theoretical assumptions of ERGM?

6. ERGM is developed to explain the dyadic interactions in an observed graph with factors exogenous to the observed graph. What is the main difference between ERGM implemented through SIENA, PNet,

or *R* and dyadic model simulated via SPSS? What are the three aspects of explanatory variables ERGM looks at while attempting to account for the observed graph?

7. Table 4.4 shows three artificial networks: friendship, classmate, and dorm-mate relationships among five students. Use any software capable of running ERGM to explain the friendship network with the classmate and the dorm-mate network matrices. Also interpret your results.

TABLE 4.4 ● Artificial Dataset About Friendship, Classmate, and Dorm-Mate Among Five Students

Dependent Matrix	Friendship among 5 students				
	A	B	C	D	E
A	0	1	1	0	1
B	1	0	0	0	1
C	1	0	0	1	0
D	0	0	1	0	0
E	1	1	0	0	0
Independent Matrix I	Classmate among the 5 students				
A	0	1	1	0	0
B	1	0	0	1	1
C	1	0	0	0	0
D	0	1	0	0	1
E	0	1	0	1	0
Independent Matrix II	Dorm-mate among the 5 students				
A	0	1	0	1	0
B	1	0	0	0	0
C	0	0	0	1	1
D	1	0	1	0	1
E	0	0	1	1	0

5

Social Network Analysis of Work and Organizations

Learning Objectives

- Explain when and why weak ties matter, as well as when and why strong ties help when people use social networks to look for jobs

- Examine the differences between Chinese Guanxi interpersonal networks and Western interpersonal networks, and how such differences affect people's use of personal networks to facilitate their job searches

- Discuss the differences between social cohesive networks that exhibit social closure and social competitive networks that exhibit a structural hole

- Demonstrate how social closure and structural holes facilitate career advancement for men and women differently

- Appraise why and how informal networks such as advice-seeking and friendship networks among co-workers may have significant impact on an organization's power structure

- Describe the antecedent factors and consequences of inter-organizational interlocking and strategic alliances

- Assess the differences between forward vertical integration and backward vertical integration, and give examples of each

Work and organizations are essential components to an economy, and the study of these two components is massive, drawing from the diverse disciplines of economics, management sciences, and sociology. In this chapter, we discuss social network studies of labor markets, intra-organizational networks, and inter-organizational relations. In labor market analyses, we focus on person-job matching, describing how social networks help job seekers find desirable jobs and help employers fill vacancies with qualified candidates. In intra-organizational networks, we examine how individuals can use personal networks to advance their careers, as well as how inter-personal networks within organizations affect the power structure of those organizations and their employees' work attitudes. Intra-organizational ties also include relationships between subunits and different departments. We discuss how organizations can achieve synergies by facilitating knowledge transfers between different internal units, which in turn can lead to innovation and high performance.

In inter-organizational relations, we describe two common forms of linkage between organizations: interlocking board directorates and strategic alliances. We investigate the antecedent factors to the formations of inter-organizational relations, as well as their consequences. We also discuss the inter-organizational relations in the context of industries such as within industrial alliances as opposed to cross-industrial partnerships.

5.1 Personal Connections and Labor Market Processes

One of the key processes in the labor market is person-job matching, in which job candidates seek out information and opportunities to obtain desirable positions. It is also a process that employers use to identify and recruit top talent to fill their job openings. In classical labor economics, such a process is automatic—the invisible hand of the market will make adjustments, depending on the demands and supplies of the candidates and the available job vacancies. When candidates outnumber jobs, the pay for a job will go down, causing a decrease of candidates to the point that the market returns to a balance (equilibrium) between supply and demand. Conversely, when jobs outnumber candidates, the pay for a job will go up, which stimulates the supply of candidates to the point that the market reaches equilibrium.

Sociologists heavily criticize such an approach, contending that such automatic person-job matching is an exception, not the rule. Often, jobs are distributed unequally among job seekers, and employers must use different strategies to recruit well-trained candidates. Personal connections and inter-personal networks, such as Guanxi in China, exert significant influences in the process of job searching for job seekers and candidate recruitment for employers. The following sections discuss some of the sociological analyses mentioned earlier. Be prepared. Some findings may be surprising to you!

5.1.1 Social Networks and Job Searches

Perhaps the most important aspect of the labor market process in advanced economies such as the ones in the United States or Europe is information distribution. For employers, information distribution focuses on disseminating their hiring ads to as many job seekers as possible. For job seekers, information distribution focuses on obtaining that pertinent information and submitting their materials to the right targets. Sometimes, job seekers take the initiative to post their ready-for-hire ads on mass media (newspapers, online job banks, or association webpages) or on their personal network sites, such as Facebook or LinkedIn. One key to this information diffusion is the recognition that it is a social process and that it happens in human society where interpersonal networks are dense, rich, dynamic, and versatile. Granted that with cutting edge technology such as the Internet and smartphone apps, information distribution is much faster and widespread than it was in pre-Internet days, the most effective way for job seekers, as well as employers, to distribute information is still simply messages passed through interpersonal networks.

Mark Granovetter (1973) interviewed professional, technical, and managerial (PTM) employees in the Boston area to study how they obtained their current jobs. Although some PTM workers found their jobs through formal means or direct applications, more than half of PTM workers in Granovetter's sample used personal contacts to obtain their jobs. The use of personal contacts to locate jobs is more pronounced for older workers (>34 years old) and managerial employees than it is for younger workers or professional/technical workers. Those job seekers obtained their jobs through personal contacts by collecting key information passing through their networks, such as the job's qualifications, specific requirements, and the time frame for the opening. And the most surprising finding from Granovetter's research is that although job seekers' strong-tie contacts, such as relatives or close friends are the most motivated to help, it is those weak-tie contacts, acquaintances or workplace friends, who pass along the most useful information for locating the jobs. The reason behind such a phenomenon is dubbed the ***strength of weak ties***. The idea behind the strength of weak ties is that one's weak-tie contacts tend to traverse different social circles than one's self. Such diversity in information embedded in one's weak-tie contacts provides the useful nonredundant information job seekers need. In contrast, one's strong-tie contacts are connected with those one already knows, so the information passing along from strong-tie contacts is already known to the job seekers. The utility of that redundant information is then lower than the utility of the nonredundant knowledge.

Let us borrow an artificial example to illustrate the operation of Granovetter's strength of weak ties in job searches. Figure 5.1 (Knoke, 2012a, p. 32) shows an egocentric network (see Chapter 2 for details on egocentric networks) of Ann, who is an engineer but was laid off recently. The solid lines denote strong ties, whereas the dotted lines represent weak ties. In the figure, Ann is strongly tied with Bob, Dee, and Cora and weakly tied to Erin, who in turn is weakly connected with Fran, Greg, and Hank. According to Granovetter, the strong-tied friends such as Bob, Dee, and Cora are

FIGURE 5.1 ● Ann's Egocentric Network With a Mixture of Strong Ties (Solid Lines) and Weak Ties (Dotted Lines)

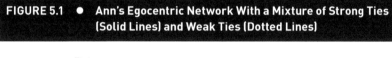

Note: Adapted from p. 32 of Knoke, D. (2012). *Economic networks*. Cambridge, England: Polity.

perhaps motivated to help Ann, but the information they provide to Ann is less useful as they are simply passing along information Ann already has. In contrast, Ann's weak-tied friends, Erin, Fran, Greg, and Hank, are not as motivated to help her, but they possess information from diverse sources and, more importantly, the information is novel, not simply a repetition of something Ann already knows. They may casually pass the nonredundant information along to Ann, who will greatly benefit from such fresh intelligence about engineering openings.

Does the "strength of weak ties" apply to other countries or other occupational groups than managerial, technical, and professional workers? The pictures get more complicated when we change the national and institutional contexts. In Germany, for example, weak ties are helpful to those who have high job prestige and want to gain further career advancement. For job shifters whose initial job prestige is low, strong intimate ties provide the structural leverage needed for career advancement (Wegener, 1991). This is because personal networks are heterogeneous, and those of low social standings have contacts of higher social standing in their networks. Connections within one's network between job seekers and their helpers are normally strong. In contrast, for those whose social standings are already high, finding helpers within their networks whose social standings are even higher is much more difficult. Job seekers must go beyond their networks to identify those helpers; hence, the ties connecting the job seekers with their ultimate helpers are commonly weak. In fact, such results correlate with Granovetter's (1973) study sample comprising only PTM workers. For those whose occupational prestige is lower than the PTM workers, strong ties matter in their job search. Occupational stratification is not the only factor distinguishing between strong ties and weak ties in affording network actors' job search leverage, but also the level of market development and legal/institutional differences also determine the kind of network ties that make a difference in finding a desirable job or improving one's income. In Section 5.1.3, we discuss how networks help job seekers in China (Bian, 1997) and Taiwan (Lin, Fu, & Hsung, 2001), respectively.

Making use of personal networks to gain valuable information is not restricted to job seekers only, though; on the other side of the fence, employers also take advantage of their employees' personal connections to recruit talent to fill their vacancies. The most commonly used method by employers is referral by current employees. In the following sections, we discuss the rationale behind an employer's decision to use referrals as opposed to other recruitment methods, and whether, and to what extent, such a recruitment method pays off.

5.1.2 Networks and Filling Job Vacancies

Employee referral is a recruiting method used by employers, in which employers encourage their current employees to nominate qualified candidates to fill the openings inside their organization. Employee referral is one of the most important recruiting strategies that has been practiced fairly extensively. For example, Harry Holzer (1987) reported that 36% of firms in his study used the method; and using a national representative sample of organizations, scholars reported that more than 51% of jobs are filled through referral (Kalleberg, Knoke, Marsden, & Spaeth, 1996, p. 138; Marsden & Campbell, 1990). Historically, referral hiring is not even a new phenomenon; studies have stated that it has been prevalent since the 1950s (Myers & Schultz, 1951; Rees & Schultz, 1970).

So what are the benefits of using referral as opposed to news media, online ads, or other recruiting methods? First of all, employee referral is less expensive than other means, such as news media, online postings, or broadcasting through association media. Although all those formal means of disseminating job information cost employers broadcasting fees, employee referral is the least expensive and tends to be a mostly cost-free recruiting method. Even when employers sometimes incur some costs by offering a referral bonus, they recoup the cost and achieve some returns to their investment by reducing recruitment expenses. Second, employee referrals serve as useful screening devices. Employers take advantage of the homophily principle that people prefer to work with others who are similar to themselves to solicit referrals from high-ability employees. The logic is that high-ability employees would recruit other high-ability candidates who are like them to the workplace, enhancing the human resources of the employers. James Montgomery (1991) named such a phenomenon *inbreeding bias*, noting that workers like to recruit others who are like them to work with them. Employers certainly exploit such inbreeding biases to increase the quality of their new hires. Third, employees who venture out to recruit qualified candidates per their employer's requests are putting their reputation on the line, and this is especially true when they receive monetary incentives for recruitment. Such employees are thus motivated to identify and recruit the best candidates as they see fit for the job at hand.

Other than the rationales discussed earlier, employers also use employee referrals to expand the scope of their reach to potential candidates to facilitate information exchange between the candidates and the employers, as well as to ease the fit-in process for new employees (Fernandez, Castilla, & Moore, 2000). For example, in a hypothetical scenario in which an employer asks 10 employees for their referrals to one opening in the organization, each employee then passes along the job information to 10 of their social contacts, and each social contact in turn passes along the information to 10 other social contacts. Thus, three steps out from the employer, 1,000 people (10^3) received the job information. Compared with the formal news media broadcast, these 1,000 job ad recipients may be a small number. Nevertheless, the recipients of the message through referral are much more trained and suitable for the opening than those targeted by the news media because employees would only refer those that they deem to be fitting candidates for the job. Employee referrals also establish an information conduit between employers and job candidates through referring employees. On the one hand, employers receive information about the candidates' hard-to-measure qualities from their referrers (he or she is truly a team player or he or she really likes to work alone). On the other hand, job candidates attain information on not only how to apply to maximize their chances, but also in case they receive the offer, how to deal with the hidden rules and informal office politics of their new workplace so they can work efficiently while playing it safe. Employee referrals also bring the extra benefit of facilitating new employees' fit-in process through their referrers. This is called the **socialization process** through which the referrers of the new employees socialize them into their new roles, avoiding the initial shock or hard landing that is commonly experienced by new employees.

Do employee referrals pay off? Do employers using employee referrals achieve those alleged economic benefits? First of all, employers using employee referrals make a $250 investment (in the form of referral bonus), receiving a return of $416 in reduced recruiting costs, at a rate of return of 67% (Fernandez et al., 2000, p. 1351). So, clearly, employee referrals carry some economic benefits to the employers. But researchers could not find direct empirical support for the inbreeding bias, informational advantages, and socialization benefits (Fernandez et al., 2000). Compared with nonreferrals, referrals do not have better job information, and they have the same propensity to turn over—referrals and nonreferrals have the same level of loyalty to their employers. Yet, between referrals and their referrers, there is strong correlation in terms of their propensities to turn over—when referrers turn over, their referrals are also likely to turn over; when referrers stay put, their referrals are also likely to stay put. The implication is that employers can take advantage of such interdependency between referrers and referrals: By keeping the referrers, they can better retain many of their new hires.

These social network studies of job matching in the labor market presumed an advanced market economy in which government plays a passive and facilitative role in the flow of and matching of jobs and candidates. Such cultural, social, and economic systems are prevalent in North America and Western Europe. With that said, how do social networks influence job matching in different social and institutional systems than those in an advanced economy? The following sections describe the process of job searching in the largest transitional economy in the world, that of China, as well as labor market processing in Taiwan.

5.1.3 Social Networks and Job Placement in Other Countries

The strength of weak ties discovered by Granovetter (1973) in the United States ignited a great deal of interest across the globe. Is the strength of weak ties universally true in other labor markets with different cultural or institutional systems than those present in the United States? In Germany, for example, both strong and weak ties benefit job changers. For those whose initial job status is low in Germany, strong ties can be used to obtain their next place of employment. Nevertheless, for those whose initial job is of high status in Germany, weak ties are the most helpful in landing them an ideal job (Wegener, 1991). In Sweden, young workers use their parents' strong social ties to land their first job, and the benefits of using strong ties are especially large when the unemployment rate is high or when the youths have low education or bad grades (Kramarz & Skans, 2014). Yet, the benefits of strong ties do not stop at the job search stage in Sweden. Those who used the strong ties to obtain their first job stayed in the positions longer and experienced faster wage growth than those who used other means to obtain their first job. But perhaps the country that has the most different cultural traditions, institutional arrangements, and historical backgrounds than those of the United States and Western Europe is China. In the following section, we discuss the job search process and the use of personal networks in China.

Unlike Western-style market economies, the labor market in reform-era China in the 1980s was characterized by strong governmental intervention—the Chinese government controlled the laborers and assigned jobs to them (Bian, 1994). Nevertheless, such models, although rigid and flawless by design, are loosely enforced. Job seekers seek out their network contacts to gain favorable conditions in the jobs they apply for. Government agents who control those job quotas scramble to respond to requests from multiple sources in their networks. The networks between job seekers and their helpers are particularly active in the Chinese labor market, providing a fascinating opportunity for scholars to study how networks afford social actors leverage in an institutional environment that is very different from that of the United States and Western Europe (Bian, 1997).

The Chinese interpersonal network, which is dubbed as the **_Guanxi network_**, exerts tremendous influence in the job search and labor-matching process. First, compared with Western interpersonal networks, Chinese Guanxi networks entail long-term orientation, greater levels of trust, and higher expectations of mutuality or reciprocity. It is also multidimensional in that it encompasses both emotional expressive contents and purposeful instrumental acts. It turns out that the strong, multidimensional Guanxi network is exactly what job seekers and their helpers need to land the job seekers desirable positions. This is because the governmental agents, who control quotas of job openings, are not supposed to exercise personal favoritism toward applicants. For them to help job seekers, a strong level of trust must be in place to minimize the later risks of governmental scrutiny regarding any malfeasance, regardless of whether there is actual malfeasance. Indeed, approximately 55% of Chinese job seekers either enter high-status work units or obtain high-status jobs by using their helpers via strong Guanxi networks (Bian, 1997).

In addition, a somewhat unique feature of Chinese job seekers is that when they lack personal connections with government agents who control the quota of a position desirable to them, they mobilize their immediate social contacts, who can in turn connect them to the governmental agents or their eventual helpers. In other words, many Chinese job seekers first identify a desirable position, then identify the agents who have control over the position, and finally find some intermediaries who can tie them to the agents. Yet, for such a strategy to work, connections between job seekers and intermediaries, and between intermediaries and agents, must be strong. Figure 5.2 depicts such a scenario, and the dotted lines denote a job seeker's cognitive knowledge of the job, as well as the government agent who controls the job. And the single arrow from the government agent to the job means that the agent has significant influence in deciding whom to hire for the job. And the double-arrowed lines connecting the government agent and intermediary, and connecting the intermediary and the job seeker, indicate strong personal ties (Guanxi) between the pairs. Figure 5.2 vividly

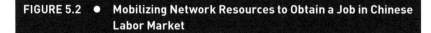

FIGURE 5.2 ● Mobilizing Network Resources to Obtain a Job in Chinese Labor Market

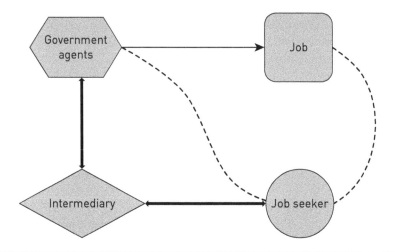

demonstrates the flow of the network mobilization: First, the job seeker obtains information of the desired job and who has the decision-making power. Then the job seeker identifies his or her strong-tied contact, who in turn has strong ties with the agent. Through such a two-step hop, the job seeker eventually is connected with the agent who may be persuaded to favor the job seeker. Such strategic mobilization of one's network contacts to facilitate one's social action is one key process in actualizing one's social capital in the Chinese labor market (Lin, 2001).

A SOCIAL NETWORK IN ACTION: THE DIFFERENCE GENDER PLAYS IN HOW THE NETWORK AFFECTS A JOB SEARCH IN TAIWAN

Certainly a social network plays a role in other labor market processes besides just finding a job or changing jobs. In Taiwan, for example, social networks, measured with a positional generator (see Chapter 2 of this book) to capture the extent to which people have personal contacts in different positions are related to job prestige and income. An interesting social phenomenon in Taiwan is that such network benefits only accrue for men. For women to attain high job prestige and income, human capital (education and training) must provide the avenue. Does the gender-based distinction in pathways to high job status only appear in Taiwan? More research is needed to answer this question.

5.2 Intra-Organizational Networks

Intra-organizational networks are those networks within the boundaries of an organization. They can refer to those networks among co-workers in terms of friendship, advice seeking, and information sharing or to those networks between subunit or departments within an organization for knowledge transfer and innovation. Intra-organizational networks, once formed, have significant consequences to the individuals in the networks, to the subunit or department, and to the entire organization. In the following sections, we discuss those intra-organizational networks and how they affect individual persons, work units in the organization, and eventually the entire organization.

5.2.1 Intra-Organizational Network and Getting Ahead: An Egoistic View

Most people engage in some kind of social activity, such as discussing important matters or socializing (dinner, lunch, drinks, coffee hours, or visitations) with other people they trust. When those social networking activities take place among co-workers in a workplace, some intra-organization networks are formed. Certainly, intra-organizational networks among colleagues can also form out of work-related activities such as authority relations with supervisors and subordinates, political support, or the securing of critical resources. The question remains, though, do those intra-organizational networks help their participants to get ahead in their career advancement within the organization? Well, it depends on how those networks are formed surrounding those given workers. The following sections discuss those network configurations in detail from the vantage point of an individual employee (Burt, 1997). Note that such network study designs are called egocentric network studies, and the questionnaire items used to collect information about workers' egocentric social networks are referred to as name generators. Both egocentric network studies and name generators receive a great deal of coverage in Chapter 2.

Social networks can be facilitative to individual actor's goal attainment by providing them with the resources flowing in those networks. Those resources can be norms that sustain strong trust among network actors (Coleman, 1990), critical information, brokerage control of the information (Burt, 1992; Burt, 1997), as well as influence from agents to advocate for network actors (Bian, 1997; Lin, 2001). Collectively, those resources are called ***social capital***. And much like the weak-ties or strong-ties debate in the previous section, researchers disagree on what network configurations are optimal for capitalizing on the social capitals in one's social network. Here, our book draws heavily from Ronald Burt's ***structural hole theory*** (Burt, 1992; Burt, 1997). But to obtain a more balanced view, readers should consult James Coleman (1990) or Nan Lin (2001) to get a glimpse of other exciting studies on this subject.

In a given network, structural holes are present between nodes or clusters of nodes that are disconnected from each other. Any individual nodes that connect to those nodes that are disconnected between them are occupying the structural hole. And the nodes that occupy many structural holes in their networks are reaping the information

FIGURE 5.3 ● Which Ties Matter? Structural Hole or Social Closure

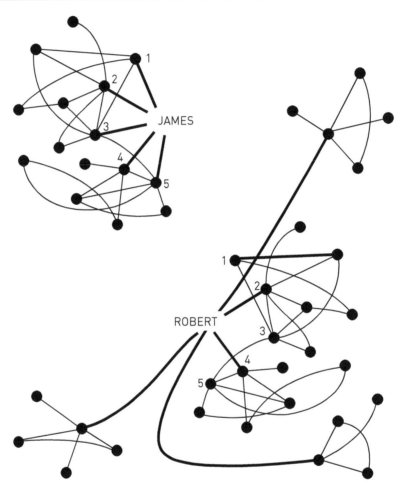

*Thick lines represent a manager's direct contacts.

Note: Adapted from p. 341 of Burt, R. S. (1997). The contingent value of social capital. *Administrative Science Quarterly, 42*(2), 339–365.

and control benefits from being the brokers of those holes. To illustrate, let's use Burt's (1997, p. 341) artificial networks, shown in Figure 5.3 with one node (Robert) full of structural holes and another (James) lacking structural holes.

When comparing James with Robert in Figure 5.3, both have five ties with others, but Robert has a network configuration that is superior to that of James because Robert's ties cross a few structural holes, whereas James's ties are all located within the same cluster. But why is crossing structural holes so important? First, structural holes provide nonredundant informational benefits to the nodes that have access to those holes. With the same number of network ties, James's information sources are homogenous: All of them come from the same cluster. Robert, in contrast, receives diverse information from sources in three different clusters. Each network tie provides additive information to Robert but redundant information to James. The second benefit of being the broker of the structural holes is the control benefits. For example, Robert can control the information flow among the three disconnected clusters. He can decide when, to what extent, and how accurately he passes information from one cluster to the others. In making those decisions, Robert can make the best use of the information at hand by playing the clusters off each other. Being able to sit on the structural holes among otherwise disconnected contacts produces tremendous opportunities that Robert can explore to gain personal benefits.

So does the structural hole benefit the network actors in reality? To investigate this, Burt (1997) studied 170 male middle managers in one of the largest American firms in electronic and computer equipment. The study surveyed each manager's key network contacts within and beyond the firm. The nine name generators used to construct the egocentric networks for the managers tap into personal relationship such as discussion and socializing, and work relationships such as political support, authority relationships with supervisors, relationships with subordinates, and critical resources buy-in. By using the egocentric networks of those managers, Burt (1997) computed the index of ***network constraint***, which is inversely related to the number of structural holes embedded in one's network. Therefore, the higher the number of structural holes, the lower the level of network constraint. For example, in Figure 5.3, the network constraint for Robert is 20 and for James is 53.6. The study (Burt, 1997) showed a clear pattern of negative relationships between the level of network constraint and career advancement. Managers with greater level of constraint (hence, fewer structural holes in their network) tend to have later promotion and receive smaller bonuses. In contrast, those with lower levels of constraint (hence, many structural holes) tend to have earlier promotion and bigger bonuses. Figure 5.4 shows the negative association between network constraint and early promotion.

SOCIAL NETWORKS IN ACTION: DO STRUCTURAL HOLES BENEFIT WOMEN?

Does the network configuration (network constraint defined with the structural holes) affect female managers in the same way it does men? In another study with the same dataset, Burt (1998) found that the effect of network configuration on female managers counters that of male managers—women managers whose networks have great network constraint (few structural holes) tend to receive early promotion (see Figure 5.5). In other words, in the men's world, Robert's network configuration is more facilitative to career advancement than that of James. In the women's world, it is the opposite—James' network configuration is more facilitative than that of Robert. So why is it that women and men have such stark differences? First, this may be a result of emotional differences between the two sexes. Although men like to seek out opportunities in competitive, sometimes rough

(Continued)

(Continued)

entrepreneurial networks, women tend to thrive in a small circle of supportive close friends. Second, compared with men, women's job status in the corporate world tends to be lower, and they tend to face a more restricted and narrow career ladder: Having an expanded network with many structural holes may not help women to get ahead within the corporate world. Third, the gender difference may stem from how men and women are being treated differently in work organizations. Women with dense networks have the advantage in breaking the "glass ceiling" in their path to advanced positions. Their network contacts will inform them of emerging opportunities and advocate on their behalf, especially in their absence.

FIGURE 5.4 ● Correlation Between Network Constraint and Early Promotion

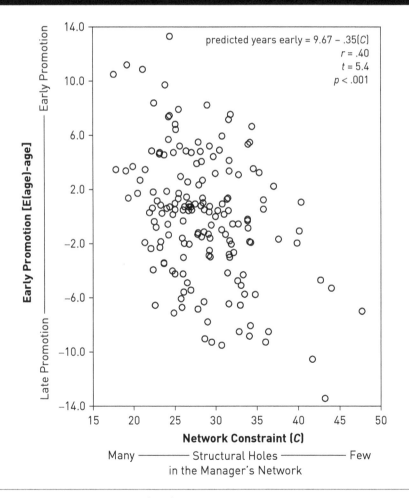

Note: Adapted from p. 348 of Burt, R. S. (1997). The contingent value of social capital. *Administrative Science Quarterly, 42*(2), 339–365.

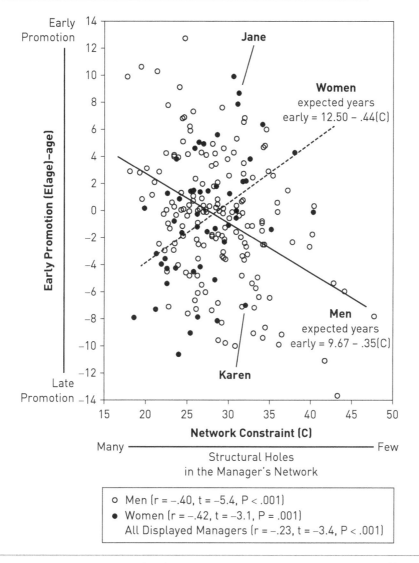

FIGURE 5.5 • Correlation Between Network Constraint and Early Promotion Between Men and Women

Note: Adapted from p. 11 of Burt, R. S. (1998). The gender of social capital. *Rationality and Society, 10*(1), 5–46.

These discussions alert us to the scope conditions for theories that all good theorizing work should carefully lay out in the scope conditions under which the theory is true. Whether it is the tie strength debate (weak ties versus strong ties in job search outcomes) or the network configuration contest (structural holes or network closure in career advancement), each theory has its unique set of conditions under which the theory holds true. In the following sections, we discuss the intra-organizational networks and work behaviors such as turnover/absenteeism, work attitudes, leadership, and the power structure within an organization. The main characteristic of those discussions is that they take a structural view as opposed to the egoistic view used in the previous discussions. In other words, rather than seeing things from an individual network node/actor's perspective, the following discussions take the structural perspective, seeing things with an aerial view. In addition to the difference in vantage point, methodologically the following studies use full network design (see Chapter 2 of this book) with a rigorously imposed boundary of work organizations or teams/groups within the organization. They commonly involve investigations of a certain type of relations (advice-seeking or friendship) among a group of co-workers within the same organization or work group (Krackhardt, 1992; Krackhardt & Brass, 1994).

5.2.2 Intra-Organizational Networks and Work Consequences: A Structural View

One issue that often intrigues scholars and practitioners is workers' turnover and job satisfaction. Why do workers choose to leave? How do those departures affect other workers' attitudes and satisfaction? Granted turnover is a multifaceted phenomenon that can be related to individual-level characteristics (race, sex, marital status, education, etc.), job features (income, flexibility, safety, health conditions, etc.), and workplace attributes (various human resources policies). Social network analyses reveal that job turnover is very much related to social networks as turnover tends to occur in clusters (Krackhardt & Porter, 1986). Those clusters are related to workers' roles in an organization. Those roles are not rooted in the formal organizational chart, but instead, they are rooted in the informal advice network among co-workers. In particular, when people see others leave who are in the same network positions (roles) as themselves, they are provided with relevant information about the nature of their jobs and the alternatives to working in their present organization. Because of this information, people in similar positions to those already leaving are motivated to consider leaving as well, resulting in clusters of employees leaving their organization within a given informal advice network.

How do researchers capture the informal advice networks among co-workers? In one study (Kranckhardt & Porter, 1986), researchers examined employees in three fast food restaurants that had 16, 27, and 20 workers each. Each worker in the restaurant was presented with a roster of all the employees of that restaurant and asked, "whom would s/he go to for help and advice at work?" Respondents not only reported his or her own network of advice but also were asked to assess each of his or her co-workers' advice networks by answering, "whom would each of the respondent's coworkers go to for help and advice at work?" Such a network study design is called a ***cognitive social*** *structure (CSS),* discussed in great detail in Knoke and Yang (2008, pp. 32–34). The advantage of having CSS data is that it not only has the respondents' self-report of network structure, but it also has a global benchmark (sometimes also called the *actual network*) created by aggregating the perceived matrices from each respondent. The disadvantage of CSS is that it imposes a huge burden on the respondents to generate large amounts of network information. Imagine a network actor in a small group of six co-workers would have to report 15 undirected relations $\left(\frac{6!}{2! \times 4!} = 15 \right)$, or 30 directed ties $\left(\frac{6!}{4!} = 30 \right)$, as he or she must report ties of all pairs in the network. For that reason, CSS datasets are generally small, comprising tens of network actors rather than hundreds or more.

How does such snowballing networked job turnover affect the work attitudes of those who stay? Contrary to the conventional wisdom that turnover hurts the work attitudes of existing workers, the co-workers of those who chose to leave experienced a greater level of commitment and satisfaction after those turnovers (Krackhardt & Porter, 1985). Perhaps it is because those would-be leavers would always complain to their co-workers, so with their departures, those complaints come to a stop, resulting in increased satisfaction within the workplace among those remaining co-workers.

Another important area in workplace dynamics is the power structure among co-workers. In this regard, the formal organizational chart delineating supervisors and subordinates only tells one side of the story. Informal networks of advising and friendship between co-workers reveal a great deal of power and negotiation in real actions. In one of the case studies of a Silicon Valley IT firm (Silicon Systems), researchers conducted a social network study of the firm's 36 employees before and after a unionization drive (Krackhardt, 1992). In particular, each employee was asked to respond to two questions: "Who would this person go to for help or advice at work?" and "who would this person consider to be a personal friend?" The "this person" in the questions refer to each respondent's co-workers, as well as the respondent himself or herself. Therefore, the study was able to produce CSS data for the friendship and advice network among the 36 co-workers. Again, the benefits of having CSS data are twofold: (1) The data reveal the actual network, in which the relationship exists only when both parties in the relationship agree that it exists. And (2) by correlating one's perceived network (friendship or advice) with the CSS network, one would receive a cognitive accuracy score, which indicates his or her ability to reconstruct the advice or friendship network. Such ability can be used to define one's *reputational power* within an organization (Krackhardt, 1992).

Figure 5.6 shows the official organizational chart of Silicon Systems, whereas Figures 5.7 and 5.8 display the actual Advice Network and the actual Friendship Network, respectively. When comparing the advice network with the friendship network, although Ev and Steve are central actors in the advice network, they are

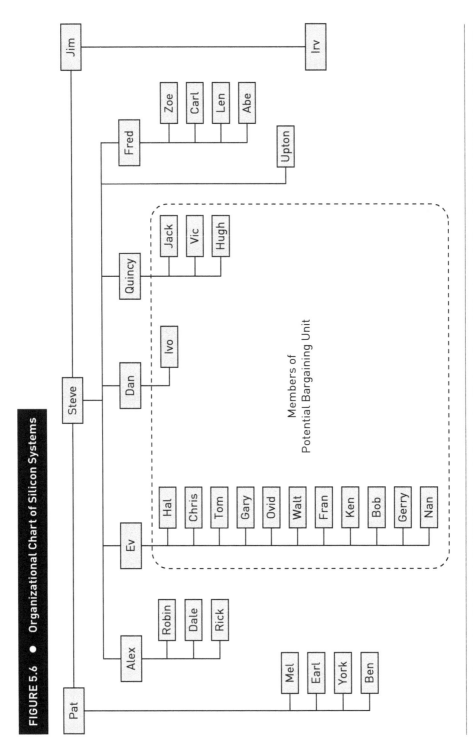

FIGURE 5.6 ● Organizational Chart of Silicon Systems

Members of
Potential Bargaining Unit

Note: Adapted from p. 226 of Krackhardt, D. (1992). The strength of strong ties: The importance of philos in organizations. In N. Nohria & R. G. Eccles, Eds., *Networks and organizations* (pp. 226–240). Boston, MA: Harvard Business School Press.

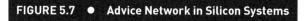

FIGURE 5.7 ● Advice Network in Silicon Systems

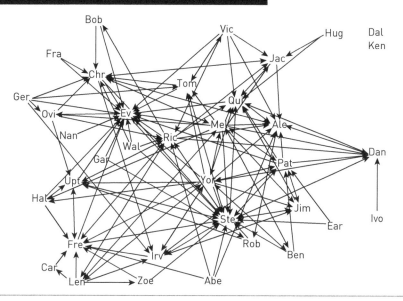

Note: Adapted from p. 228 of Krackhardt, D. (1992). The strength of strong ties: The importance of philos in organizations. In N. Nohria & R. G. Eccles, Eds., *Networks and organizations* (pp. 226–240). Boston, MA: Harvard Business School Press.

FIGURE 5.8 ● Friendship Network in Silicon Systems

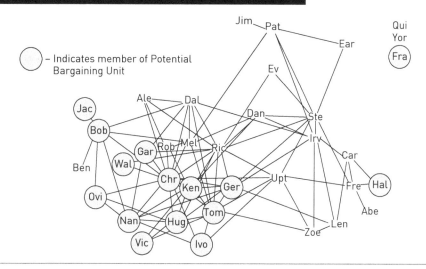

Note: Adapted from p. 226 of Krackhardt, D. (1992). The strength of strong ties: The importance of philos in organizations. In N. Nohria & R. G. Eccles, Eds., *Networks and organizations* (pp. 226–240). Boston, MA: Harvard Business School Press.

relatively much more peripheral in the friendship network. It suggests that the centralities of Ev and Steve in the advice network simply reflect their leadership roles in technology (Ev is the technical lead) and the organization (Steve is the founder). In contrast, Chris emerged as the leader in the friendship network, having the highest centrality score. More to the point, although Chris has the second highest reputational power (the ability to reconstruct the actual network), Ev and Steve have lower than average reputational power. The unionization drive ultimately failed mainly because the union representatives did not contact and convince Chris, the influential player in the network. And Chris was ambivalent about the union, torn between his original pro-union stance and influences from his two close allies Robin and Mel, who are strong union opponents. Instead, the union representatives spent much of their time with Hal and Jack, two peripheral and less influential players in the friendship network. Had the union representatives understood the informal friendship network structure among the co-workers, they could have revised their plan to wage a much more effective campaign.

An interesting case in point is Steve, who is the founder and president of Silicon Systems. His centrality in advice network is high, but in his friendship network, his centrality is low. He likes to stay in touch with company operations, but he only connects himself with managers of the company. His lack of connections with the company's rank and file contributes to his relatively low reputational power (large discrepancy between his perceived network and the actual network in friendship structure). So when he was informed by union representatives that a unionization was underway in his company, he encountered an overwhelming sense of shock and betrayal. Steve's case points to the issue of effective leadership, to which we turn in the following sections.

By default, a leader occupies the center and top of the formal organizational chart; all employees report to their leader. In reality, different leaders exercise different leadership styles from the most rigid style (only listen to the immediate subordinates) to the most egalitarian type (connecting to a wide range of employees at different levels). From a network point of view, the former represents ineffective leadership that eventually will drive the leader out of touch (much like Steve in Silicon Systems). Yet, the latter is simply impractical as leaders normally have limited time and attention to details. An effective leadership requires that the leaders establish strong connections with those having high centrality scores in the informal network. The central players tend to be more powerful and tend to have access to more relevant information that could be passed back to the leader (Brass & Burkhardt, 1992). When the intra-organizational structure is divided into many subsets, which resembles most cases in reality, it is imperative that leaders establish strong ties with at least one member of each subgroup (Krackhardt. 1994). By making connections to diverse subgroups, the leader receives nonredundant information. Also, subgroups with strong connections to leaders tend to be allies of the leaders. By spreading ties with diverse subgroups, leaders maximize their allies, minimizing the chance that a disfranchised group will resist or rebel.

But how do leaders identify those subsets of workers and those with high centrality scores in the informal network? This is where the reputational power (Krackhardt, 1990, 1992) becomes relevant. The reputational power comes from the leaders' abilities to reconstruct accurately the informal network structure of their organization. The earlier recommendations for effective leadership only work when leaders have great reputational power (their perceived informal networks resemble their actual informal networks). With that said, how do leaders improve their reputational powers? The answer is by making connections. Essentially this is an iterative and fine-tuning process in which leaders constantly improve their network connections to achieve optimal connections. When leaders stop making connections, the leadership ceases to exist.

Intra-organizational networks may derive from a random process in which individual employees establish informal personal networks with their co-workers for advice-seeking or friendship purposes. Once formed, those informal networks are consequential to individual career advancements and overall workforce activities in terms of turnover, job satisfaction, power structure, and effective leadership. In for-profit business firms, intra-organizational networks may also come from more or less formalized resource flows between different subunits within a given firm (Knoke, 2012a; Tsai, 2000). And formation and configuration of those intra-organizational networks exert influences on the firm's performance by improving knowledge transfer between organizational subunits and increasing their innovativeness (Wijk, Jansen, & Lyles, 2008). Note that although intra-organizational networks in business firms often refer to cross-unit linkages, those connections ultimately derive from those boundary-spanning personnel or agents. And the personal networks of those agents strongly influence the formation and evolving of those inter-unit relations (Galaskiewicz & Zaheer, 1999; Tsai, 2000).

5.2.3 Intra-Organizational Networks and
Competitive Advantage: An Organizational Utility View

At the beginning of the new millennium, a new form of organization, often called the *networked organization*, emerged as a prominent mode of control and coordination (Knoke, 2001). Compared with the traditional hierarchical mode of structure, networked organizations emphasize vertical and lateral collaborations between subunits in different levels and different functional areas. Consultative ties between subunits replace administrative fiats in regulating those intra-organizational relations. Often short-term projects supersede long-term hierarchical commands to coordinate different departments or functional areas in delivering customized goods and services. Networked organizations exhibit in several main forms (Knoke, 2001: chap. 6). In the following sections, we discuss one of those main intra-organizational networks: the

internal network organization. Then we examine the intra-organizational network within multinational corporations (MNCs) and knowledge transfers between different subunits in an organization.

An internal network organization represents one extreme form of networked organization where all hierarchical command lines are replaced with lateral exchange relations. Figure 5.9 (Knoke, 2001, p. 207) illustrates an artificial example of one such internal network organization. The double-headed arrows denote recurrent communication exchanges, resource transfers, or collaborative projects involving inter-unit teams. Perhaps the production unit has the most exchange relations with six other internal departments. For example, production would have to secure resource input (hence, its tie with the Purchasing Department), but it also must deal with sales (hence, its tie with the Sales Department). Note that the absence of the traditional top-down

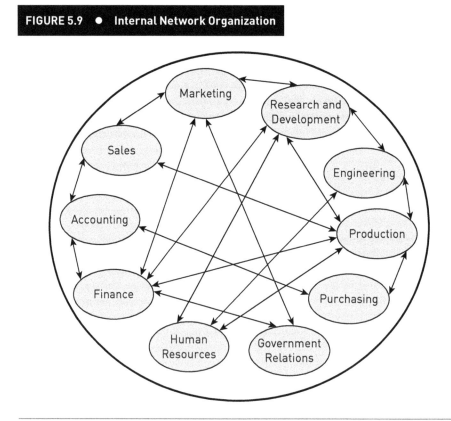

FIGURE 5.9 ● Internal Network Organization

Note: Adapted from p. 207 of Knoke, D. (2001). Changing organizations: Business networks in the new political economy. Boulder, CO: Westview Press.

organizational chart is conspicuous. In this internal network organization, commands from CEOs or other executives only exist nominally. Senior managers lack detailed information to manage and monitor inter-departmental transactions, leaving them to the discretion of functional managers.

SOCIAL NETWORKS IN ACTION: DIRECT FROM DELL

One such internal network organization is Dell Computer, founded by Michael Dell in his dorm back in the 1980s. Dell's method runs counter to the traditional mode of production, in which manufacturers make and assemble the parts, ship them to distributors/retailers, and end with products sitting in the shelf to be purchased by customers. Instead, Dell uses the "Direct from Dell" model, in which a customized order from a consumer triggers the production process. Dell relays orders of parts to the suppliers, which ship the parts to Dell for final assembly and shipment to customers. Through such virtual integration of different segments of a production network, Dell ensures fast delivery of customized goods, while minimizing costly inventory.

The second most common intra-organizational network exists in MNCs. Figure 5.10 shows such multinational differentiated networks that depict the relations among various organizational subsidiaries and between those subsidiaries and their headquarter offices. One of the most researched MNCs is Philips N.V., which is headquartered in the Netherlands and has subsidiaries operating in more than 60 countries that are heterogeneous in their political regimes and economic developments (see Figure 5.11 for the geographic links among its subsidiaries). Subsidiaries exhibit a great level of variability in the complexity of their internal structures and sizes; some are small and single function, employing tens of workers, whereas others are large and complex, hiring thousands of employees. Ultimately, controlling and coordinating diverse acts between such a wide range of subsidiaries is a daunting task for headquarter officials. One line of research propagates the requisite complexity hypothesis, stating that optimal MNC structural complexity closely matches environmental complexity (Nohria & Ghoshal, 1997). The study in question investigated 41 MNCs, reporting that the 17 MNCs with good structure-environment fit achieve much better organizational performance than the 24 MNCs with poor fits to their environments.

Among all of the data flowing between different subunits within a given organization, knowledge or intelligence perhaps represents the most important resources. Knowledge transfers between units improve organizational and departmental performance by fostering capacity development and taking advantage of current competencies (Lane, Salk, & Lyles, 2001). Although knowledge transfers occur in both inter-organizational

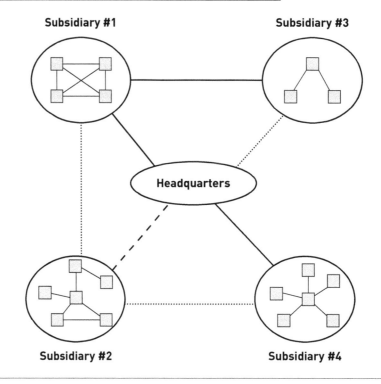

FIGURE 5.10 ● Multinational Differentiated Network

Subsidiary #1   Subsidiary #3

Headquarters

Subsidiary #2   Subsidiary #4

Note: Adapted from p. 14 of Nohria, N., & Ghoshal, S. (1997). *The differentiated network: Organizing multinational corporations for value creation.* San Francisco, CA: Jossey-Bass.

and intra-organizational contexts, transfers within an organization are much more conducive to high organizational performance than are transfers between organizations. It is perhaps because firms can easily identify the relevancy of the knowledge transferring within the organizations and thus can refine and exploit the knowledge (Wijk et al., 2008).

Within a given organization, the extent to which knowledge transfers benefit subunits varies, depending on the network location and absorptive capacity of those subunits. In constructing the intra-organizational knowledge transfer network, researchers asked a representative of the subunit, "which units provide your unit with new knowledge or expertise when your unit is seeking technical advice inside your organizations" (Tsai, 2001, p. 1000)? The representative was presented with a list of all other business units within the company. The procedure was then repeated for all the business units within the company. In using such data, researchers constructed an intra-organizational knowledge transfer network. Another important variable is

FIGURE 5.11 • Organizational Units and Some Interlinkages Within Philips N. V.

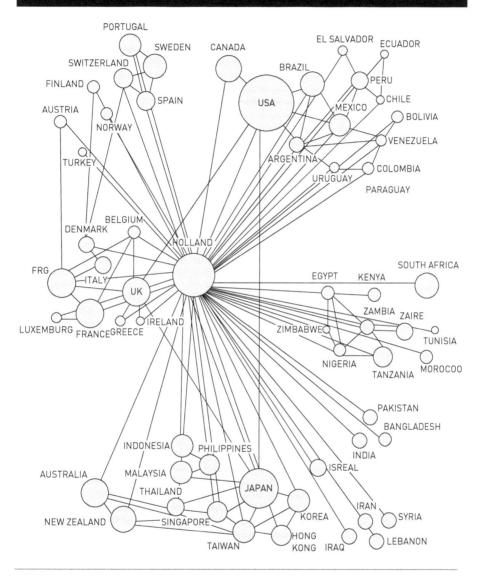

Note: Adapted from p. 605 of Ghoshal, S., & Bartlett. C. A. (1990). The multinational corporation as an interorganizational network. *The Academy of Management Review, 15*(4), 603–625.

absorptive capacity, measured with the research and development (R&D) investment by the subunit. The results are intriguing—having high centrality in intra-organizational knowledge transfer network increases a subunit's performance and innovation.

FIGURE 5.12 ● Contingent Effect of Absorptive Capacity on the Associations Between Network Centrality and Performance, and Between Network Centrality and Innovation

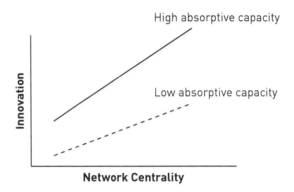

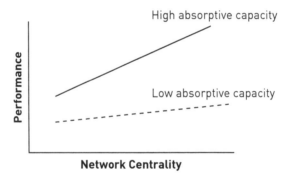

Note: Adapted from p. 1002 from Tsai, W. (2001). Knowledge transfer in intraorganizational networks: Effects of network position and absorptive capacity on business unit innovation and performance. *The Academy of Management Journal*, *44*(5), 1002.

But the extent to which the high centrality increases the performance and innovation depends on the absorptive capacity. Figure 5.12 shows that for subunits with high absorptive capacity, the payoffs (in terms of having high levels of performance and innovation) to having high network centrality are great. Nevertheless, for those units with low absorptive capacity, the returns to having high network centrality are not that great. It seems such differentials in returns to network centrality between high and low absorptive capacity are much more pronounced for performance than they are for innovation. The business units are better able to benefit from the intraorganizational knowledge transfer when they invest in their own knowledge absorption and creative abilities.

Although intra-organizational ties between different units are conduits for knowledge transfers, a high number of ties between subunits does not necessarily lead to efficient exchanges for all knowledge. An increase in intra-organizational ties only raises passages of codifiable knowledge. For tacit, complex knowledge, the strength of the ties, rather than the sheer number of them, matters in facilitating exchanges and absorptions (Maurer, Bartsch, & Ebers, 2011). So in addition to knowledge transfers, knowledge assimilation is a critical process the subunit must go through to capitalize on the benefits in the intra-organizational network of knowledge.

5.3 Inter-Organizational Relations

Before we discuss inter-organizational relations, we want to stress that the intellectual distinction between an intra- and an inter-organizational network only exists for conceptual clarity. Many intra-organizational exchanges, such as information flows, work flow interdependence, or even friendship and authority can be extended to inter-organizational relations. In fact, many inter-organizational relations perhaps start with inter-personal ties between boundary spanning personnel of different organizations. Those preexisting ties between boundary spanning personnel across different organizations are not only precursors of inter-organizational alliances, but also afford a competitive edge to those organizations seeking strategic partners (Galaskiewicz & Zaheer, 1999).

Despite the great variety of inter-organizational relations, we state that they can be grouped into two main forms: ***interlocking boards*** and ***strategic alliances***. Interlocking boards connect organizations together as board members at one organization may come from multiple other organizations. It can occur unilaterally, such as organization A appointing personnel from organizations B and C to its board. It can also occur in mutuality, such as organizations A, B, and C appointing each other's personnel to their respective boards. Strategic alliances are another major form of inter-organizational relation, by which organizations join hands to deal with the primary strategic opportunities or challenges they are facing. The following two sections discuss these two main forms of inter-organizational relations in great detail.

5.3.1 Interlocking Board Directorate

Large organizations, especially those in the financial sector, would like to exercise control over macro-economic conditions. They often try to accomplish such goals by appointing to their boards of directors key personnel from other main organizations in the national economy. For example, by sharing board members with other key players in the field, large financial institutes receive rich and timely information on economic conditions, giving them guidance in making investment decisions (Mintz & Schwartz, 1985).

Do interlocking boards result in a congregation of power into the hands of a few social elites? After all, one may envision such interlocking boards would link social elites from multiple domains, such as large corporations, military branches, and governmental agencies. Those at the top of those important social institutions would come to know each other, socialize with each other, and eventually develop a shared vision and agreement over many important issues. But in reality, such concerns are unwarranted as issues dividing social elites as numerous as those united them (Mills, 1956). Financial companies especially experience decline in their corporate powers as many companies are increasingly relying on the market for their commercial loans. This is the main reason behind banks' move into the securities underwriting business.

So what are the reasons that organizations engage in interlocking board relations? The most important reason is the information benefit: Board interlocks are a primary source of information. Companies linked with board interlocks are conducting "business scans" of the political economy to identify problems and come up with solutions (Useem, 1984). Second, companies may use interlocking boards to fine-tune their operating environments. For example, companies often invite executives from key suppliers or client firms to serve on their boards. By doing so, companies secure key suppliers and establish friendly ties with customers. In other words, the inter-organizational resource flows determine with which companies a focal company would like to have interlocking board relations (Pfeffer & Salancik, 1978).

The third reason behind corporate interlocking may relate to the power struggle between the current board and executives. Although CEOs like compliant board members, active boards may want to recruit assertive, outspoken members. Who eventually gets in depends on the outcome of battles between CEOs and the board. For example, Edward Zajac and James Westphal (1996) analyzed 491 large companies between 1985 and 1992, reporting two types of boards: low-control boards that add passive, management-oriented members and high-control boards that recruit active shareholder-oriented directors. Most companies have either low-control or high-control boards. Fourth, board members sometimes are being recruited simply because they are well connected. Those who serve on a lot of boards are likely to be mentioned as potential candidates (Davis, Yoo, & Baker, 2003). Often CEOs are targeted to be potential board members for other companies by virtue of their high visibility in business. Do CEOs adopt a pro-management style when they serve on other companies' boards, just to give their fellow CEOs a break? Not necessarily. They generally do adopt such a style, but with an important qualification: that they experience active board control in their own companies (Westphal & Zajac, 1998).

Does corporate interlocking generate economic benefits? Well, it depends on national origins and institutional differences, and research has produced mixed results. In the United States, although organizations may recruit outside board members to manage their operating environment, board interlocking does not seem to increase their profitability (Mizruchi, 1996). In transitional economies such as China, firms with interlocking boards outperform their peers without interlocking boards in sales, net assets, profits, and worker productivity (Keister, 2000; also see Figure 5.13). Besides economic performance, board interlocking is very consequential to other aspects of

FIGURE 5.13 ● Interlocking and Performance of Chinese Firms

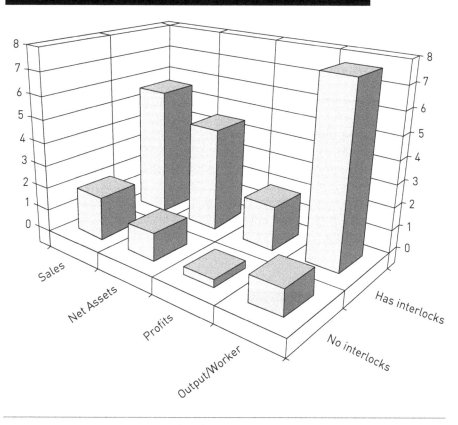

Note: Adapted from p. 182 of Keister, L. A. (2000). *Chinese business groups: The structure and impact of interfirm relations during economic development.* New York, NY: Oxford University Press.

organizational life. Well-connected CEOs engaged in more acquisitions in the 1960s and 1980s than their less-connected counterparts (Haunschild, 1993; Palmer & Barber, 2001). Executives of the companies in Minneapolis/St. Paul who have many contacts with philanthropists tend to make greater donations than do their peers with fewer contacts. Companies also adopt similar business practices to those with whom they have interlocking relations. For example, the adoption of a ***poison pill*** diffuses among organizations linked via interlocking boards (Davis & Greve, 1997). The so-called M-form structuration also spreads among organizations with interlocking board ties (Palmer, Jennings, & Zhou, 1993). Companies listed on Nasdaq often defect to the New York Stock Exchange when their interlocking partners have done so. Interlocking ties are an important medium by which organizations imitate each other's practice, a process vividly called a contagion, much like a contagion among individuals (Scott & Davis, 2006).

5.3.2 Strategic Alliance

A strategic alliance refers to a strategic partnership involving at least two partnering firms. It is strategic in the sense that the alliance is formed as a direct response to major strategic challenges or opportunities that the partner firms face (Child & Faulkner, 1998, p. 5). After the alliance is formed, the partner firms remain independent, share benefits and managerial control over the performance of assigned tasks, and make continuing contributions in one or more strategic areas (Yoshino & Rangan, 1995). Strategic alliances take on a variety of different forms, but we found that John Child (2005, p. 224) provided one of the best typology maps of inter-firm links in general, and strategic alliances in particular, which is shown in Figure 5.14. In the figure, inter-firm links run from left to right as partnering firms engage in the least intensive relations (arm's length contracts, franchising, licensing, and cross-licensing) to the most intensive relations (mergers and acquisitions). Strategic alliances take the form of nontraditional contracts, to equity agreements including those leading to the creation of no new entities and those leading to the creation of new entities. The following sections discuss those different types of strategic alliances in detail.

FIGURE 5.14 ● Typology of Inter-Firm Relations

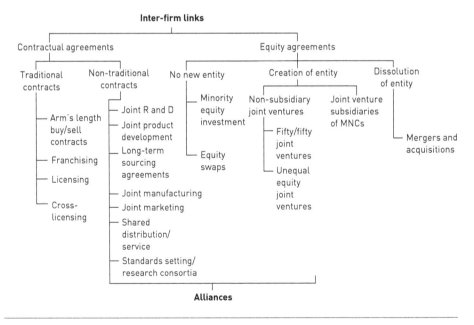

Note: Adapted from p. 224 of Child, J. (2005). *Organization: Contemporary principles and practice.* Chichester, West Sussex, England: Wiley.

The most intensive partnership is ***joint venture***, defined as "two or more legally distinct firms pool a portion of their resources within a jointly owned legal organization that serves a limited purpose for its parents" (Inkpen, 1995, p. 1). Joint ventures may involve 50:50 ownership between two parents or unequal shareholding among multiple partners. The Chinese government, for example, adopted the joint venture format to encourage collaborations between foreign companies and domestic Chinese firms to benefit from a foreign firm's capital and technologies.

SOCIAL NETWORKS IN ACTION: A JOINT VENTURE BETWEEN MOTOROLA AND PANDA ELECTRONIC GROUP

One of these joint ventures was between Motorola and the Panda Electronic Group of Nanjing China. Established in 1995, the joint venture drew a 60% equity investment from Motorola and a 40% investment from Panda Group. For Motorola, this was an opportunity to expand its market in China, whereas for Panda Group, the joint venture allowed them to absorb more capital and advanced technology in the wireless industry. The Motorola–Panda Group joint venture, however, ended in 1997 when Motorola was unable to reach a license agreement with Apple Computer (Luo, 2000).

Equity investment occurs when one firm buys a direct financial stake in another through a direct stock purchase. It can be either majority stake purchase (more than 50%) or minority stake purchase (less than 50%). An ***equity swap*** occurs when two firms mutually purchase each other's stocks. Equity investment or equity swaps do not create new entities. Instead, they provide a partner some financial stake in another company's affairs. Equity investments or equity swaps often occur in high-tech industries such as computer or biotechnology when large corporations use financial means to gain access to key technologies held by small firms. A famous minority equity investment, however, happened between two airlines, KLM and Northwest (later merged with Delta). The two airlines announced their alliance in 1989 when KLM invested US$400 million in the Minneapolis-based company. Despite the economic success of the alliances, the partners developed distrust of each other over the disagreement of policies, and the alliance ended in 1997 when Northwest spent US$1 billion to buy back the shares from KLM (Knoke, 2001, pp. 120–121).

Strategic alliances also embody various forms of nontraditional contracts, such as joint R&D, joint product development, joint manufacturing, joint marketing, standard setting, shared distribution/services, and long-term sourcing agreements. The joint R&D alliances occur often in the high-tech fields such as biotechnology and the IT industry. Technologies in those industries are fast changing, engendering individual firms to pool their resources for R&D to stay current while avoiding the prohibitive costs associated with the R&D. Standard setting is another commonly occurred alliance between members trying to establish a standard for industrial product.

FIGURE 5.15 ● Strategic Alliances Among 13 IT Firms 1990

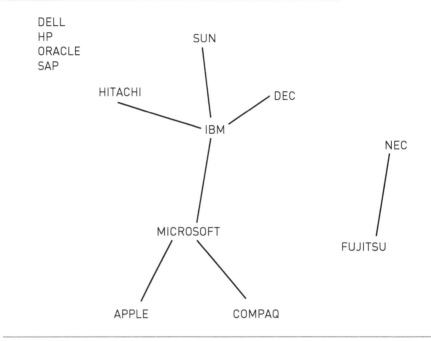

Note: Adapted from p. 147 of Knoke, D. (2012). *Economic networks*. Cambridge, England: Polity.

SOCIAL NETWORKS IN ACTION: ORGANIZATIONAL ALLIANCES FOR ESTABLISHING INDUSTRIAL STANDARDS

The famous battle between Betamax and VHS for the standard of the home entertainment industry illustrates the importance of strategic alliances. Although Sony was behind Betamax and persuaded the Japanese Ministry of International Trade and Industry to endorse it as the industry standard, the strategic alliance led by JVC, which backed the VHS, joined by powerful allies Hitachi, Mitsubishi, and Sharp was a much stronger force than Sony. In the end, VHS won as the industrial standard format.

The strategic alliance as a new way to coordinate between groups of organizations to achieve collected outcomes has been flourishing since the 1980s. For example, in Knoke's (2012a, pp. 146–147) study of the Global Informational Sector, strategic alliances among 13 computer and software companies in 1990 appeared to be spotty, with a network density (see Chapter 3 for details of computing network density) of only 0.09 (see Figure 5.15). Nevertheless, ten years later in 2000, every firm was connected

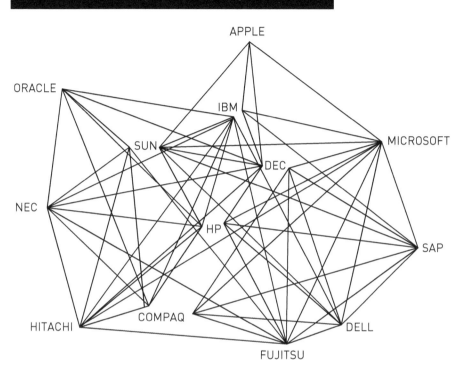

FIGURE 5.16 ● Strategic Alliances Among 13 IT Firms 2000

Note: Adapted from p. 149 of Knoke, D. (2012). *Economic networks*. Cambridge, England: Polity.

with other firms among the set, and the density reached 0.79 (see Figure 5.16). With the thriving of strategic alliances among companies, the traditional methods such as vertical integration (to be discussed in the following section) have been fading away as less viable choices for managing organizational operating environment. The chief reason behind such a transformation is the standardization of many previously complicated business practices. Such standardization enables the frictionless combination of many different aspects of a business, and integrating them into a unified whole.

SOCIAL NETWORKS IN ACTION: CIVIL AVIATION

Take civil aviation as example: The industry went through government deregulation post-911, which was intended to encourage competition. Many contractors rushed to offer the kinds of services needed for new start-ups, from writing applications for

(Continued)

(Continued)

government certification, to selling tickets, to staffing gates at airports, to catering the food, to even flying the airplanes. Many secondhand airlines also scattered in the Arizona desert, waiting to be purchased (Scott & Davis, 2006, p. 294). Venture capitalists seized the opportunity to provide seed money for the start-ups. As a result, small discount airlines flourished by the mid-2000s, with JetBlue, Allegiant Air, Frontier, Southwest, Spirit, and Sun Country airlines providing convenient daily flights connecting thousands of mid- to small-size metros across the United States.

Strategic alliances seem to be consequential to a firm's performance. For example, those investment banks involved in many strategic alliances tend to have the best long-term performance (measured by dollar amount underwritten). The active network alliances also lead to higher popularity and expanded participation in stock deals (Chung, 1996). Biotech firms with diverse portfolios of strategic alliances tend to become more central, grow much faster, and are faster to go public through IPO than their peers without such a level of strategic alliances (Powell, Koput, & Smith-Doerr, 1996). Nevertheless, the greater diversity in the format of strategic alliances makes the issue of how those alliances improve partnering firms' performances hard to assess. For example, when multiple partnering firms pool their resources to develop new products or technology, such an alliance may dissolve before or after the new product/technology is fully developed. Little is known about how each firm in the alliance could benefit from such a new collective outcome, and little is known as to whether such a collaboration yields higher returns than those available from alternative resources expenditures. Researchers tend to emphasize the positive synergies from networking, ignoring the potential risks of inter-organizational relations. Although lack of network connections may dampen firms' profitability, over-embeddedness (having too many network connections) is also detrimental to a firm's performance by limiting firm's adaptability (Uzzi, 1996). What is the optimal level of network connections for firms or organizations? Such questions will inspire much research and study in the variety of contexts defined by the combination of markets, institutions, and industries.

5.3.3 Inter-Organizational Relations Across Industries

At the industrial level, inter-organizational ties can occur within the same industry or across different industries. For example, a car manufacturer can establish ties with other manufacturers, or it can forge relations across industries with either supplier firms or client companies. Sometimes, the relationship between two firms becomes so intense that a merger takes place to integrate the two firms into one entity. Such a process is called ***vertical integration***, and depending on the positions of two firms in the value chain, it can be either *backward vertical integration* (a car manufacturer merges its part suppliers) or *forward vertical integration* (a car manufacturer purchases a car rental firm). Vertical integration was prevalent among business firms during the early and mid-20th century. The famous Ford River Rouge Complex built in the 1920s serves as a classic example of vertical backward integration. Facing tremendous demands of its cars, the Ford Motor Company purchased the supplier firms of rubber, glasses, and metal and made them internal subsidiaries of the company. Such backward integration ensured the input of key resources, while preventing integrated suppliers from holding out for higher prices or providing inferior products to Ford.

The process of vertical integration can also be reversed. For example, to expand shares in the rental car market, Ford purchased Hertz Rental in 1994 (forward vertical integration). But by 2005, financial hardship compelled Ford to sell Hertz to a group of private equity firms, which is a reversed vertical integration or vertical disintegration. The trend of disintegration accelerated so much that by the 1990s and 2000s, many companies experienced some forms of spin-off, disintegration/de-integration, or outsourcing. Several reasons may account for such a wave of restructuring: increasing customized markets, financial hardships, or stock market pressures. Nevertheless, from the corporate governance point of view, the chief reason for corporate disaggregation is the emergence of the network as a viable structure to deal with the issue of interdependence between companies (Powell, 1990). In other words, companies no longer have to face a binary choice between an arm's length market and vertical integration when it comes to managing interdependence. When recurring transactions between two companies necessitate a tie that is warmer or closer than the arm's length market, networked forms of governance replace vertical integration as a superior way (in many regards) to manage the relationship between the two companies. Many different forms of alliances (discussed in the previous sessions) replace vertical integration to regulate inter-firm relations.

At the industry level, the structural characteristics of a given industry have significant influences on its organizations' performance. One of the key industrial characteristics is the ***four-firm concentration ratio***, defined as the proportion of an industry's output accounted for by the four largest producers in the industry. The four-firm concentration ratio is a measure of monopoly: the higher the ratio, the higher the monopoly, and the lower the competition of the industry. Different industries have different concentration ratios, and for a given firm, a desirable situation it wants to be in is that its own industry is concentrated (hence, less competition) while the industries of its suppliers and client firms are dispersed (low concentration ratio, hence, high competition). With such a structural configuration, a firm can maximize its interests by playing its suppliers or clients off each other, while facing little constraint within its own industry. Basically, companies can have structural autonomy to the extent their own industries are concentrated while their suppliers' and clients' industries are dispersed. An empirical study found exactly the predicted result that firms with great structural autonomy command higher profit margins (Burt, 1982).

SOCIAL NETWORKS IN ACTION: STRUCTURAL AUTONOMY AND PROFITABILITY

One real-life example is the Sealed Air Corporation (a manufacturer of bubble-wrap packaging materials) in the late 1980s. Its main suppliers were from the commodity chemical industry, and its buyers were every home or business that shipped fragile items. The company also had patents that protected it from significant competition from other firms within the same industry. Such structural autonomy allowed the company to reap a high profit margin of 50% in the 1980s (Scott & Davis, 2006, p. 302).

End-of-Chapter Questions

1. Social networks matter in job search processing. Under what conditions are weak ties important, and under which conditions are strong ties critical in facilitating job searching?

2. Discuss the four reasons why employers often use referrals for recruiting.

3. What are the main differences between the Chinese Guanxi network and Western interpersonal network? How do Chinese job seekers strategically use the Guanxi network to facilitate their job search?

4. Based on Burt's (1997) study, how do structural holes affect male and female managers' career advancement differently? Why there is such a difference?

5. How does employee turnover affect co-workers in the same or similar positions within the same company? How does turnover affect those who stay?

6. What is reputational power? How does reputational power affect leadership effectiveness?

7. Discuss the main reasons that organizations engage in interlocking board relations with each other.

8. How do the interlocking boards' ties affect organizations involved in the interlocking with each other?

9. Strategic alliances include equity investment, joint ventures, and organizational coalitions that establish industrial standards. Rank the three strategic alliances based on the involvement of partnering firms. Which one is the most intensive, and which one is the least intensive?

10. Based on Burt's (1982) research, what kind of structural position in an industry is conducive to high profitability for a given firm, and why?

6

Social Network Analysis in Crime and Terrorism

●

Learning Objectives

- Describe how social ability model and social inability model explain the connection between youth networks and juvenile delinquency

- Discuss how social network scholars use various methods to separate effects of peer influence from peer selection in juvenile delinquency

- Identify the three network characteristics in Robert Sampson and Byron Groves's (1989) study that affected community crime and delinquency

- Examine how, in social disorganization theory, non-network characteristics such as socioeconomic and demographic factors measured at the neighborhood level impact delinquency and crime in a neighborhood

- Appraise Andrew Papachristos's (2009) study of gang murders that highlighted the structured relations between gang members in gang violence

- Examine network-based approaches in understanding the structure (including "key players"), evolution, and consequences of criminal networks

- Demonstrate SNA's applications to characterize the structural features of terrorist networks and to improve counterterrorism effectiveness

This chapter focuses on applications of social network analysis in the research of crime and terrorism, and it illustrates how social network perspectives and methods help us understand why crimes are being committed, or how to best disrupt a terrorist network. Delinquents are influenced by their peers, and terrorists are often recruited through acquaintances; both coordinate their actions along personal ties that can be analyzed by using social network analysis (SNA). In this chapter, we first discuss how personal networks among peers, the family, and the neighborhood contribute to delinquency and crime. We then use network analysis to understand how criminal and terrorist groups organize. Finally, we turn to the question of how best to disrupt their activities.

6.1 Personal Networks, Delinquency, and Crime

6.1.1 Social Ability Model Versus Social Inability Model

The social ability model and the social inability model provide two very prominent explanations for youth delinquency—and relationships play an important role in both. The **social inability model**, best presented by Travis Hirschi's *control theory*

(1969), argues that deviant behavior is caused by a lack of bonding or attachment to family or school. In other words, this theory considers delinquents as *lacking* social abilities, unable to establish and maintain meaningful social relationships because they are selfish, unreliable, and display little regard for the feelings and opinions of others (Gottfredson & Hirschi, 1990). Strong affective ties to family or school constrain the adolescents' behavior and prevent them from becoming delinquents. Hirschi's (1969) emphasis on the constraining influence of social integration is therefore consistent with a social network perspective (Krohn, 1986): We should expect delinquents to report fewer and weaker ties to family members and classmates or teachers.

Proponents of the ***social ability model***, on the other hand, would disagree with this portrayal of delinquents as isolated individuals. For example, Edwin Sutherland's ***differential association theory*** (see Sutherland, Cressey, & Luckenbill, 1947/1992) emphasizes the role of relationships with peers in fostering attitudes and beliefs conducive to delinquent behavior and in acquiring the necessary skills and abilities for such behavior. Together with Albert Cohen's (1955) *subcultural theory* and Ronald Akers's (1998) *social learning theory*, these theories posit that delinquent behavior is learned through social interactions with others (Hansell & Wiatrowski, 1981). We would thus expect to observe homophily—that delinquents are more likely to have social ties to others that either have similar attitudes or, as Mark Warr and Mark Stafford (1991) found, also engage in forbidden behavior.

SOCIAL NETWORKS IN ACTION: SOCIAL ABILITY OR SOCIAL INABILITY?

So does social ability or social inability explain adolescents' delinquent behaviors? Several empirical studies have seemed to lend support to social ability, refuting the social inability model. For example, Peggy Giordiano, Stephen Cernkovich, and Meredith Pugh (1986) examined numerous friendship characteristics and found that delinquent and nondelinquent adolescents were similar in their social relationships. They found no differences in the stability and frequency of their contacts, and, more importantly, in the trust, caring, and self-confirmation in those relationships. The delinquents even reported a slightly higher level of loyalty and self-disclosure. Denise Kandel and Mark Davies (1991) investigated friendship networks among adolescents who did and did not use illicit drugs and found little difference in terms of intimacy. In fact, frequent drug users shared more intimate friendships than did adolescents with lower or no drug consumption. Similarly, Michel Claes and Raymonde Simard (1992) reported no differences between incarcerated delinquent adolescents and nondelinquent adolescents in trust, communication, and levels of intimacy. They did find, however, that delinquents were more likely to feel different from others and to be ridiculed or even rejected by their peers.

It should be noted that the quality of personal relationships in each study was based on the respondents' own *perceptions* rather than on direct measures of actual quality. Furthermore, as Chris Baerveldt, Ronan Van Rossem, Marjolijn Vermande, and Frank Weerman (2004) pointed out, concepts such as "peers" and "friendship" were not clearly defined and instead left to the respondents to interpret subjectively. Mattias Smångs (2010) avoided the problem of subjectivity by examining co-offending networks, networks in which a tie indicates that the two actors commit crimes together. He also drew on social network concepts, in particular Mark Granovetter's (1973) notion of **the forbidden triad** (i.e., the claim that if there is a strong tie between actors A and B, and A and C, there should also be at least a weak tie between B and C).

Smångs (2010) reasoned that if the social inability model is correct and delinquents do lack social skills, then their weak and strong ties should form different patterns than those of nondelinquents. He reported that the Swedish juveniles in his three-year dataset formed strong and weak co-offense ties in a manner predicted by the social ability model, a development that ran contrary to the predictions of the social inability model. In the research, delinquents also seemed to introduce common friends to each other, thereby avoiding the creation of forbidden triads. Results from an analysis that uses the quadratic assignment procedure (QAP; see Chapter 4 for details) also showed that the number of offenses two actors allegedly commit together is correlated with the number of friends they share. This finding suggests social learning and influence among juveniles again more in line with the social ability model. Smångs's (2010) study also demonstrated the value of using social network analysis for traditional criminological theory. The evidence, thus, suggests that the social inability model is incorrect and that juvenile delinquents and nondelinquents are equally able to develop, negotiate, and maintain social relationships.

6.1.2 Peer Influence Versus Parenting Influence

That adolescents are subject to peer influence has long been established in delinquency research; several of those are reflected in studies by Marvin Krohn and colleagues (1986, 1988, 1993) examining the peer influences with adolescents' friendship network properties such as *muliplexity*, which is defined as the number of activities in which individuals participate jointly, and *network density*.

It was in this vein that Dana Haynie (2001) used detailed social network information on high-school–age adolescents from the **National Longitudinal Study of Adolescent Health (Add Health)**. Unlike most previous work, this study uses self-reported measures of peer delinquency rather than friends' perceptions. More importantly, its network data allow researchers to test the extent to which the strength of the delinquency–peer association depends on the density of the peer network and the adolescent's **centrality** or **popularity** (i.e., the number of times they were named as friend, in-degree) among network members. The results show that peers' delinquency has a stronger association with an adolescent's delinquency when the latter scores high on all three measures. In other words, adolescents that are central, popular, and embedded in dense friendship

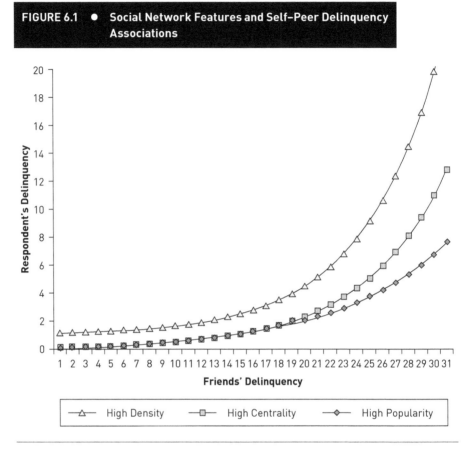

FIGURE 6.1 ● Social Network Features and Self–Peer Delinquency Associations

Note: Adapted from p. 1046 of Haynie, D. L. (2001). Delinquent peers revisited: Does network structure matter? *American Journal of Sociology, 106*(4), 1013–1057.

networks are more likely to engage in delinquent behavior if their friends are delinquents. Among these network characteristics, network density, which signifies network cohesion, emerges as the most important moderator of peer delinquency. Figure 6.1 demonstrates that the association between a respondent's delinquency and his or her friends' delinquency tends to be strong when the three indicators (density, centrality, and popularity) of the respondent's network are high. Criminological research should thus incorporate network cohesion when studying delinquency-peer association.

But we would usually think that parents and family influence adolescents as well, not just their peers. Machteld Hoeve et al. (2009) reported that the link between parenting and delinquency does exist after conducting a meta-analysis of 161 published and unpublished studies that varied on the delinquency type and parenting dimensions examined, as well as in how these concepts are operationalized, and in the populations from which the samples are drawn. The parenting dimensions that have the strongest impact on delinquency are parental monitoring, psychological control, and negative aspects of support, such as rejection and hostility. The magnitudes of these effects are moderated by factors such as gender of the child, the child's age, and the delinquency type. The authors also noted that fewer than 20% of the studies reviewed focused on the fathers' behavior, despite the fact that the effect of poor paternal support was larger than poor maternal support, particularly for sons.

Do parents or peers exert a greater influence over adolescents? According to Hirschi's (1969) social control theory, strong social bonds with parents reduce delinquent behavior. By using data from a three-wave panel study of more than 400 youths with data on both parents and friends available, Robert Aseltine (1995) examined the relative influences of parents and peers on adolescent delinquency. The study concluded that friends are the primary source of influence on youths' behavior although the magnitudes of peer influence are grossly overstated in analyses relying on respondents' perceptions of their friends' behavior. In contrast, parental supervision and attachment are weakly related to adolescent delinquency, offering limited support to Hirschi's (1969) social control theory of deviance.

6.1.3 Selection Versus Socialization

The problem with the literature discussed so far is that it cannot answer the question of causality: Do adolescents learn delinquent behavior from their friends? Or do adolescents who are prone to delinquency become friends with delinquents—a phenomenon sometimes known as *assortative selection*, a process exemplified in the expression "birds of a feather flock together" (Cairns, Cairns, Nekerman, Gest, & Gariepy, 1988; Patterson & Dishion, 1985)?

Cross-sectional data usually cannot distinguish between these two explanations for observed homophily. Nevertheless, as Haynie (2001) pointed out, if selection were the main driving force of homophily, we would not expect that the network characteristics would moderate this delinquency-peer association. For example, network measures, such as density of the peer network or centrality of one's position in the peer network, should not have an impact on the strength of the association if adolescents join peer networks that are most fitted with their delinquent inclinations. Longitudinal data can be used to test explicitly whether self-selection or socialization is the primary mechanism responsible for the association. Research employing longitudinal data has shown that both influence and selection are responsible for similarities in adolescent behavior (Bauman & Ennet, 1996; Elliott & Menard, 1996).

In the statistical analysis of networks, homophily is also known as ***network autocorrelation*** (Doreian, 1989). To address the problem adequately, researchers should model this as a dynamic process that uses longitudinal network data (Valente, 2003). In one such effort to model both the behavior changes caused by current friends in the network and the formation of new friendships due to behavioral similarity, Christian Steglich, Tom A.B. Snijders, and Michael Pearson (2010) proposed a novel method that formalizes the simultaneous, joint evolution of the social networks and the behavioral characteristics of the network actors in an explicit, stochastic model.

Their model requires ***network-behavior panel data,*** in which complete networks as well as changeable attributes are measured over time. The proposed actor-based model separates what drives network change and what drives behavioral change, thus, allowing us to draw separate conclusions about selection and influence while assuming that both of these processes occur simultaneously. Steglich and his associates use their model on data from Scottish secondary school pupils and find evidence for significant peer influence on drinking behavior, as well as a slightly weaker effect on smoking. Partner selection, on the other hand, is only weakly related to substance use.

By using longitudinal data and the SIENA program, Weerman (2011) analyzed a longitudinal social network data of more than 1,000 Dutch students to examine the interplay between network evolution and delinquency. He found that engaging in similar types of delinquency does not increase the chance of forming a friendship once other network dynamics are controlled for. Nevertheless, the average delinquency level of someone's friends in the school network has a significant, although relatively small, effect on the delinquent behavior of the respondents. The results also show that leaving or joining informal street-oriented youth groups has a substantial effect on changes in delinquency. Both studies, thus, concluded that peer socialization is more important than peer selection, while illustrating the utility of the actor-based model on network-behavior panel data for distinguishing between the two.

The latter study may raise the question of whether there is a unique contribution of street-oriented youth group membership to delinquency above and beyond having delinquent peers. Sarah Battin and colleagues (1998) drew on data from the Seattle Social Development Project and found that gang membership independently explained both self-reported and officially recorded delinquency beyond the effects of having delinquent friends and prior delinquency.

6.2 Neighborhood Networks

6.2.1 Neighborhood and Contextual Effect

School and family ties are not the only networks that influence adolescents and adults. Neighborhood is another social setting that shapes adolescents and adults. According to Park's (1916) classic work that laid the foundation for urban study, a ***neighborhood*** can be defined as a collection of both people and institutions occupying a spatially defined area influenced by ecological, cultural, and sometimes political forces. For a long time, researchers have relied on geographic boundaries defined by the U.S. Census Bureau or other administrative agencies (e.g., school districts and police districts) to operationalize the concept. It was not until recently that social networks of neighbor interactions or street patterns were used to define neighborhoods. Neighborhoods or "tertiary communities" defined by residential street patterns correspond more closely to resident's cognitive maps of their neighborhoods and areas of social interaction, that is, how they define the neighborhood (Grannis, 1998).

Neighborhood-level variables, such as average household income, residential stability, home ownership rate, density, and ethnic heterogeneity, have been associated with a wide range of child and adolescent outcomes, including low weight birth, teen child-birth, high school dropouts, child maltreatment, and adolescent delinquency (Brooks-Gunn, Duncan, & Aber, 1997; Morenoff, Sampson, & Raudenbush, 2001, Wilson, 1987). The literature on neighborhoods, thus, has examined not only whether local contexts affect the behaviors of individuals but also through which mechanisms those contexts work. Barbara Entwisle, Katherine Faust, Ronald Rindfuss, and Toshiko Kaneda (2007) posited at least four ways in which patterns of social interaction relate to features of neighborhoods and communities and affect individual behavior: (1) ***Social cohesion***. The concept has its origin in Émile Durkheim's (1949) concept of solidarity and can be defined as "the social forces that draw and bind men [and women] together" (Schacter, 1968). In network analysis, the social cohesion of the neighborhood can be measured by the relational structures of the community, such as the strength and nature of social ties in the neighborhood as a whole. (2) ***Social capital***. This concept refers to social structural components that can be used by individuals or groups to achieve certain goals (Bourdieu, 1986; Coleman, 1988; Lin, Cook, & Burt, 2001; Putnam, 1993). Neighborhood social capital can be measured by the extent and nature of social ties to neighbors, as well as by the composition and density of these locally based social networks. (3) ***Informal social control***. Clifford Shaw and Henry McKay's (1942) social disorganization theory argues that poor structural characteristics of neighborhoods (i.e., poverty or high residential mobility) reduce social control and allow for deviant behaviors in neighborhoods (see also Sampson and Groves, 1989). (4) ***Collective efficacy***. This concept is defined as "the linkage of mutual trust and the willingness to intervene for the common good" in a neighborhood (Sampson, Raudenbush, & Earls, 1997, p. 919). In empirical research, it is often operationalized as a combination of two scales. One measures neighborhood residents' willingness to intervene in certain instances (i.e., social control), and the other measures residents' perceptions of the closeness, friendliness, and trustworthiness of the people in the neighborhood (i.e., social cohesion).

In this section, we focus in particular on social disorganization theory, which is perhaps the most influential and productive line of research in understanding the impact of neighborhood effects on delinquency and crime. Rather than trying to identify certain "kinds of people" to explain crime, social disorganization theory focuses on the effects of "kinds of places"—specifically, different types of neighborhoods—in creating social contexts that encourage or discourage crime and delinquency (Kubrin & Weitzer, 2003). First formulated by Shaw and McKay (1942), it emphasizes the importance of community-level characteristics, including social networks, for developing informal social control and decreasing area crime rates. The local community is viewed as a complex system of friendship, kinship, or acquaintance networks (Bursik, 1988; Bursik & Grasmick, 1993; Kasarda & Janowitz, 1974).

In a study testing the social disorganization theory, Sampson and Groves (1989) measured a community's level of social organization in terms of local friendship networks, control of street-corner teenage peer groups, and prevalence of organizational participation. Based on two large-scale samples from England and Wales, respectively, the analysis showed that communities with sparse friendship networks, unsupervised teenage peer groups, and low organizational participation had much higher rates of crime and delinquency. Non-network factors that could influence crime rates, such as average socioeconomic status, residential mobility, ethnic heterogeneity, and family disruption, are largely mediated by these three network factors.

Pamela Rountree and Barbara Warner (1999) posited that not all social ties are equally effective in producing informal social control and decreasing crime rates. By drawing on data from 100 Seattle neighborhoods, they showed that although women and men have similar levels of local social ties, their effect is gender specific: Female social ties are more effective in controlling crime, particularly in communities with few female-headed households. In another related neighborhood research study, Gregory Zimmerman and Steven Messner (2010) found that the gender gap in violent crime decreases as the level of neighborhood disadvantage increases. And although neighborhood disadvantage increases exposure to peer violence for both sexes, peer violence has a more pronounced impact on women's violent behavior. The authors explain this with the fact that compared with males, females tend to have more close friendships. In other words, at least in this particular setting, strong ties might increase crime.

The notion that strong social ties in a neighborhood network automatically prevent crime has also been challenged in other ways. By drawing on data from 60 urban neighborhoods in medium-sized U.S. cities, Paul Bellair (1997) tested ten measures of social interaction among neighbors by asking respondents how often members of their household visited neighbors or were visited by them. Both frequent and infrequent social interaction among neighbors helped establish community control (Bellair, 1997). Since infrequent interaction among neighbors signals the existence of weak ties, weak ties, thus, also help strengthen community organization by creating important linkages across individual networks.

In taking the criticism further, Jeffrey Morenoff, Robert Sampson, and Stephen Raudenbush (2001) argued that, under certain neighborhood contexts, strong ties may impede efforts to establish social control. Instead, dense local ties may foster the growth of gang-related networks (Pattillo-McCoy, 1999). In an analysis of homicide in Chicago neighborhoods, Morenoff et al. (2001) found there was no independent association between social ties and neighborhood homicide rates after controlling for collective efficacy, which was a combined measure of the neighborhood capacity for informal social control and social cohesion. Other research has provided further evidence that although social networks contribute to neighborhood collective efficacy, they also provide a source of social capital for offenders, potentially diminishing the regulatory effectiveness of collective efficacy (Browning, Feinberg, & Dietz, 2004).

Neighborhood research has also looked at the influence of local culture. From a social network perspective, culture is not merely adaptive but relational (Hannerz, 1969); individuals acquire culture through their interactions in social networks. In exploring the effects of **_legal cynicism_**, a cultural frame whereby people perceive the law as illegitimate, unresponsive, and ill-equipped to ensure public safety, David Kirk and Andrew Papachristos (2011) argued that although direct experiences with harassing police may influence an individual's cynicism, this cynicism becomes cultural as it is transmitted through social networks. By compiling data from multiple sources, including the Project on Human Development in Chicago Neighborhoods (PHDCN), the Chicago Police Department, and the U.S. Census Bureau, they showed that neighborhood rates of homicide are positively associated with legal cynicism after controlling for structural and social factors. Kirk and Papachristos saw this as the cause behind the unexpected change in the homicide rate in Chicago from the early 1990s to the early 2000s. Future research on neighborhood networks, thus, may need to consider both social-structural and cultural mechanisms to understand in full the bases of neighborhood rates of crime.

6.3 Criminal Networks

6.3.1 Structure and the Evolution of Criminal Networks

Most of the research presented so far has focused on ego-networks or complete networks of a population of criminals and noncriminals. Another important application of social network analysis to the study of crime is the examination of the structure of various illegal groups, tracing that structure's evolution, and understanding its consequences. Papachristos (2009), for instance, posited that gang murder should best be studied by examining the social network of actions and reactions between different gangs. As the author forcefully argued, "Gang members do not kill because they are poor, black, or young or live in a socially disadvantaged neighborhood. They kill because they live in a structured set of social relations in which violence works its way through a series of connected individuals" (p. 75).

Papachristos's (2009) study illustrated the interactional quality of gang murder by applying descriptive and statistical network techniques to analyzing homicide records in Chicago from 1994 to 2002. His findings suggest that individual murders between gangs create an institutionalized network of group conflict—stable patterns of retaliation—independent of any individual's participation or motive. Murders spread through the network in a process similar to social contagion as gangs respond to threats by evaluating the highly visible actions of others in their local networks.

But the most common network studies of criminal groups examine the internal structure and interactions of, for example, drug dealers and political conspirators (Athey & Bouchard, 2013; Faulkner & Cheney, 2013; Natarajan, 2006). Based on 2,408 wiretap conversations collected over the course of prosecuting heroin dealers in New York City in the 1990s, Mangai Natarajan (2006) used social network analysis to identify a large, loosely structured group of 294 individuals who comprised one segment of the heroin market in the city. This study also revealed that organized crime, such as drug trafficking, is mostly carried out by small groups of loosely linked entrepreneurs rather than by large, highly structured criminal syndicates.

Analyzing hidden networks such as criminal networks has its methodological difficulties. One major problem is ensuring that no important actor or tie is missing (Berlusconi, 2013; Sparrow, 1991). Researchers have tried to address this problem by using a variety of data sources. One example for this approach is a study that investigated the notorious Bay Area Laboratory Cooperative (BALCO) scandal involving the production and distribution of an undetectable steroid to professional athletes, including baseball player Barry Bonds and track and field star Marion Jones. Nicholas Athey and Martin Bouchard (2013) drew on four different data sources to code the network data, including 1) a tell-all book written about the scandal (which was based on extensive amounts of court documents and 200 interviews), 2) media articles associated with BALCO, 3) a TV news program interviewing BALCO executives, and 4) multiple court documents involving the main actors in the scandal. They uncovered six communities in the BALCO network of 97 individuals, including three structures oriented around athletic interests (baseball, football, and boxing), one containing BALCO's chemist, one around the eventual whistle-blower, and a "broker" community at the core of the whole network. The broker community functioned as a bridge between the others because of the diversity of the actors involved and the presence of BALCO's founder, the main broker in this particular network.

Another fascinating analysis of a criminal and political conspiracy is Robert Faulkner and Eric Cheney's (2013) examination of the Watergate scandal using archival network data. Instead of explaining the breakdown of the conspiracy as a result of external forces, for example the investigation by journalists and the subsequent media exposure, the study suggested that political conspiracies collapse because of their internal structural relations. The study showed that specific positions in the multiplex networks of discord and corrupt action among the conspirators were associated with a key measure of conspiracy collapse, that is, finger pointing at trial. In addition, social network analysis used in this study also vividly depicted the structural relations of who testified against whom and why (Faulkner & Cheney, 2013).

Although criminal networks are often characterized as fluid, flexible, and adaptive, most studies on criminal networks have examined them at a single time point. One effort to examine the dynamic and evolutionary dimension of criminal networks over time was a study of the growth and evolution of a drug trafficking network over a period of eight years by Bright and Delaney (2013). The authors found that the density of the network remained relatively stable over time but that the network became more decentralized. Centrality scores for actors changed significantly over time as they adopted new roles according to the changing needs and focus of the network. Frederic Ouellet, Remi Boivin, Chloe Leclerc, and Carlo Morselli (2013) explored the relationship between co-offending and rearrest by using data from seven years of arrest records involving 415,350 offenders in the province of Quebec, Canada. They showed that a higher degree of centrality is associated with a higher risk of rearrest, whereas a higher individual clustering coefficient is associated with a lower risk of rearrest. In other words, engaging with more individuals in more criminal activities unsurprisingly increases the chance of being arrested, but being ensconced in a dense local network provides some protection.

6.3.2 Key Players Problem in Criminal Networks

Another important application of social network analysis in criminology is to identify the critical actors of a criminal network. This line of work is practical for law enforcement as it can help them decide who to arrest or investigate more closely. Most network specialists assume that network centrality is the most important factor, but debates abound as to what other network measures are important.

Stephen Borgatti (2006) developed a particularly useful network-based approach to identify central actors or "key players" as he called them. This approach made a critical distinction between enforcement and intelligence. Borgatti proposed the novel key-player measures of *fragmentation* (to maximize disruption of networks) and *reach* (to maximize the spread of information). As illustrated in Figure 6.2, although Node 1 has the highest centrality on all standard centrality measures, deleting Node 1 has no effect on fragmenting the network. In contrast, deleting Node 8, which has a lower centrality on all measures, splits the network into two components. Nevertheless, if we formulate the problem in terms of reaching the most nodes in as few steps as possible, then Node 1 makes the best target.

Which node to target may, thus, depend on whether the attacker wants to collect as much information about the network as possible or to disrupt its functioning. Another aspect to consider is whether the attacker can target multiple individuals at the same time. Martin Everett and Stephen Borgatti (1999) demonstrated that

FIGURE 6.2 ● Hypothetical Network in Which Removing the Most Central Node (1) Does Not Fragment the Network

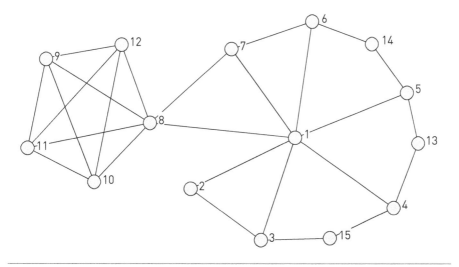

Note: Adapted from p. 23 of Borgatti, S. P. (2006). Identifying sets of key players in a network. *Computational & Mathematical Organization Theory, 12*(1), 21–34.

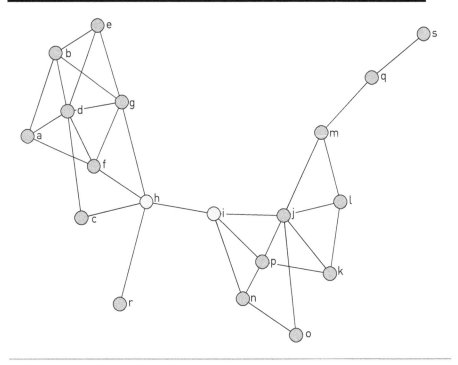

FIGURE 6.3 ● Network in Which Removing the Two Most Central Nodes (i and h) Is Not as Disruptive as Removing a Different Pair of Nodes (m and h)

Note: Adapted from p. 25 of Borgatti, S. P. (2006). Identifying sets of key players in a network. *Computational & Mathematical Organization Theory, 12*(1), 21–34.

selecting a set of *k* nodes that, as an ensemble, is optimal for fragmentation or reach, is quite different from selecting the *k* nodes that individually are optimal. Figure 6.3 shows a graph in which Nodes *h* and *i*, individually, make the best enforcement priorities as the removal of either fragments the network. Yet, deleting both Node *h* and *i* is not as good as removing Node *h* and *m* together even though Node *m* does not rank as high as Node *i* in terms of centrality because removing both Node *h* and *i* is redundant.

The success of optimal disruption strategies may also depend on the target network's various structural features. When a high level of clustering characterizes a network, repeated attacks on multiple nodes are most likely to disrupt the network. Scale-free networks are best disrupted by hub attacks, which target the nodes that receive and send the most ties. Networks characterized by many brokers between subgroups are most vulnerable to attacks that disrupt these bridges (Malm & Bichler, 2011).

Most research in this line of work has been theoretical, either based on theoretical considerations or computer simulations on network data from closed cases. Nevertheless, as law enforcement agencies increasingly make use of these models, the application becomes less innocuous: What if innocent individuals are arrested or killed based simply on their association with or position in a network? Those ethical issues need to be addressed when applying these theoretical models.

6.4 Analyzing Social Networks of Terror

6.4.1 Network Structures Among Terrorists

Social network analysis has been credited with the discovery of Osama bin Laden's hideout in Abbottabad, Pakistan (Knoke, 2013). *It takes a network to defeat a network* has become a new U.S. Army counterinsurgency doctrine in that intelligence agencies have applied network analysis to identify and map links among terrorists and insurgent organizations, as well as in that the intelligence forces operate as a network to destroy the enemies. As General Stanley McChrystal noted, "It became clear to me and to many others that to defeat a networked enemy we had to become a network ourselves" (McChrystal, 2011, p. 67).

But even before that, in the aftermath of 9/11, social network experts in academia and government agencies such as the National Security Agency increasingly began using network analysis to make sense out of the intercepted communication data between individuals (Keefe, 2006). As terrorist organizations often operate in a loose network form in which individual terrorists cooperate and collaborate with each other to carry out attacks (Sageman, 2004), we gain valuable knowledge by studying the structural properties of those networks. And visualization and mathematical measures of network analysis allow analysts to "evaluate the best responses and tactics in attempting to disrupt the cell to the point at which it is no longer able to function" (Koschade, 2006, p. 572).

In a pioneering study on the terrorist network of the 9/11 attacks, Valdis Krebs (2002) used the information published in major newspapers and available through Internet sources during the weeks after the attack. His analysis showed that the terrorist network was composed of 37 participants, including 19 hijackers who executed the attacks and an additional 18 co-conspirators who were not directly involved in executing the attack (Figure 6.4). Krebs referred to the hijackers as the network's *action segment* and to the co-conspirators as *complementary participants* in the network. After the Madrid bombing in 2004, Joseph Rodríguez (2005) conducted a similar analysis when he used public sources to map the March 11 terrorist network. His study revealed diffuse networks based on weak ties among the terrorists.

Using public sources, Marc Sageman (2004) collected biographies of 172 Islamic terrorist operatives affiliated with the Global Salafi Jihad (GSJ). The GSJ network consists of many terrorist groups with members from different countries, through which

FIGURE 6.4 ● **9/11 Hijackers' Network**

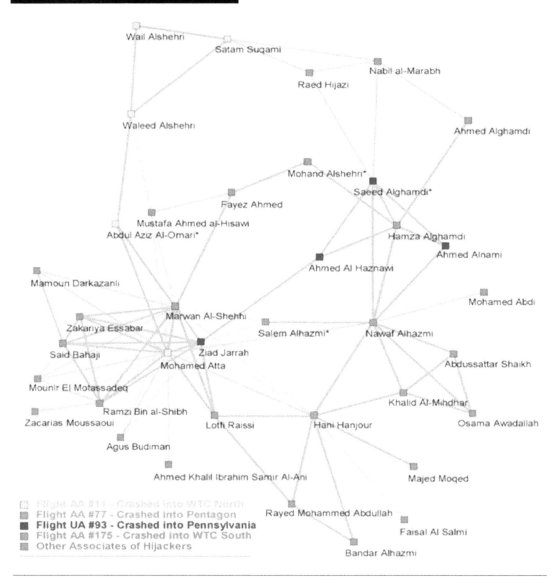

Wail Alshehri
Satam Suqami
Nabil al-Marabh
Raed Hijazi
Ahmed Alghamdi
Waleed Alshehri
Mohand Alshehri*
Saeed Alghamdi*
Fayez Ahmed
Mustafa Ahmed al-Hisawi
Abdul Aziz Al-Omari*
Hamza Alghamdi
Ahmed Alnami
Ahmed Al Haznawi
Mamoun Darkazanli
Mohamed Abdi
Marwan Al-Shehhi
Salem Alhazmi*
Nawaf Alhazmi
Zakariya Essabar
Said Bahaji
Ziad Jarrah
Mohamed Atta
Abdussattar Shaikh
Mounir El Motassadeq
Khalid Al-Mihdhar
Ramzi Bin al-Shibh
Zacarias Moussaoui
Lotfi Raissi
Hani Hanjour
Osama Awadallah
Agus Budiman
Ahmed Khalil Ibrahim Samir Al-Ani
Majed Moqed
Rayed Mohammed Abdullah
Faisal Al Salmi
Bandar Alhazmi

☐ Flight AA #11 - Crashed into WTC North
▦ Flight AA #77 - Crashed into Pentagon
■ **Flight UA #93 - Crashed into Pennsylvania**
▦ Flight AA #175 - Crashed into WTC South
▦ Other Associates of Hijackers

Note: Adapted from p. 50 of Krebs, V. E. (2002). Mapping networks of terrorist cells. *Connections*, 24(3), 43–52.

many large-scale attacks against civilians across different countries have been executed, including the 9/11 tragedy in 2001, the bombing in Bali in 2002, and the bombing in Morocco in 2003. Sageman identified four large terrorist clusters among the al-Qaeda operatives since 1998. The first cluster resides in the Pakistan–Afghan border and consists of the central staff of al-Qaeda and the GSJ movement. The second cluster is a group of operatives located in core Arab states, such as Saudi Arabia, Egypt, Yemen, and Kuwait. The third cluster is known as the Maghreb Arabs who, although they come from North African nations, currently reside in France and England. The final cluster is centered in Indonesia and Malaysia and is affiliated with Jemaah Islamiyah.

Figure 6.5 displays the GSJ network as examined by Jialun Qin, Jennifer Xu, Daning Hu, Marc Sageman, and Hsinchun Chen (2005), who collected extensive data from various sources, including transcripts of court proceedings involving GSJ terrorists, reports of court proceedings, and corroborated information from people with direct access to the information provided. In addition to corroborating Sageman's (2004) findings about the four clusters, the Qin et al. (2005) used three centrality measures (degree, betweenness, and closeness degree) to identify the leaders of each cluster. They found that members with high degrees are likely to be the leaders of their local networks, whereas individuals with high betweenness are usually the contact persons among several terrorist groups and play important roles in coordinating terrorist attacks. They also found that outliers with particularly low closeness can be the true leaders of local networks, only appearing to be marginal while directing the whole network from behind the scenes to evade the attention of intelligence agencies. The key members identified by these measures matched the experts' knowledge on the GSJ.

Qin and his associates (2005) also applied block-modeling analysis on the GSJ network involved in the Strasbourg cathedral bombing plot, which was a plan to blow up a cathedral in Strasbourg, France, in December 2000. The analysis revealed three interconnected subgroups of terrorists: 1) the group that conducted the Strasbourg plot, 2) the group that orchestrated the LAX airport (Los Angeles, CA) bombing plot in 2001, and 3) the group that carried out the Russian embassy bombing plot. The leader of the Strasbourg plot, a high-ranking member of al-Qaeda and close associate of Osama bin Laden named Zubaydah, connected the Strasbourg group to the other two groups in the network. Intelligence collected by authorities during the investigation of the Strasbourg plot closely matches with the SNA results.

A similar block-modeling analysis on the 9/11 attacks reveals Osama bin Laden as the leader and gatekeeper of the September 11th attack. Four major actors (bin Laden, Zawahiri, Hambali, and KSM), who have the highest betweenness values among all GSJ members, connect the 19 hijackers who directly participated in the attacks to all four clusters of the GSJ network, which indicates a worldwide level of planning and coordination used to carry out the attacks (Figure 6.3). A further analysis using the PageRank algorithm (Podolny & Page, 1998), which is also used by Google to rank search results, indicates that the GSJ network functions in a "holding company" model with al-Qaeda as the "headquarters" in charge of planning, and many small independent groups as "operating divisions." Such a model allows effective planning of attacks by having al-Qaeda as the "master brain" of the whole network, and reduces the risk of being disrupted by leaving the operations to the smaller groups that have minimum interactions with the core members. Other studies of terrorist networks also indicated a concentrated structure that consists of a core and periphery

FIGURE 6.5 ● Terrorist Network of the September 11th Attack

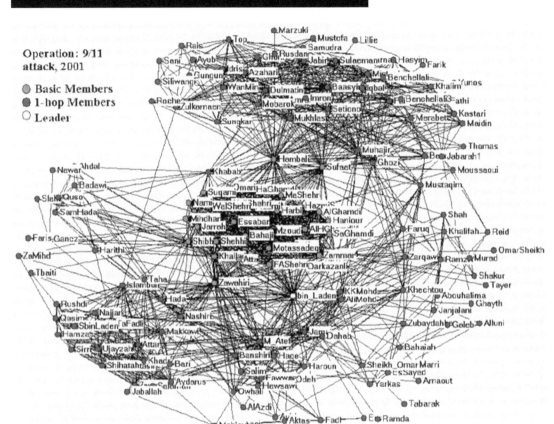

Operation: 9/11
attack, 2001

◉ Basic Members
● 1-hop Members
○ Leader

Note: Adapted from p. 297 of Qin, J., Xu, J. J., Hu, D., Sageman, M., & Chen, H. (2005). Analyzing terrorist networks: A case study of the global salafi jihad network. *Intelligence and Security Informatics*, 287–304.

groups of actors (Demiroz & Kapucu, 2012). The core group tends to have a strong connectedness with each other, whereas the network density is lower in the peripheral groups. Peripheral actors are often separated into subgroups, which are necessary for operational purposes.

The network structure is often associated with advantageous features such as adaptableness, resilience, superior information processes, and learning capabilities (Barabasi, 2003). Nevertheless, Mette Eilstrup-Sangiovanni and Calvert Jones (2008) also demonstrated its limitation for terrorist networks in particular. They argued that in terrorist networks, information is "compartmentalized" to safeguard the identities of individuals, in particular about the larger objective and resources. Although compartmentalization may keep individuals safe from detection, it limits personal interaction and compromises coordination and learning across the network. Information often takes longer to circulate, and restrictions on information impede the types of improvisations that make networks flexible. Moreover, in compartmentalized terrorist networks, subgroups often act autonomously; the lack of leadership or direction may contribute to poor decision-making. Eilstrup-Sangiovanni and Jones, therefore, argued that al-Qaeda may be less threatening than many assume.

Nevertheless, the reality of terrorist networks may be quite different from these theoretical considerations. By drawing on the John Jay & ARTIS Transnational Terrorism Database (JJATT), the first open-source database for the empirical study of terrorist networks, Scott Helfstein and Dominick Wright (2011) traced the evolution of six attack networks. Their exponential random graph models (ERGMs) show that the attack networks become increasingly dense and cohesive as they enter the execution phase. This finding suggests the limitation of the compartmentalization model.

6.4.2 Network Analysis in Counterterrorism

As studies on the structural features of terrorist networks progress, researchers will explore ways to destabilize terrorist groups. Including the aforementioned key-player strategy developed by Borgatti (2006), destabilization strategies targeting a terrorist network can be roughly categorized into two types: one aiming at isolating or decapitating particular actors or leaders, and the other aiming at destroying the network's infrastructure, such as weapons or training facilities and transportation or communication channels.

Kathleen Carley (2003) maintained that terrorist organizations are structured at the operational level as *cellular networks,* characterized by sets of quasi-independent cells, distributed command, and the ability to build larger cells rapidly from subcells whenever needed. The cells in cellular networks are often small but functionally self-sufficient, only loosely interconnected with each other, spread out geographically, and may take on entirely different tasks. Information flow in the network is kept minimal and on a need-to-know basis. This makes each cell expendable. The removal of a cell generally does not inflict great damage on the overall network.

SOCIAL NETWORKS IN ACTION: NEW COUNTER-TERROR NETWORK TECHNIQUES

An example of the increasingly sophisticated use of computer technology and social network analysis at the intersection of academia and government is the collection of large-scale multiagent network models developed for counter-terrorism purposes by

(Continued)

(Continued)

Kathleen Carley and colleagues (Carley, 2004; Diesner & Carley, 2004; Dombroski, Fischbeck, & Carley, 2003).

(1) **BioWar**, a city-scale, dynamic-network, agent-based model for understanding the spread of disease and illness that are a result of natural epidemics, chemical spills, and weaponized biological attacks.

(2) **DyNet**, a tool that traces the change in covert networks, naturally and in response to attacks, under varying levels of information uncertainty.

(3) **RTE**, a model designed for examining state failure and the escalation of conflict at the city, state, national, and international levels.

The previously mentioned structural characteristics of the cellular networks means that a successful attack should not only dismantle the command-and-control infrastructure but also fully disconnect cells from crucial operational information or resource flow. To achieve such goals, precise and detailed knowledge of the network structure and resource distribution within the network is needed. On the other front, a successful attack on key actors involves the isolation of actors, ranging from the disabling of communication, to the discrediting of actors, to even the assassination of actors. As intuitive as the idea of targeting key players is, Maksim Tsvetovat and Kathleen Carley's (2005) study suggested it is much more complicated in reality. For example, they found that when there were structural equivalencies around, isolating central individuals was not effective because the structurally equivalent actors quickly move to take the vacancy.

A recent and dangerous trend of terrorism is the "leaderless jihad" (Sageman, 2008), in which individuals and small groups are no longer affiliated with the major terrorist organizations and use information technology, such as the Internet, to learn about jihad and to connect with others. These groups consist of numerous, small, self-organized cells, as few as two or three people receive no financial support or training from established groups, but they are formed to carry out terrorist acts. The complete network exhibits low density and low social cohesion and therefore is highly resilient to loss of any key players (Knoke, 2012b). The optimal strategy to combat terrorism is therefore far from clear.

End-of-Chapter Questions

1. Based on your experience and observation, do peer groups or parents exert greater influence on your "deviant" behavior, if any, such as smoking or cheating on tests? Why?

2. What do you think of Parachristos's (2009) argument that, "Gang members do not kill because they are poor, black, or young or live in a socially disadvantaged neighborhood? They kill because they live in a structured set of social relations in which violence works its way through a series of connected individuals"?

3. What are the advantages and limits of identifying and removing "key players" in criminal networks?

4. In what sense do people think that terrorist organizations operate in a network form? Can you name some structural characteristics of terrorist networks?

5. What do people mean when they say that "it takes a network to defeat a network" in counterterrorism?

7

Social Network Analysis in Emotional and Physical Health

Learning objectives

- Explain how social support and social influence from one's social network affect emotional health, such as happiness, loneliness, and depression

- Examine how longitudinal social network analysis helps sort out interdependent social processes such as induction, homophily, and shared environment resulting in clustering of people with similar physiological and behavioral characteristics

- Appraise the mechanisms through which one's social networks affect one's propensity to drink or smoke, and even one's body mass index (BMI)

- Discuss how one's social network features are associated with initiation and cessation of illicit drug use

- Explain the gender difference between men and women in network composition of injection drug users (IDUs)

- Describe how understanding the network as a whole as opposed to a respondent's direct contacts helps to curb the spread of sexually transmitted diseases (STDs)

- Assess the research finding of the HIV/AIDS epidemic network that is contradictory to the common assumption of the HIV/AIDS prevention program

That people's health is interconnected (Smith & Christakis, 2008) has become especially obvious during the outbreak of new dangerous diseases such as Ebola: Doctors and investigators scramble to track the contact network of a patient in the hope of isolating anyone who might have contracted the disease before they become contagious themselves. But there are many less dramatic applications of social network analysis (SNA) in the areas of emotional and physical health. Not only do deadly viruses spread along social ties, so do emotions or new ways of treating diseases (DiMaggio & Garip, 2012). In addition, researchers have identified a variety of mechanisms through which social networks affect health, including the provision of both perceived and actual social support, social influence (e.g., norms and social control), social engagement, person to-person contact, and access to resources such as money, jobs, and information (Berkman & Glass, 2000). In this chapter, we look at a variety of SNA applications on topics related to health: We start out with emotional well-being and mental health, and then we move on to peer effects for smoking, alcohol use, and obesity. In a third section, we discuss drug use and needle sharing before examining the spread of **sexually transmitted diseases (STDs)**, in particular, HIV/AIDS.

7.1 Social Network Analysis and Emotional Health

We all have experienced moments when our friends have lifted our spirits or their unhappiness has rubbed off on us. But our relations do not just influence our short-term mood. They can also have an impact on long-term mental health, in particular, depression. Researchers have long examined not only the role of social networks in the development and treatment of mental disorders (Bergin & Lambert, 1971; Erickson, 1975) but also their importance in maintaining good mental health and preventing mental disorders (Caplan, 1974; Kelly, Snowden, & Munoz, 1977). In the following sections, we showcase both of these research traditions by examining social networks' roles in affecting one's happiness, loneliness, and likelihood of depression.

7.1.1 Happiness

Before we turn to serious health issues, let's first look at the effect of the social network on simple emotional well-being. Social species need companionship. Research on happiness has consistently shown that friends and a good family life are the main sources of increased happiness and that married people are happier than singles (Layard, 2006). One indicator of emotional health is ***subjective well-being (SWB)***, the positive evaluation of one's life associated with good feelings. One's social network affects SWB in different ways. First, being respected by others and receiving positive social feedback is an important source of self-esteem and SWB (Atchley, 1991). Second, social support from one's social network helps buffer life stress (Antonucci & Akiyama, 1991; Thoits, 1986). Nevertheless, not all kinds of contacts provide the same level of protection. For instance, contact with friends is more strongly related to SWB than is having contact with family members (Pinquart & Sörensen, 2000). Moreover, research has shown that the absence of family in the context of friends is less detrimental than is the absence of friends in the context of family (Fiori, Antonucci, & Cortina, 2006). Finally, social relationships are not always beneficial: They can overburden or even hurt individuals (Ingersoll-Dayton, Morgan, & Antonucci, 1997). Researchers have tried to explain these contradictory findings on the effect of social ties by positing the ***social comparison theory***. They claim that happiness depends on how individuals compare themselves with others close to them (Brickman, Coates, & Janoff-Bulman, 1978; Easterlin, 1974; Van Praag & Kapteyn, 1973). For instance, the increase in happiness that one may expect from an increase of one's personal income in the wake of an economic upturn may be offset by observing that everyone else's income is also (or even more rapidly) increasing.

Although strong evidence exists that our happiness is indeed influenced by how our situation compares with those around us, researchers have also repeatedly found that egos surrounded by happy alters tend to be happier themselves. This raises the question of whether happiness can spread from person to person or whether happy people are more likely to form ties with each other in social networks. To tackle this question,

James Fowler and Nicholas Christakis (2009) conducted a longitudinal social network analysis on 4,739 individuals in the ***Framingham Heart Study*** for an observation period from 1983 to 2003. Their goal was to distinguish among three processes through which the clustering of happy and unhappy people could come about. The first process is *induction*, meaning that happiness in one person causes the happiness of his or her network neighbors. The second process is *homophily*, whereby happy individuals are more likely to become friends. They call the third process the *confounding effect*, meaning that connected individuals may be exposed to the same happiness-increasing or -decreasing events or circumstances.

To distinguish among these processes, they took advantage of the directionality of the ties and the fact that both the network ties and the happiness of each subject were measured repeatedly over time. They did indeed discover clusters of happy and unhappy people in the network. In fact, they found that an individual's happiness is not just correlated with his or her immediate neighbors but with those up to three steps away, that is, the friends of one's friends' friends. People surrounded by many happy people and those who have high centrality tend to become happier as time goes on. The results also show that the clusters of happiness are mainly the result of the spread of happiness and not of homophily, the tendency of people to associate with similar individuals. In particular, a person is 25% more likely to report being happy if a friend who lives within a mile becomes happy. Similar effects are observed in spouses, siblings who live within a mile of each other, and next-door neighbors. But, the effects are not observed in co-workers. Christakis and Fowler's (2009) claims, although widely reported on in popular news, have not gone unchallenged. Cosma Shalizi and Andrew Thomas (2011) showed that their method cannot in fact distinguish among the three processes. Russell Lyons (2011) pointed out that the respondents likely did not report all their friends to the researchers. It is therefore possible that the alter of the alter, whose happiness supposedly influences the ego, does in fact have a direct tie with ego through which he or she exerts this influence. Although it seems likely that happiness is indeed "contagious," the statistical evidence provided so far is not conclusive.

7.1.2 Loneliness and Depression

The flip side of social networks transmitting emotions is that social contact can also have negative effects. For example, research on spouses caring for their sick or disabled partner has shown that the patient's poor mental health affects the physical and mental health of his or her caregiving partner, and that depression is associated with caregiving (Kiecolt-Glaser, Dura, Speicher, Trask, & Glaser, 1991; Mittelman et al., 1995; Pruchno & Potashnik, 1989; Shaw et al., 1997; Zarit, Todd, & Zarit, 1986). This effect occurs more often in women than in men: Caregiving wives are more likely to report psychological fatigue and strain than are caregiving husbands (Barusch & Spaid, 1989; Collins & Jones, 1997).

But low emotional well-being is even more commonly associated with the absence of ties or at least with the perception of such an absence. A sizable amount of literature has documented that perceived social isolation (i.e., loneliness) is a more important

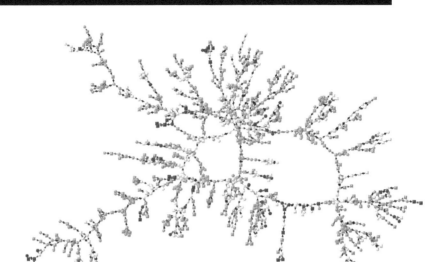

FIGURE 7.1 ● Loneliness Clusters in the Framingham Social Network

Notes: This graph shows the largest component of friends, spouses, and siblings. There are 1,019 individuals shown. Each node represents a participant, and its shape denotes gender (circles are female, squares are male). Lines between nodes indicate relationship (grey for siblings, black for friends and spouses). Node color denotes the mean number of days the nodes felt lonely in the past week, with light grey being 0–1 days, grey being 2 days, and dark grey being greater than 3 days or more. The graph suggests clustering in loneliness and a relationship between being peripheral and feeling lonely. Reprinted from p. 981 of Cacioppo, J. T., Fowler, J. H., & Christakis, N. A. (2009). Alone in the crowd: The structure and spread of loneliness in a large social network. *Journal of Personality and Social Psychology, 97*(6), 977–991.

predictor of a variety of adverse health outcomes than is objective social isolation (Cole et al., 2007; Hawkley, Masi, Berry, & Cacioppo, 2006; Penninx et al., 1997; Seeman, 2000). By using the same data as in the previous section, John Cacioppo, James Fowler, and Nicholas Christakis (2009) examined the structure and spread of loneliness through social networks. They found that loneliness, similar to happiness, occurred in clusters and extended up to three degrees of separation. But loneliness is not just a matter of perception: In contrast to the findings that happy people tend to be central in the social network, lonely people are disproportionately represented at the periphery of social networks (see Figure 7.1).

Cacioppo et al. (2009) again claimed to find evidence that loneliness spreads. Moreover, the spread of loneliness is stronger for friends than for family members, and stronger for women than for men. The analysis also reveals that loneliness shapes social networks; people who felt lonely in earlier time periods are less likely to have friends in the next period. Loneliness is thus both a cause and a consequence of becoming disconnected from the rest of society.

Prolonged loneliness can lead to depression, which is a mental health illness. In the United States, a lifetime incidence of depression is estimated between 13.3% and 17.1%, and a yearly cross-sectional prevalence ranges from 2.3% to 4.9% (Fava & Cassano, 2008). Niels Rosenquist along with Fowler and Christakis (2011), therefore, also used the same data to analyze the spread of depressive symptoms. These symptoms, measured by ***CES-D scores (the Center for Epidemiological Studies Depression Scale)***, were associated with similar scores in friends and neighbors but not in co-workers, siblings, or spouses. They also found that depression spreads more easily from women than from men. When a female friend becomes depressed, it increases the probability that the ego also becomes depressed by 142%. No such effect exists for male friends. This finding, therefore, corroborates the conventional wisdom that women are more effective at communicating mood states than men.

But the negative consequences of social networks do not stop there. A growing body of research has linked social isolation to suicide attempts (Berkman, Glass, Brissette, & Seeman, 2000). Peter Bearman (1991) suggested that adolescent suicidality may be a product of network positions characterized by either relative isolation or structural imbalance. Bearman along with James Moody (2004) analyzed friendship data on 13,465 adolescents from the National Longitudinal Survey of Adolescent Health (Add Health) to explore the relationship between friendship and suicidal ideation (entertaining thoughts about suicide) and suicide attempts. Having friends who have attempted suicide does indeed increase the likelihood of suicidal ideation and attempts for both male and female students. But other network causes of suicide vary strikingly by gender. Among young women, the likelihood of suicidal ideation increases substantially when they are socially isolated from peers or have intransitive friendships, that is, when they have friends who are not friends of each other. Moreover, attending a school with dense social networks lowered their odds of thinking about suicide. In contrast, these variables did not have any significant impact on the odds of suicidal ideation among young men. It may thus be possible to lower suicide rates among women through interventions that increase the density of their and their friends' networks.

7.2 Social Network Analysis in Physical Fitness

Social networks also influence physical health. A stream of research has examined the importance of social integration—one's membership in a diverse social network—for health and longevity (Berkman & Syme, 1979; Cohen & Janicki-Deverts, 2009). Studies in this line of research have found that individuals with diverse social networks live longer (Berkman & Glass, 2000), retain their cognitive skills when aging (Fratiglioni, Paillard-Borg, & Winblad, 2004), have greater resistance to infectious disease (Cohen, Doyle, Skoner, Rabin, & Gwaltney, 1997), and enjoy a better prognosis when facing chronic life-threatening illnesses (Kop et al., 2005; Rutledge et al., 2004).

7.2.1 Alcohol Use and Smoking

Two of the most studied social behaviors relevant to physical fitness are smoking and alcohol use. Sheldon Cohen and Edward Lemay (2007), for instance, found that those with more diverse social networks reported that they smoked and drank less when interviewed at the end of the day. Nevertheless, within-subject analysis found that the number of people with whom the subjects interacted during a day was positively associated with drinking and smoking on that day. This was particularly true for those low in network diversity, whereas those with high network diversity were not influenced by the increased interactions. The authors suggested that individuals with diverse social networks are used to interacting with a broad range of people and are therefore less emotionally responsive to being with others. The diversity of their networks may also make them less subject to social pressures from specific sub-groups to drink or smoke. Individuals with diverse networks overall may be more socially adept and, therefore, less dependent on alcohol and cigarettes to facilitate social interaction.

But the right social ties can also help resolve drinking problems (McCrady, 2004). Being involved with others and receiving high levels of support from even one person prior to treatment leads to better outcomes for quitting drinking. Unsurprisingly, the reverse is also true: Having a social network that includes many other drinkers or even just contains one such person increases the risk of relapse (Havassy, Hall, & Wasserman, 1991). Individuals combating drinking problems are therefore often asked to identify and cope with high-risk individuals, social settings, and activities that may undercut recovery efforts. Programs, such as ***Alcoholics Anonymous (AA)***, not only offer a social network with role models that encourage sober and rewarding activities, but they also help reshape participants' social network by reducing pro-drinking social ties and increasing pro-abstinent social ties (Groh, Jason, & Keys, 2008; Kelly, Stout, Magill, & Tonigan, 2011; Moos, 2007).

Christakis and Fowler (2008) also studied the smoking behavior among the individuals of the Framingham Heart Study. Their analysis once again revealed discernible clusters of smokers and nonsmokers who tended to stop smoking around the same time. Specifically, they claim that smoking cessation by a spouse decreased a person's chances of smoking by 67%. The effect size for a sibling quitting is 25%, 36% for a friend, and 34% for a co-worker working in the same small firm. Results also show that better-educated friends tend to influence one another more than those with less education. Smokers are more likely to be found in the periphery of the social network and tend to move further to the periphery of the network over time. The authors also observed that the network becomes increasingly segregated between smokers and nonsmokers, with fewer social ties between these groups. Findings from such studies help to explain why cessation programs that provide peer support, effectively modifying a person's social network, are more successful than those that do not afford peer supports (Malchodi et al., 2003; McKnight & McPherson, 1986).

7.2.2 Obesity

Obesity is yet another affliction that has a strong social component, as Christakis and Fowler (2007) showed by using the same data and similar methodology mentioned earlier. They claimed that obesity spreads in a manner reminiscent of an infectious disease or a fad (Figure 7.2), and they found similar clusters and influence on neighbors up to three degrees removed. Specifically, Christakis and Fowler claimed that having a friend who is obese increases one's likelihood of becoming obese by 57%, with larger effects observed for friends of the same sex. Among pairs of adult siblings, one sibling becoming obese increases the other's chance of obesity by 40%, and an effect size similar to that among spouses (37%). The friend or sibling effect does not vary over how far away the friends or siblings live from each other, which makes it less likely that shared environmental factors are the true cause of this correlation.

FIGURE 7.2 ● Largest Connected Subcomponent of the Social Network in the Framingham Heart Study in the Year 2000 With Distinct Clusters of Obese or Nonobese Individuals

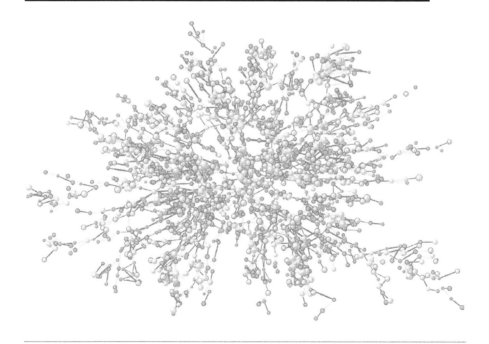

Notes: Large, light grey nodes denote obese persons with BMI > = 30; smaller, grey nodes stand for non-obese people. Reprinted from p. 373 of Christakis, N. A., & Fowler, J. H. (2007). The spread of obesity in a large social network over 32 years. *New England Journal of Medicine, 357*(4), 370–379.

With obesity increasing among children and adolescents over the past several decades, researchers have wondered whether these findings can be generalized to children and adolescents. Research on childhood obesity has focused on parental influences, food prices, the built environment, and school nutrition policies (Koplan, Liverman, & Kraak, 2005). To examine the role of peers in determining adolescent weight, data from Add Health and defined peer groups including nominated friends within schools were used (Trogdon, Nonnemaker, & Pais, 2008). The results show that an alter's average body mass index (BMI) is correlated with that of the ego. Young women are again more likely to be influenced by peer BMI and overweight status than are their male classmates. In addition, peer weight is more influential for adolescents who are already at the higher end of the BMI scale.

What is the mechanism behind this influence? Existing literature has suggested that shared attitudes or norms and weight-related behaviors may explain it. What body weight is considered "normal" depends on peer opinion, and close adolescent friends engage in similar behaviors. Weight loss programs are therefore most effective with peer involvement (de la Haye, Robins, Mohr, & Wilson, 2010; Eisenberg, Neumark-Sztainer, Story, & Perry, 2005; Jelalian & Mehlenbeck, 2002; Paxton, Schutz, Wertheim, & Muir, 1999). In short, the social contagion of obesity appears to start at a young age, and social affiliations by obesity status may have far-ranging consequences for health outcomes.

7.3 Social Network Analysis and Illicit Drug Use

Another health area in which SNA has been often applied is the use of illicit drugs. Illicit drug abuse is a significant public health problem because of its numerous negative health and social consequences. Compared with the topics treated so far, it has additional SNA applications because the drugs and utensils used to consume them are often acquired and shared through a social network. Understanding the role of social networks in propagating or curbing drug use has thus emerged as a promising new avenue of research.

7.3.1 Initiation and Cessation of Illicit Drug Use

There has been substantial literature explaining the role social networks play when individuals decide to start using illicit drugs. Differential association theory (Sutherland & Cressey, 1974) maintains that adolescents learn such behavior from close friends or family who use or have a favorable attitude toward drugs. Empirically, illicit drug use is often initiated and supported in social networks that already involve drug use, providing a context that reinforces and sustains the behavior (Valente, Gallaher, & Mouttapa, 2004).

Peer influences from one's social network have a strong impact on one's initial drug use. One longitudinal study followed a random sample of 996 adolescents aged 14 to

19 years in Sydney, Australia, for one year. The study found that the characteristics of one's social network and drug use in the social network in particular were associated with a likelihood of initiating marijuana use (Levy & Pierce, 1990). Another study, by following a random sample of 2,446 youth in Munich, Germany, for four years, found that peer drug use was associated with incidental cannabis use (von Sydow, Lieb, Pfister, Höfler, & Wittchen, 2002). Ronald Rice, Lewis Donohew, and Richard Clayton (2003) also provided longitudinal evidence based on data collected in the United States that suggested adolescents who had friends using illicit drugs were more likely to start using drugs.

SOCIAL NETWORKS IN ACTION: HOW NETWORKS CAN HELP DRUG USERS TO QUIT

Although peer influences induce people to use drugs, disassociating from drug-using peers and receiving support from non–drug-using friends often facilitates quitting drug use. During the Vietnam War, an estimated 43% of U.S. Army male personnel used narcotics and 20% became dependent on them. But 8 to 12 months after returning home, only 5% among the latter remained addicts (Robins, Davis, & Goodwin, 1974). In one of the few studies that investigated natural cessation—recovery without undergoing treatment—Carl Latkin, Amy Knowlton, Donald Hoover, and Wallace Mandell (1999) examined the relationship between network characteristics and cessation of heroin, cocaine, and crack use in a sample of 335 underclass, inner-city, injection drug users in Baltimore, Maryland. The researchers found that having a smaller proportion of drug users in one's personal network was associated with becoming clean (Latkin et al., 1999). As far as a treatment program is concerned, a study of 252 methadone maintenance patients found that continued injection drug use was highest among those who had a drug-using, live-in partner or reported relations with drug users. Among the drug injectors, those who reported having more emotional support were less likely to share needles (Gogineni, Stein, & Friedmann, 2001). Intervention programs that help drug addicts to develop social networks of nonusers may thus help them to become clean.

7.3.2 Needle-Sharing Among Drug Users

Drugs that are consumed through injection pose the additional danger of spreading diseases when the tools used are shared among users. For instance, it is estimated that 37% of adult AIDS cases are linked to drug use, with nearly three quarters of new HIV infections associated with injecting drugs (Holmberg, 1996). Needle-sharing is one primary pathway of HIV transmission in the United States, and drug users' social network characteristics, such as tie strength, network position, and composition are associated with both. By drawing on a sample of 330 injecting drug users (IDU) in Baltimore,

Maryland, Latkin and his colleagues (1995) found that the larger and denser a person's drug network was, the more likely they were to share needles. It seems plausible that such a large and dense network exerts strong social pressures or provides greater opportunities to share needles.

This finding is supported by another study, which employed both ethnography and social network analysis, of approximately 800 IDUs in Brooklyn from 1990 to 1993. The researchers identified three categories of IDUs in a street-level drug market: (1) a core, and (2) an inner and (3) an outer periphery. Core members were those considered by others as "regular" members in the network; inner-periphery members were defined as those who had shared drugs with a core member in the past 30 days but were not in the core, whereas outer-periphery members were those who did not have direct links to the core. The researchers found that a higher percentage of core and inner-periphery members were HIV positive and involved in risky behaviors, such as sharing needles, than were outer-periphery members (Curtis et al., 1995).

Nevertheless, a small, closely knit group of IDUs may be insulated from pathogens coming from the outside. This is particularly true when disease prevalence is low. A study of IDUs found that IDUs tend to share syringes with close friends more than with new friends or weakly connected friends (Valente & Vlahov, 2001). Such selective risk-taking behaviors by IDUs may minimize their short-term risk exposure but not the long-term risk. For example, weak ties to IDUs outside the group provide pathways for the entry of pathogens. Once a disease infiltrates this tightly closed network, it can spread rapidly. Research has shown that peripheral members of IDU networks contribute to the overall risk of blood-borne infections for the networks by bridging high- and low-risk networks as a result of their needle-sharing practices (Curtis et al., 1995).

IDU networks with high turnover are associated with a higher rate of needle-sharing. A study of social networks of IDUs in Chicago and Washington, DC, examined changes in individual behavior and network characteristics over time and found few changes in network density or network size over time. Nevertheless, significant movement of network members over time led to a greater likelihood of needle-sharing over time among network members (Hoffmann, Su, & Pach, 1997).

As in other health-relevant social networks, there are gender differences. For male IDUs, syringe sharing tends to occur more often between frequent injectors who are also kin or drinking buddies (Sherman, Latkin, & Gielen, 2001). In contrast, networks of female IDUs are smaller and more homogeneous than that of their male counterparts (Pivnick et al., 1994). Female IDUs share syringes with a significantly higher percentage of injecting partners compared with males; their IDU networks have a higher level of density. Females share needles with their intimate partners more frequently than men do because they do not view sharing a needle with a regular sex partner as a risky practice (Friedman et al., 1997; Sherman, Latkin, & Gielen, 2001).

7.4 Social Network Analysis and Sexually Transmitted Disease

Another risky behavior that can lead to the transmission of diseases is unprotected sex. STDs, including human immunodeficiency virus (HIV) infections, pose a major reproductive health burden to sexually active individuals. STDs are associated with genital and other cancers, pelvic inflammatory disease, ectopic pregnancy, infertility, spontaneous abortion, stillbirth, and low birth weight for infants (Aral, 2001). Historically, the primary focus of STD epidemiology has been on the attributes and behaviors of individuals and on the risk of acquiring, rather than on transmitting infection. Network analysis has been used to investigate the spread of STDs, HIV/AIDS, and other infectious diseases. Because network analysis is particularly useful in revealing the underlying transmission structure of an STD outbreak, it can also be used for planning interventions against STDs.

7.4.1 Network Effects on STD Dynamics

Richard Rothenberg and colleagues (1999) published one of the first network analyses for understanding STD transmission. In the spring of 1996, a nurse at an STD clinic in an affluent Atlanta suburb detected a syphilis outbreak in a small cluster of people. Relevant information collected by the county STD control program revealed the sexual network of 99 teenagers, among whom 10 were diagnosed with syphilis. The researchers could show that this network was centralized, which facilitated the spread of the disease. Figure 7.3 shows the sexual network of those 10 persons diagnosed with syphilis (denoted with S) and their sexual contacts who do not have syphilis (denoted with N). One infected person (S30) has no known contact with other infected persons. Several persons (N41, N26, N18, N10, N42, and N13) are not infected despite having sexual contacts with two or three infected persons, suggesting that the STD may have been prevented with epidemiological treatments. The most sexually active person S11 is having sex with five other infected persons; she is diagnosed with secondary syphilis.

Social network analysis was also used to explain the puzzling racial disparity in the STD infection rate: African Americans have up to 10 to 20 times higher infection rates of selected STDs than do other groups. Edward Laumann and Yoosik Youm (1999) analyzed sexual behavior and sexual network data from the **National Health and Social Life Survey (NHSLS)**, a nationally representative probability sample of 1,511 men and 1,921 women in the United States. The authors found that the higher rates of sexual contact between the "core" and the "periphery" among the African Americans' social network facilitate the spread of infection among them. "Peripheral" African Americans—defined as those who had only one sexual partner in the past year—were five times more likely to choose "core" African Americans (with four or more partners) than "peripheral" Whites were to choose "core" Whites. Sexually transmitted infections also stay within the African American population because their partner choices are more segregated (assortative mating). Such pioneering studies are considered to be paradigm-shifting research in STD epidemiology (Aral, 1999).

FIGURE 7.3 ● **Sexual Network of Those With Syphilis and Their Sexual Contacts**

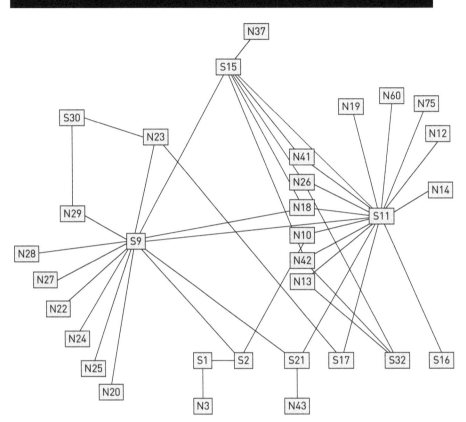

Note: Rothenberg, Richard B., Claire Sterk, Kathleen E. Toomey, John J. Potterat, David Johnson, Mark Schrader, and Stefani Hatch. (1998). "Using social network and ethnographic tools to evaluate syphilis transmission." *Sexually Transmitted Diseases 25*(3): 158.

SOCIAL NETWORKS IN ACTION: STOPPING THE SPREAD OF STDs

Examining the whole network as opposed to only the respondent's direct connections can thus help design interventions to limit the spread of disease. For example, Peter Bearman, James Moody, and Katherine Stovel (2004) examined the sexual and romantic network of 800 adolescents in a midsized, predominantly White, midwestern U.S. high school between 1993 and 1995. They found that 52% of all romantically involved students constituted one large component with structural characteristics of a "spanning tree" (Figure 7.4). This network is characterized by a few cycles and a lack of redundant ties, meaning that most adolescents are connected to the large component by only one pathway. In contrast, prior models of STD transmission, such as that among African Americans mentioned previously, had found higher activity cores that disseminated disease to lower activity individuals and sustained epidemics by functioning as reservoirs of infection. But in this network, removing a few links may well break the network into two, potentially halting the spread of an STD. This "spanning tree" network should thus be highly vulnerable to broad-based STD control programs that target the entire population rather than the assumed cores.

FIGURE 7.4 ● Romantic/Sexual Relationship Structure at Jefferson High

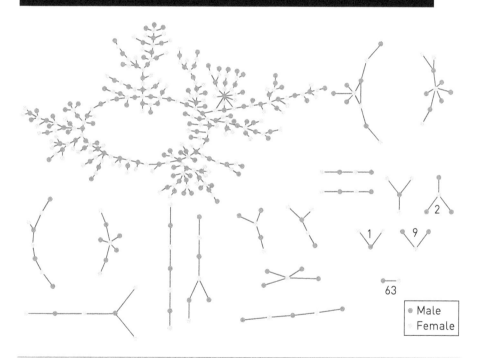

Note: Reprinted from p. 58 of Bearman, P. S., Moody, J., & Stovel, K. (2004). Chains of affection: The structure of adolescent romantic and sexual networks. *American Journal of Sociology, 110*(1), 44–91.

STD epidemics can be categorized into five phases: (1) introduction, (2) establishment, (3) growth, (4) maintenance, and (5) decline (Wasserheit & Aral, 1996), all of which require different intervention mechanisms. Researchers have used the characteristics of the sexual network to infer the phase of STD. John Potterat and his colleagues (2002a, 2002b) explored the sexual network structure of a community-wide genital chlamydia infection over a four-year period and contrasted the network picture with one generated by case surveillance reports. They concluded that network information provided a quicker and more reliable indicator of an STD epidemic phase than did information based on routinely collected, secular-trend data of case reports.

Besides sexual networks, researchers have also examined social network effects on the transmission of information about STDs. Such research is crucial for creating effective primary interventions that may prevent infection from occurring in the first place. People often do not acquire information about STDs from the media but through their informal social networks, especially their friends. Data from the National Health and Social Life Survey in the United States shows that approximately 40% of the adult population relied on close, informal, nonkin networks (friends or sex partners) for learning about sexual matters when they were growing up, whereas only 8% primarily relied on school instruction and only 1% on TV or medical clinics (Laumann, Gagnon, Michael, & Michaels, 1994).

But the effect of those informal social networks goes beyond transmitting information about sexual practices. Other effects of informal social networks include social control exercised by network members over the ego's choice of sex partner(s) and behavior and the information flow about the risks posed by particular sex partners, behaviors, and meeting places. For instance, Youm and Laumann (2002) found that friendship networks affected not only the transmission of STDs, even after controlling for other risk factors, but also that this effect varied based on the number of sex partners. Among people with fewer lifetime partners (1 to 12 partners), those with no close social friends were less likely to be infected, suggesting they focus their energy and social resources on their sex partners, which leads to strong mutual control and influence over one another. On the other hand, among people who had many lifetime sex partners (more than 12), those with many friends but weak ties to them were less likely to be infected than were those with either fewer friends or stronger ties to their friends. In this case, the egos do not profit from tight control, but their large network of weak ties may provide them with the necessary information to prevent the spread of STDs.

7.4.2 Network Analysis on HIV/AIDS

In this final section, we focus on one particular STD, which is also closely associated with drug abuse. "If there ever was a health issue in the modern era that has changed the course of history and left a social impact, it would have to be HIV/AIDS," Gabriel Stover and Mary Northridge (2013, p. 199), the editors of the *American Journal of Public Health*, wrote in an editorial of the journal. HIV-related behaviors are embedded in social networks. The characteristics of these networks, such as size, composition, and density, have been associated with HIV risk behaviors such as sharing injection equipment, maintaining concurrent sexual partnerships, practicing unprotected sex, and exchanging sex for money or drugs (Barrington et al., 2009; Lakon, Ennett, & Norton, 2006; Neblett, Davey-Rothwell, Chander, & Latkin, 2011).

In a breakthrough study of the early spread of HIV/AIDS, David Auerbach, William Darrow, Harold Jaffe, and James Curran (1984) used a diagram of 40 AIDS patients from ten cities to depict the sexual network linking them. This was one of the first pieces of evidence that AIDS was an infectious, sexually transmitted disease. Alden Klovdahl (1985) later reanalyzed Auerbach et al.'s (1984) data; his conceptualization of AIDS transmission as a social network marked a transition to wider use of network concepts and methods for studying infectious diseases.

In studying the HIV/AIDS epidemic among 18- to 35-year-old residents from Likoma Island in Lake Malawi, Stephane Helleringer and Hans-Peter Kohler (2007) found most of their subjects, directly or indirectly, shared more than one sexual partner. Like Bearman et al. (2004), this study did not find high-activity hubs. These findings call into question the assumption behind many HIV/AIDS prevention programs that the epidemic is driven either by a high-activity core made up of sex workers and their patrons or by other high-activity individuals transmitting disease to a low-activity periphery. Methodologically, the Bearman et al. (2004) and Helleringer and Kohler (2007) studies also demonstrated the value of collecting global network data rather than egocentric network data. Global network data provide a fuller picture and more accurate insights into the macrostructure through which infectious diseases flow (Smith & Christakis, 2008).

End-of-Chapter Questions

1. How could the friends of your friends' friends, whom you may not know or have met, affect your happiness or weight? Speculate about some mechanisms in the process.

2. Why do friends have more influence on your subjective well-being than do your family members? To what extent do you think this finding can be generalized to other outcomes, such as happiness and depression?

3. What do you think about the comparison theory of happiness, that the happiness of individuals depends on how they compare themselves with others close to them? Does it contradict the finding that whether an individual is happy depends on whether others in the individual's social network are happy?

4. Have you or someone close to you ever had any problems with alcohol use or smoking? Have you learned anything useful from this chapter that could help you solve the problem?

5. What are the similarities and differences between behavioral contagions (e.g., smoking) and biological contagions (e.g., sexually transmitted diseases) in social networks?

8

Political Networks

Learning Objectives

- Examine how social networks affect people's political behaviors when they vote, form their political opinions, or protest

- Discuss several ways in which networks among politicians can be measured

- Explain how donor networks help predict the success of different presidential candidates

- Describe the role of policy networks in U.S. politics

- Compare the three different ways nations can exercise power (power as access, power as brokerage, and power as exit)

- Appraise the differences between networks formed through bandwagon and homophily effects in trade and military networks

- Assess the hierarchical structure of nations and cities, how networks can help measure that hierarchy, and why different ways of measuring the ties can lead to different assessments

I n its broadest sense, *political science* examines the state: Political scientists in the field of American politics try to predict who will win the next U.S. presidential election because they want to know who will represent the state, what actions he or she will have the state organs execute, and what consequences those policies will have. Political scientists study the behavior and attitudes of individuals toward the state, wondering why people vote or participate in a revolution, or why members of the U.S. Congress sponsor a bill. In *comparative politics*, they explore how political systems—the state's organizational structure—restrict and enable political actors and make certain outcomes more likely: They try to explain why some countries democratize, grow at a faster rate, or adopt specific policies. In *international relations*, they examine how states interact with each other: Why do they go to war or trade goods?

In this chapter, we show that many of these examples are inherently network phenomena and we explain how social network analysis can help us answer these questions. In the first section, "American Politics," we discuss how people vote because of how their friends and families do. Their social contexts not only influence their candidate choice but also their level of trust in government, volunteerism, or even political knowledge. Of course, political elites also engage in networking. For example, in Congress, legislators try to find support for their bills by asking peers to co-sponsor them. We present studies that have thus created a network of legislators connected through the (number of) bills they have sponsored together. Who is the most popular congressperson when it comes to finding a co-sponsor, and whose co-sponsorship influences the chance of a bill being passed?

We also discuss the political campaign-financing network between presidential candidates. In a network of campaign financing between presidential candidates, the value of the tie between two politicians is the number of individuals that have donated money to both their campaigns. This is useful because we could assume that such individuals would be willing to switch their support between the candidates if one of them drops out of the race. If a party's two main candidates do not share a strong tie in such a network, then the party might lose a lot of the voters who favored the runner-up after the preprimaries.

Members of Congress or presidential candidates are not the only ones who form coalitions to garner support. Network coalitions are also common between ***nongovernmental organizations (NGOs)***, or ***international nongovernmental organizations (INGOs)***. They often form networks to address global issues, such as fighting the spread of deadly diseases (HIV, Ebola, or SARS) and environmental problems (global warming) or advocating for human rights. Political scientists and sociologists have interviewed NGO representatives about their cooperation and information exchanges with other organizations, and they have used social network analysis to understand how those different networks manage to coordinate and achieve their goals. We briefly discuss those policy networks in the last parts of this section.

Political networks do not just connect individuals or organizations; they can also emerge between states in the form of networks of trade, alliances, or wars. In the second section, we investigate networks in international relations, addressing the issues of network power, network diffusion, network formation, and the world network of cities. Although in the world network of nations, power is not as well defined, as it is under hierarchical structure in formal organizations, power has been omnipresent in the international networks. In this section, we discuss power being exercised in three forms—***power as access, power as brokerage,*** and ***power as exit***. In discussing network diffusion, we examine how democracy spreads from one state to the other. But how are international networks formed in the first place? In network formation, we look at the ***preferential attachment (PA)/bandwagon effect*** and the ***homophily principle*** that undergird trade networks and military pacts respectively. Finally, at the level of the state, an international trade network connects different nations, creating a globalized web that sustains the flow of merchandise across borders. Examining those networks can reveal a global hierarchy and dependency structure among different cities or nations: It may become obvious that certain countries receive most of their goods from only a handful of other countries, which may or may not be their direct trading partners. If that is the case, then that country can be vulnerable to a boycott, for instance. The following sections discuss these topics of social network analysis in political science in more detail.

8.1 American Politics

In this section, we discuss social network analysis as it is often employed in American politics, concentrating on four areas: (1) political behaviors and attitudes, (2) networks between politicians, (3) presidential campaign networks, and (4) policy networks.

8.1.1 Political Behavior: Opinions, Voting, and Protest

8.1.1.1 Attitudes and Opinions This chapter discusses a wide range of behavior in and attitudes toward political processes, such as voting, participating in demonstrations, obtaining political knowledge, joining political or even civil organizations, or trust in government. Our political behavior, much like other social behavior, is influenced by those around us: Friends, family members, classmates, or co-workers often have a direct influence on our political view and behavior. Political scientists have long subsumed this influence under the term *social environment*. They've noted that parents' social economic status, measured by education, occupation, and income, affects their children's political participation and views, as does their civic engagement, political knowledge, and political participation. Network analysts tend to see this as a contagion effect more than as influence by a vaguely defined environment: David Nickerson (2008) found, for example, that college students living with someone who frequently discusses politics become more likely to do so as well. Casey Klofstad (2011) found that college students who have more political discussions with their roommates are more likely to vote or participate in civic associations.

The social network affects political attitudes and activities through multiple means. Being socially connected, in and of itself, is important for individuals to develop prosocial behaviors, which in turn leads to a greater level of civic and political engagement. Social integration in a friendship network also encourages social capital development and fosters norms of political participation. Social networks formed during adolescence affect civic and political engagement in adult life, embodied as trust in governments, volunteerism, voting, and partisanship (Settle, Bond, & Levitt, 2011).

It is often thought that homogeneous social networks have a stronger effect as the individual will not experience cross-cutting (i.e., contradictory) pressures. But even ***politically heterogeneous social networks***, in which members of the networks hold different political views, tend to increase political interests and activity among its members. Along this line, researchers consistently have reported that political disagreement within a community network sparks greater political engagement (Anderson & Paskeviciute, 2005; Campbell, 2006; Oliver, 2003).

8.1.1.2 Voting Perhaps the most studied political behavior is voting. Other than the question of partisanship (i.e., who an individual votes for), political scientists are also interested in why voters vote in the first place. A large-scale study (Bond et al., 2012) revealed that voting is contagious, and that all voters can thus potentially start a "voting" ***cascade*** in their social networks: Their act of voting might be enough to convince their hesitant friends to vote, whose trip to the ballot box then causes their friends to join, and so on.

SOCIAL NETWORK IN ACTION: NETWORKING AND VOTING

Bond et al. (2012) used Facebook as a venue to conduct their experiments, randomly assigning millions of users into three different groups: (1) the social message group, (2) the information message group, and (3) the control group. On November 2, 2010, the day of the U.S. congressional elections, members in the social message group saw in their "News Feed" a message encouraging them to vote, with a link to help them find their local polling station, a clickable button reading "I Voted," a counter showing how many other Facebook users had previously reported voting, and up to six randomly selected "profile pictures" of friends who had already clicked the "I Voted" button. The information message group saw the same post but was not told which of their friends had already clicked the "I Voted" button. The control group did not receive any special message in their "News Feed." The Facebook users in the social message group were more likely to claim to have voted and to seek political information (i.e., about the location of the polling station). The social message thus produced many more votes: It directly encouraged an additional 60,000 Facebook users who received it to vote. But by posting information about their political behavior, those users then induced an additional 280,000 friends to go vote as well. The finding of the indirect effects of voting confirms existing studies (Nickerson, 2008), which claimed that each act of voting on average generates three votes as the behavior spreads through the network. It is not clear whether this is a case of online political mobilization, though: The study speculates it works mainly through strong ties, which exist offline but have an online representation.

But traditional, offline mobilization through door-to-door campaigns seems to have indirect effects as well. In Denver and Minneapolis, Nickerson (2008) sent assistants to two-person households, encouraging some of them (in the treatment group) to vote and others (in the control group) to recycle. Individuals in the treatment group who opened the door were 10% more likely to vote. But the other people living in the same household were also 6% more likely to vote. Thus, 60% of the effect on the persons who answered the door is passed to their flatmates who had never directly interacted with the canvasser.

Exactly what type of network configuration is conducive to such ***contagious or cascading effects*** for voter turnout? Nicholas Christakis and James Fowler (2009) investigated network data from studies conducted in Indianapolis and St. Louis and found that the cascading effect is the strongest when the network transitivity is at

FIGURE 8.1 ● **Visual Illustration of Transitivity in Egocentric Network**

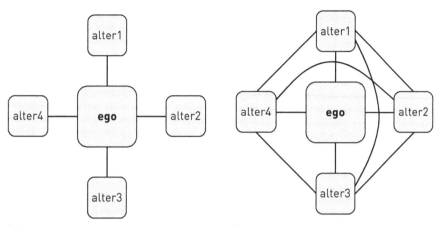

(a) Egocentric network in which
network transitivity is 0

(b) Egocentric network in which network
transitivity is 1

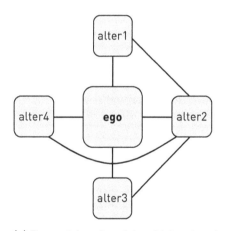

(c) Egocentric network in which network
transitivity is 0.5

0.5, when half of an individual's friends know each other. The cascading effects are weak when the network transitivity is at 0 and none of the ego's alters know each other or at 1 and the individual is surrounded by a network of contacts who all know each other as well. When the network transitivity is at 0, the network is disjointed and no communication or cascading can materialize. But when transitivity reaches 1, the network becomes too tightly knit to connect with the outside world. Figure 8.1 illustrates these different situations through the depiction of an ego with four alters. In Figure 8.1a, none of the alters know each other, and transitivity is therefore 0, whereas in Figure 8.1b, all six pairs among the four alters have a direct link (transitivity = 1). Cascades are more likely to happen in Figure 8.1c, where only three out of the six pairs have a direct link, and transitivity is therefore intermediate (0.5).

8.1.1.3 Protesting   Among the many other forms of political behavior, protest has attracted the most attention from analysts of social networks. This attention is hardly surprising given recent events like the Arab Spring or the Occupy Wall Street movement, in which social media has played an important role, not just in informing the world about the existence of dissenters and their demands but also in their coordination. The exact role and influence of online social networks is still hotly debated: Would the so-called "Twitter revolutions" in Egypt, Tunisia, Bahrain, and other countries of the Middle East have occurred even without the eponymous social media platform? Can governments prevent protests by shutting down the Internet? If participation in such protests "cascades" through the network, who are good initiators of such collective action? Although little consensus has emerged beyond the conclusion that protests are "contagious" and social networks important, some researchers have revealed interesting preliminary findings: Sandra González-Bailón, Javier Borge-Holthoefer, and Yamir Moreno (2013), for instance, found that "hidden influentials" exist. These Twitter users look like ordinary users (i.e., have few followers but follow a lot of others), but they are often mentioned by others and, thus, could be driving forces of the movement. David Siegel (2009) showed theoretically that certain network-level characteristics make it easier for the opposition to coordinate and that having a denser network can— counterintuitively—sometimes decrease political participation. The network structure also influences how government repression influences the movements: whether it falls apart or reacts with a backlash (Siegel, 2011).

8.1.2 Political Elites Among Themselves: Congress

Most people recognize that politicians spend a lot of time networking because being well connected is important to succeed in politics. But can we identify the most talented networkers among the members of the House or the Senate? And are those individuals really more successful when it comes to pushing through their agenda? In Chapter 3, we learned that centrality in a network often marks powerful individuals. So can we use social network analysis to identify the most influential members of the Congress?

Some early studies used the record of agreement in roll call votes to examine the interpersonal ties in the House and the Senate. But voting together is probably more suggestive of ideological similarity on the liberal–conservative axis than of personal sympathy (Poole & Rosenthal, 1997). Recent studies, thus, looked at bill co-sponsorship instead, assuming that when two congresspersons co-sponsor a bill, they may have drafted it together because they are political allies or friends even outside the political arena. Such co-sponsoring bills may not just reveal preexisting interpersonal networks, but they may also let us observe the political process and strategic actions. In some cases, legislators may form new alliances to recruit co-sponsors to increase the chance that the bill will pass. Sometimes, the content of the bill draws support from legislators to whom the terms of the bill are appealing. Finally, there may be norms of reciprocity or even backroom dealings: You have been supportive of my bills in the past, so I will vote for your bill; in other words, you scratch my back, I'll scratch yours.

SOCIAL NETWORK IN ACTION: PERSONAL ENMITY INTERFERES WITH POLITICAL ASSOCIATION

Social network analysis not only reveals personal affinity but also personal enmity. For instance, despite close ideological and geographical affiliations, New Jersey Democratic senators Frank Lautenberg and Bob Torricelli have a long-term personal feud, which erupted in one closed-door meeting in 1999 as both inflicted verbal insults on each other. Thus, the two senators rarely co-sponsor each other's bills (Christakis and Fowler 2009: 200).

Despite the influence of such informal factors, it turns out that formal structures still influence the tie formation in the co-sponsorship network in Congress. Congresspersons that are more likely to co-sponsor bills have a similar ideological view, which of course means that they are also often in the same party. Being on the same committee also makes co-sponsorship more likely (Christakis & Fowler, 2009). But one recent study (Cranmer & Desmarais, 2011) also found evidence for the importance of informal politics, pointing to the high level of reciprocity and transitivity in those networks. In other words, not only do members of Congress return favors by sponsoring bills of those that have sponsored their bill (reciprocity), they may also help their co-sponsor find supporters among the other individuals they have co-sponsored a bill with in the past. The authors therefore argued that researchers who do not take these effects into account may overestimate ***partisanship homophily***, that is, the importance of belonging to the same party when recruiting co-sponsors.

But does this wheeling and dealing pay off? Are central players in this co-sponsorship network more likely to have their bill approved? It seems so. Empirical studies have found evidence that, in the House, members in the center of the co-sponsorship network are three times as likely to see their amendments passed as those in the periphery, whereas in the Senate, the difference is seven times (Hall, 1992). Christakis and Fowler (2009) found that the best-connected representatives can collect 10 more votes than

FIGURE 8.2 ● Most and Least Connected Legislators in the 108th House

TOP 20

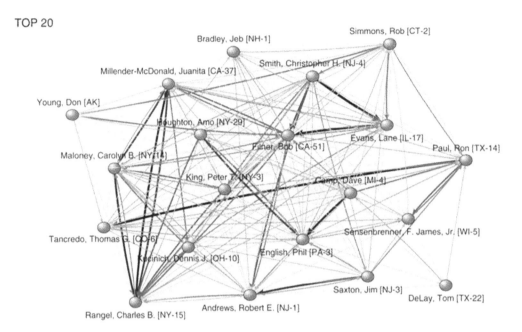

BOTTOM 20

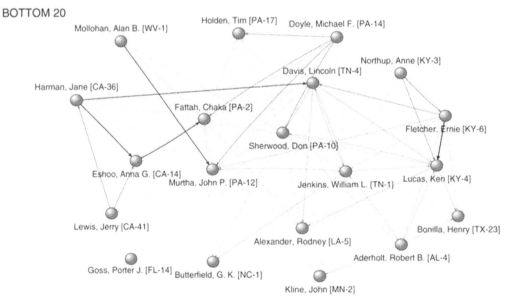

Notes: These graphs only show connections among the 20 most connected (top 20) and among the 20 least connected (bottom 20). Adapted from Fowler, James H. "Connecting the Congress: A Study of Cosponsorship Networks," *Political Analysis*. 14.4 (2006): 475. Reprinted by permission of Oxford University Press.

the average member of the House, whereas in the Senate, the best-connected senators can garner 16 more votes. Figure 8.2 shows the network among the most and least connected legislators in the 108th House from Fowler's (2006) study.

Research on Congress is continuing, and there are lively debates about what is the best way to measure the relevant network: Co-voting has been criticized as reflecting mainly party affiliation, but co-sponsorship has come under fire on the same account. Bruce Desmarais, Vincent Moscardelli, Brian Schaffner, and Michael Kowal (2015), therefore, argued that examining which representatives hold press conferences together is a better measure for cooperation because co-signing a bill is an almost costless act, whereas coordinating a press conference requires much more interaction and commitment.

Social network analysis of co-sponsorship networks divulges more than just the dynamics of pairs or positional characteristics of individual legislators: We can also examine how the external environment shapes or is shaped by the structure of the whole network. Justin Kirkland and Justin Gross (2014) explored changes in the co-sponsorship network over time and found that they are correlated with congressional approval rates. When the rating declines, legislators become willing to work across the aisle; the co-sponsorship networks become less clustered, more spread out; and there is less homophily along partisan lines. The increased partisan bickering after Barack Obama's election produced a negative public view of Washington, which results in a low approval rating for Congress. Thus, we should expect less partisanship and more working across the aisles between politicians under Obama's administration. On the contrary, a recent article in *The Economist* (Lucioni, 2013) reported increasing partisanship in co-voting between congresspersons over the decades (Figure 8.3). Perhaps more studies are needed to uncover the complex relations between Congress's approval rating and collaborative patterns between politicians.

The structure of the co-sponsorship network also affects legislative productivity, which is measured by the amount of important legislation passed (Cho & Fowler, 2010). Well-connected co-sponsorship networks, indicated by high density, are conducive to high legislative productivity because the connections between representatives enhance trust, communication, and collaboration, which makes it easier to pass new important laws.

Network analysis of legislators and other political elites is also one topic that has been picked up by the field of comparative politics (see, e.g., Franziska Keller's studies of the Chinese Communist elites [2015 and 2016a] or Thomas Metz and Sebastian Jäckle's 2016 analysis of the German opposition in the Bundestag), where SNA has been underrepresented so far: Paolo Parigi and Laura Satori (2014) analyzed co-sponsorship networks among members of the Italian parliament in the 1970s and showed that politicians from the same region tended to cooperate with each other but did so continuously only if they also belonged to the same party. The authors argued that this was a strategic decision on the part of the members of parliament: Working across the aisle with individuals from the same region would have weakened the party and thereby undermined the national reach with which it provided the members of parliament.

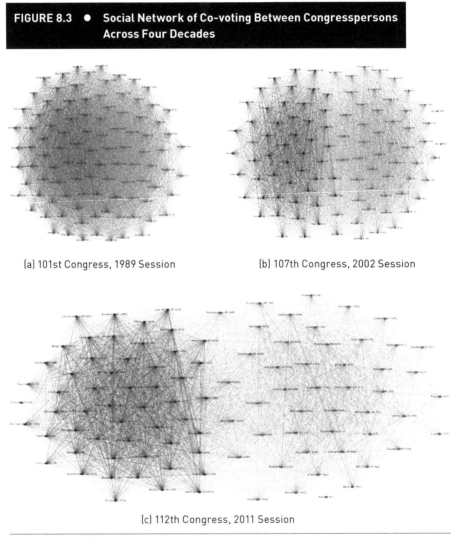

FIGURE 8.3 ● Social Network of Co-voting Between Congresspersons Across Four Decades

(a) 101st Congress, 1989 Session

(b) 107th Congress, 2002 Session

(c) 112th Congress, 2011 Session

Note: Dark grey = Democrats; light grey = Republicans. © The Economist Newspaper Limited, London (12/7/2013).

8.1.3 Political Elites and Donors: Social Network Analysis of Presidential Campaign Financing

Predicting the outcomes of elections is the bread and butter of what could be called "applied" political science, with correct predictions of the U.S. presidential elections probably being the most coveted prize of all. The most commonly used tools for this are voter polls. But especially during the stage when parties decide which candidate to nominate, when voters are not yet familiar with all candidates, other factors apart from voter popularity affect a politician's success: support from important organizations and individuals, a policy program that appeals to the right actors, and of course the ability to raise funding for an expensive electoral campaign. A candidate's network and ties to other elites influence these factors. It is with such a network—that between potential candidates within a party—that recent research by Andrew Dowdle, Scott Limbocker, Song Yang, Patrick Stewart, and Karen Sebold in 2013 and 2015 (Dowdle et al., 2013; Yang et al., 2015) explained why the Democrat's contender, Barack Obama, won the last two presidential elections. But before we turn to the elite networks, it is worth analyzing Obama's election campaign in the light of the online experiments discussed in the previous section.

In both elections, Obama's team made great use of social media for the campaigns (Chadwick, 2013). In the 2008 election, for instance, they used YouTube for free advertising worth $47 million, a strategy other candidates were unable to emulate successfully. In the 2012 reelection, President Obama and his team pushed their success in raising money through online campaigns further: They invented a one-click program for campaign donations and reached out to 5 million young voters via Facebook. They also developed the capacity to analyze large amounts of data on political participation and activism, which allowed them to motivate select individuals to act on Obama's behalf.

One reason for Team Obama's success is, thus, the ability to tap into the power of social media and its cascading or contagious effect on political mobilization. This is not just important for getting out the vote on election day: Political activists or engaged citizens also make campaign donations. Although the proportion of donations from individual political activists is small, their analysis can reveal patterns of ideological endorsement by the general public. Note that there is a marked difference between the donations from individuals and those from corporate or union interests. Individual donors are usually motivated by ideological values and policies, whereas interest groups are transaction oriented in seeking favorable policy decisions in return for their financial contributions. The studies discussed here only look at individual donors, therefore, revealing the ideological-drive behaviors.

Fortunately, information on campaign donations is publicly available: Since 2000, the Federal Election Commission (FEC) has required all presidential candidates to file their donor information electronically. Social network scholars have used these data to create a network among both parties' candidates during the ***preprimary period***, defined as the time frame from January 1 to December 31 in the year prior to the general election (Dowdle et al., 2013; Yang et al., 2015).

In this network, the ties between two candidates indicate the number of shared donors. Why would the position in that network matter? Imagine the presidential election as a network on contested terrain, with presidential candidates competing against each other to attract voters and donors. At the same time, there is also a level of coordination and coalition because once the intraparty competition is settled, the winner needs to convince voters and donors of those candidates who did not obtain party nominations to rally behind him or her. If Candidate A shares a lot of donors with Candidate B, then she can hope to "inherit" some of B's support in case he drops out.

8.1.3.1 2007 Preprimary: A Tale of Two Networks   Top Democratic contenders during the 2007–2008 presidential election cycle were Senators Joe Biden of Delaware, Hillary Clinton of New York, Barack Obama of Illinois, and the 2004 Vice-Presidential candidate, John Edwards of North Carolina. On the Republican side, candidates were careful to distance themselves from the incumbent President, George W. Bush, unpopular because of the war in Iraq and a stagnant economy. Among the top contenders were Senator John McCain of Arizona, former Governor Mitt Romney of Massachusetts, and former New York City Mayor Rudolph Giuliani. Commonly used predictors diverged over who would likely be the most successful candidate, but the ultimate winner of the Republican nomination, John McCain, was neither leading the rankings in terms of number and amount of donations, nor the polls. But by analyzing the donation network via dendogram, we gain a clearer sense not only of the ranking of candidates (ranking in terms of actor centrality measure; see Chapter 3 for the methodology) but also of the cohesion and cleavage of the parties (Dowdle et al., 2013; Yang et al., 2015).

In a dendogram (discussed in Chapter 3), candidates who received funding from the same, or similar, subsets of donors will quickly merge, whereas candidates with fewer shared donors join later, as the merging criteria are weakened. Individuals at the center of a cluster have the biggest chance of ending up victorious: As other candidates give up the race, they are most likely to "inherit" the supporters of those drop-outs.

Figure 8.4 shows that the dendogram of the preprimary shared donation networks for the Democratic Party and the Republican Party in 2007 have marked differences: In the Democrat's dendogram, the top contenders Obama and Clinton share the most donors and, thus, merge first. The remaining candidates join this "core" one after the other. In contrast, the Republican Party witnesses two competing cores, with Duncan Hunter, Tom Tancredo, and Ron Paul remaining in a separate cluster from that with the most promising candidates (Mitt Romney, Rudy Giuliani, and John McCain) until the second-to-last step. The Republican camp, therefore, had a potentially troublesome cleavage between the two groups of candidates, whose respective supporters might not be easily convinced to join the other camp.

It is, thus, easy to imagine that donors to some of the more peripheral Democratic candidates would have little difficulty supporting the party nominee during the general election. In contrast, the Republican structure suggests a much more divisive financial campaign. It is plausible that those donating to the losing "cluster" around Tancredo, Hunter, and Paul would not be willing to switch their allegiance to the party nominee, John McCain.

Figure 8.5 uses multidimensional scaling (MDS) (see Chapter 4) to plot the donor networks of Republicans and Democrats combined. The MDS analysis positions pairs

FIGURE 8.4 ● Dendogram of Democratic Party (above) and Republican Party (below) Presidential Candidates in Their Shared Donor Network 2007

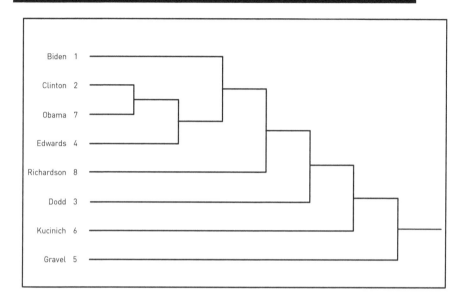

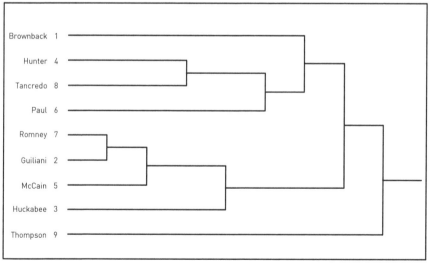

Note: Adapted from p. 79 of Dowdle, A., Limbocker, S., Yang, S., Stewart, P. A., & Sebold, K. (2013). *The Invisible hands of political parties in presidential elections: Party activists and political aggregation from 2004 to 2012*. New York, NY: Palgrave McMillian.

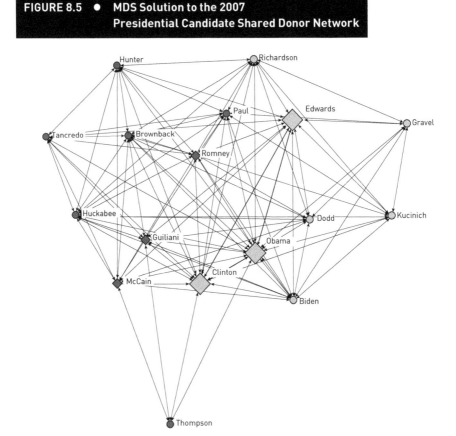

FIGURE 8.5 ● MDS Solution to the 2007 Presidential Candidate Shared Donor Network

Note: Adapted from p. 78 of Dowdle, A., Limbocker, S., Yang, S., Stewart, P. A., & Sebold, K. (2013). *The Invisible hands of political parties in presidential elections: Party activists and political aggregation from 2004 to 2012*. New York, NY: Palgrave McMillian.

with many shared donors close to each other and pairs with few shared donors far apart. Candidates with many shared donors tend to occupy central positions, and those with few shared donors tend to be located in the peripheral positions.

Unsurprisingly, the two parties' candidates are clearly separated, with Republicans on the left side and Democrats on the right. The size of the nodes reflect the candidate's coreness measure, thus, indicating not just how central they are but also whether they are connected to other actors that have high centrality (Borgatti & Everett, 1999). The three main Democratic candidates, Obama, Clinton, and Edwards, have much greater coreness than do their Republican counterparts, McCain, Guiliani, and Romney, because the Democratic contenders are connected with candidates who have high centrality as opposed to Republican contenders who are connected with candidates with low centrality.

FIGURE 8.6 • Agglomerative Hierarchical Dendrogram of the 2007 Shared Donor Matrix Between Democratic Party and Republican Party Presidential Nominees

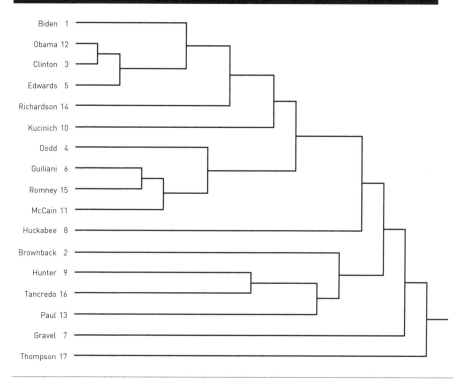

Note: Adapted from p. 78 of Dowdle, A., Limbocker, S., Yang, S., Stewart, P. A., & Sebold, K. (2013). *The Invisible hands of political parties in presidential elections: Party activists and political aggregation from 2004 to 2012.* New York, NY: Palgrave McMillian.

Figure 8.6, the dendogram of this combined network, shows three core groups: (1) Obama, Clinton, and Edwards; (2) Giuliani, Romney, and McCain; and (3) Hunter, Tancredo, and Paul. Strikingly, the two core groups with the main Republican (2) and Democratic (1) contenders merge before the Hunter, Tancredo, and Paul group. In other words, Giuliani, Romney, and McCain share more donors with Obama, Clinton, and Edwards than with their co-Republicans Hunter, Tancredo, and Paul. In addition, Obama, Clinton, and Edwards merge before any of the Republican contenders do, which suggests more coherence among the Democrats.

SNA has, thus, helped us discover the relative coherence among the apparently heterogeneous (in terms of racial background or gender) Democratic candidates, and it has revealed the divide in the Republican camp. The Democrats may have been more successful in raising donations, but if their donors had been as divided as Republicans' donors, the amount might not have translated into such a landslide victory for Barack

Obama. Ultimately, the latter carried the day against both Republican and Democratic opponents because of his team's sophisticated online campaigns, which took advantage of contagious behavior and activism cascading along network ties—another classic concept in SNA. In short, it pays off to be deeply embedded in the extended party network of donors—a finding that also applies to politicians running for seats in Congress (Desmarais, Raja, & Kowal, 2015).

8.1.4 Policy Networks

Another network that connects the government and its elites with the wider population is that of lobbyists advocating specific policies, as well as NGOs and different administrative units trying to implement them: If you are a leader of an advocacy group or a local administrator, who should you team up with when trying to influence a government's policy? Who is most likely to know and inform you about the latest developments in the complex negotiations that take place when new laws are hammered out? And who can help you coordinate different branches of the administration in multiple counties? These issues and questions are investigated by policy network analysts, researchers who seek to explain the formation of state-interest organization networks, their persistence and change over time, and the consequences of network structures for public policy-making outcomes (Knoke, 2011). According to David Knoke (2011), the following four features are typical for policy networks: (1) Their connections are short-lived and formed for specific narrow goals; (2) partners in the coalition change depending on the specific issue; (3) organizations that lobby together succeed more often than the soloists; and (4) broad cleavages can emerge within some policy domains.

One such instance of lobbying—and illustration of the third feature—occurs when the U.S. Supreme Court decides on the interpretation of the laws enacted, and different groups support the litigants by writing *amicus curiae* briefs. Judges are swayed, not necessarily by the number of supportive groups, but by how well-connected those groups are with other "amici" (Box-Steffensmeier et al., 2013). These central groups are especially influential when the two litigants are evenly matched.

Figure 8.7 illustrates the fourth feature mentioned earlier. David Knoke, Franz Urban Pappi, Jeffrey Broadbent, and Yutaka Tsujinaka (1996) used MDS and blockmodel analysis (see Borgatti, Everett, & Johnson, 2013, pp. 215–218) to study cleavages in a communication network among interest groups in the national labor policy domain. The analysis revealed clear political divides between two pro-labor blocks (blocks 1 and 2) and two pro-business blocks (blocks 3 and 4) but also that two pro-labor organizations (House Democrats and Teamsters) seem to be closer to the two pro-business blocks.

In the analysis of policy networks, researchers often collect data from interviews or questionnaires sent to the groups and individuals involved, asking them whom they trust, whom they ask for information, or whom they coordinate activities with. An example is a study on the protection of estuaries, a policy area in which there are many different stakeholders, from conservation societies to local governments to agricultural and industrial interests (Berardo & Scholz, 2010). The study found that despite

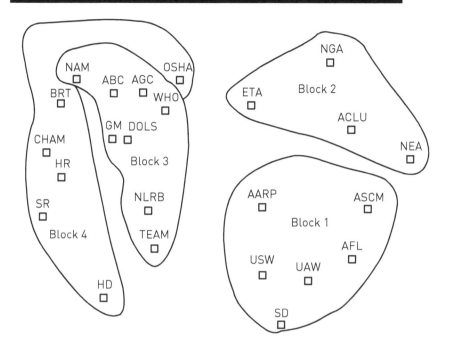

FIGURE 8.7 • MDS With Blocks in U.S. National Labor Policy Domain (Stress = 0.20)

AFL:	American Federation of Labor	AARP:	American Association of Retired Persons
ASCM:	American Federation of State, County, And Municipal Workers	ACLU:	American Civil Liberties Union
		UGA:	National Governors Association
TEAM:	Teamster Union	DOLS:	Department of Labor Secretary
UAW:	United Auto Workers	ETA:	Education & Training Administration
USW:	United Steel Workers	OSHA:	Occupational Safety & Health Administration
ABC:	Association of Builders and Contractors	NLRB:	National Labor Relations Board
AGC:	Association of General Contractors	WHO:	White House Office
BRT:	Business Roundtable	HR:	House Labor Committee Republicans
CHAM:	Chamber of Commerce of the U.S.	HD:	House Labor Committee Democrats
GM:	General Motors	SR:	Senate Labor Committee Republicans
NAM:	National Association of Manufacturers	SD:	Senate Labor Committee Democrats
NEA:	National Education Association		

Note: Adapted from p. 91 of Knoke, D., & Yang, S. (2008). *Social network analysis*. Thousand Oaks, CA: Sage.

the fact that problems with estuary management are raised and solved in a relatively decentralized manner, the network is hierarchical: Actors do not cooperate with their partner's partner (low transitivity) and instead prefer to interact with highly connected alters, who can then act as central brokers in the network. Such policy networks have also been studied outside the United States, in particular, in various European countries (see Keller, 2016b).

8.2 Networks in International Relations

Even though this field deals, as its name implies, with relations, SNA has only recently been applied to its study of conflicts, trade, treaties, or alliances. Up until then, most statistical research has examined simple country-dyads; in other words, it has looked at the United States and the Soviet Union, the United States and the United Kingdom, the United Kingdom and the Soviet Union, and so on. But surely it makes more sense to examine those relationships together? If America is an ally of Great Britain, but has bad relations with the Soviet Union, then this will probably influence the relationship between Great Britain and the Soviet Union. SNA is, thus, a natural way to explore how wars, alliances, or trade between other countries affects a country.

But as in other contexts, network analysis can go beyond a more accurate analysis of individuals and individual relationships. The international system is an ideal candidate for the "networked form of governance" discussed in earlier chapters. Networks as a governance structure represent a different kind of practice and reflect a different underlying logic than that of the market or the formal hierarchy (Podolny & Page, 1998; Powell, 1990). Actors in a given network pursue repeated, enduring exchange relations with one another, unlike the one-off meetings under the market logic. They also lack a legitimate organizational authority of the formal hierarchy to arbitrate and resolve disputes that may arise. Concerns for reputation and the fear of being excluded from the network of beneficial transactions in the future induce network members to follow the norms adopted in the network (Granovetter, 1985).

This is particularly pertinent to the international environment: It is true that in any period of history, few countries have wielded considerably more power than the others, sometimes resulting in a system in which one country's position was hegemonic. Nevertheless, and despite the presence of such organizations like the United Nations or international courts, the international system does not have an ultimate arbitrator or ruler in the same way as functioning states have in the form of the government and its monopoly of power. At the same time, countries are too enduring and too few for a perfect market logic with transactions among anonymous actors.

But the absence of a formal hierarchy among states doesn't prevent the emergence of an informal hierarchy, as we will see. In fact, Danielle Jung and David Lake (2011) argued that especially in a hostile environment with many uncooperative or opportunistic players, countries will try to join a (potentially informal) hierarchy to protect themselves. We might, thus, again ask how positions in the overall networks affect states: Do some governments wield more informal power than others (Hafner-Burton, Kahler, & Montgomery, 2009)? Does war or democratization spread through the network of nations? International relations scholars also study the network of intergovernmental organizations (IGOs), nongovernmental organizations (NGOs), cities (Derudder & Taylor, 2005; Taylor, 2004), or individual persons and agents, such as those in terrorism networks (Krebs, 2002; Stohl & Stohl, 2007).

8.2.1 Power in International Relations Networks

The traditional view of power in international relations has equated it with a country's attributes: its gross domestic product (GDP), its economic (e.g., oil) resources, or its military resources. But as we saw in Chapter 4, power is often relational. In networks between countries, power can be defined in three ways: power as access, power as brokerage, and power as exit options (Hafner-Burton et al., 2009).

In power as access, power is the prominence in networks where valued information and scarce resources are transferred from one actor to another (Knoke, 1990). Thus, power reflects the extent to which actors in a social network have access to valuable information and resources flowing in the network. The conventional degree centrality measure discussed in Chapter 4, for instance, reflects a country's power in so far as it captures the amount of valuable information and resources it is likely to receive directly (Hafner-Burton & Montgomery, 2006). Powerful states can withhold benefits from many others, enacting sanctions. According to Jason Beckfield (2003), such states can set agendas, frame debates, and promulgate policies that benefit them, creating structural inequalities between nations.

● ### SOCIAL NETWORK IN ACTION: WHY CHINA WANTS TO BE PART OF THE WTO

China's successful bid to become a member of the World Trade Organization (WTO) in 2001 is a good case in point. Although China had to make some concessions (reduce tariff and open market further), the WTO membership benefits China by integrating it with the world economy and establishing deep economic ties with major economies such as the European Union and the United States.

Network power can also be embodied in a node's brokerage position, which is the extent to which a country can act as an intermediary between other countries. In Figure 8.8, for instance, China holds such a brokerage position, as the only country with access to North Korea and Iran. In some situations, the other countries can thus only rely on China to put pressure on those countries or to intervene on their behalf. Note that the graph reflects the full network of shared IGOs among the five nations of United States, France, China, Iran, and North Korea only. If more countries were to be added to the network, Iran and North Korea would have more connections than their only ties to China in the graph.

So far we've associated power with network centrality, but paradoxically, being peripheral (i.e., being located at the outer border of a network or having only a few ties to other actors) brings its own power. This third type of network power is called the power to exit. Less embedded actors can sometimes leave the network much more

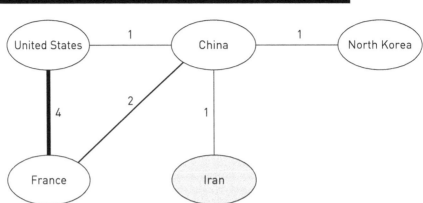

FIGURE 8.8 ● Network of Five Nations in Co-Affiliation in IGOs

Note: Adapted from p. 564 of Hafner-Burton, E. M., Kahler, M. & Montgomery, A. H. (2009). Network analysis for international relations. *International Organization, 63,* 559–592.

easily because they only have to sever a few ties, and they may have little at stake in the flow of network. Both North Korea and Iran in Figure 8.8 are such examples, but in practice, this sort of power seems particularly pertinent to North Korea: With its limited trade relations and few international agreements, the international community has often no tools at its disposal to put pressure on this country.

● SOCIAL NETWORK IN ACTION: WHY CENTRAL ACTORS HAVE TO CARE ABOUT THE MARGINAL NODES

From Hirschman (1970), we know about the power of threatening to exit or leave either from a marginalized employee at a work organization or from isolated countries in the world network of nations. This is because the existence of those structures, either work organizations or world systems, depends on the participation of their components. Although those marginal/isolated actors in a network have little to lose from their departure, it is up to those central activists of the network to reengage the marginal ones.

Being a peripheral node does not automatically grant the node exit power, however, because an exit may not be a viable option. Many colonies in the British Empire were located at the periphery of its trade network, but London would never have allowed the colonies to sever their trade links. This configuration, thus, produced tremendous structural leverage for England during the colonization era (Hafner-Burton et al., 2009)—and even afterward, as we see in the next section.

8.2.2 Network Diffusion Processes

Earlier we saw that people adopt political behavior and attitudes from those they interact with on a regular basis. Such social contagion or diffusion process does not just happen between individuals, however; they also occur between countries or U.S. states when adopting new policies (Desmarais, Harden, & Boehmke, 2015). Magnus Thor Torfason and Paul Ingram (2010) showed that the interstate network through joint memberships in IGOs is a fundamental power grid behind the diffusion of democracy. States that come in contact with more democratic states in this IGO network are more likely to democratize themselves. The authors argued that this is mainly the result of what they call ***normative isomorphism***—the message that democracy is the only legitimate form of government spreads through interactions within those IGOs until the participating authoritarian countries accept this view. But the authors also found some evidence for a potentially more ***coercive isomorphism***, as interaction with powerful or richer democracies in the IGO network makes democratization even more likely. In other words, the democratizing countries might be bowing to the economic or military might of the countries they encounter.

8.2.3 Network Formation Processes

So far we have taken the network between countries as given and inquired about the effect of holding a specific position in that network. But we can also examine how those networks came into existence. How do states decide who they want to trade goods or form alliances with? Zeev Maoz (2012) answered these questions by looking at the shape of the trade and the alliance network and found that they correspond to network formation processes that we have discussed earlier: the principle of preferential attachment (i.e., egos prefer to be connected to already well-connected alters) and homophily (i.e., egos prefer to be connected to alters that have similar characteristics). These processes each reflect a different logic in forming alliances and choosing partners. The preferential attachment process resembles that of a bandwagon effect: Countries aim to connect with the most central—and therefore presumably most powerful—actors in the network. The underlying motivation for this behavior is that (1) the central country allows indirect connections to a large number of other countries in the network via a fairly short path and that (2) the country in question can join a large coalition by attaching itself to such a central actor, which can be used to deter potential enemies. The central actors have an incentive to accept those pacts to increase their power and competitiveness against opposing powers, while preventing those new nonaligned nodes from joining opposing coalitions.

Homophily represents a different logic. It assumes that countries establish connections less for strategic considerations but because of intrinsic similarities. Maoz (2012) suggested three relevant dimensions of similarity: the level of democracy, shared enemies, and cultural similarities. He then showed that the interstate trade network operates according to a preferential attachment logic, whereas the military pact or alliance network follows the homophily principle. In particular, when it comes to choosing military alliances, democratic states trust each other, as their political system is built on contractual sustainable arrangements, whereas nondemocratic states are suspicious of each other, as they are likely to exploit each other. Therefore, democratic states use democracy as the main criteria to choose partners, whereas nondemocratic states prefer to ally themselves against common enemies. This is of course just a general rule, and exceptions do exist: The recent U.S.-led airstrikes against ISIS were joined by five nondemocratic Arab nations that are nondemocratic nations (Saudi Arabia, Jordan, United Arab Emirates, Bahrain, and Qatar), for instance.

SOCIAL NETWORK IN ACTION: FORMATION OF WARSAW PACT

A good case in point indicating that "nondemocratic states prefer to ally themselves against common enemies" would be the Warsaw Pact, which comprised eight communist states led by the Soviet Union. It was formed as a direct response to the North Atlantic Treaty Organization's (NATO's) inclusion of Western Germany in 1954. Both Eastern Germany and the Soviet Union were so wary about the inclusion that they felt compelled to form an alliance to counteract NATO's move.

In contrast to the homophily principle, the bandwagon effect characterizes trade networks: In trade networks, newcomers are eager to form short trading routes to many other countries. The most efficient way to accomplish this is by establishing trade relations with the central core. Such dyadic-level motivation then produces the star-like configuration in the international trade network commonly associated with preferential attachment networks.

Maoz (2012) also discussed how else those two networks differ: The preferential attachment process results in a network with few components, low density, and high graph centralization, which, as discussed in Chapter 4, indicates great differences between nodes in their degree centralities and, therefore, a strong hierarchy. In contrast, the homophilic network has many components, high transitivity, and low graph centralization. Structurally, the former produces a network with one core consisting of a few well-connected nodes and other peripherals connected to the core. The latter may have multiple cores, each of which is surrounded by a few peripheral nodes of their own. Figures 8.9 and 8.10 from Maoz's (2012) study illustrate these two configurations, respectively.

8.2.4 World Network of Nations and Cities

So far we have looked at ties between states that mostly came about through (or are at least maintained by) a conscious decision by the state's government. But sometimes networks between nations reflect historic legacies or many small decisions made

FIGURE 8.9 • **International Trade Network 1974—Illustration of Bandwagon Effect**

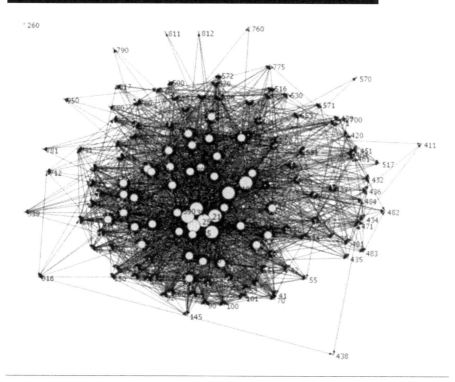

Notes: Sizes of circles represent centrality level: large = highly central state; medium = moderately central state; small = marginal state. Adapted from p. 345 of Maoz, Z. (2012). Preferential attachment, homophily, and the structure of international networks, 1816-2003. *Conflict Management and Peace Science*, 29(3), 341–369.

by individuals living in those nations—for instance, in the case of trade networks (as opposed to trade agreement networks). Both political activists and scholars have argued that there are strong hierarchies among the different nations and that trade networks established by different colonial powers as early as the middle-to-late 1400s created and perpetuated these hierarchies. The most famous proponent of this "world-systems theory" is Immanuel Wallerstein (1974).

In Chapter 4, we discussed how networks can create and measure informal hierarchies. In particular, the concept of "brokerage" is relevant here: Many of the long-distance trade routes established first by Portugal and then Spain, the Netherlands, or Great Britain passed through their Empire's capital. They served to bring primary resources from the colonies to the center, where those resources were processed and then sent back to the colonies, the periphery, along the same trade connections. The capital of the respective colonial empires was thus located in the structural hole between the

FIGURE 8.10 ● Alliance Network 2002—Illustration of Homophily Effect

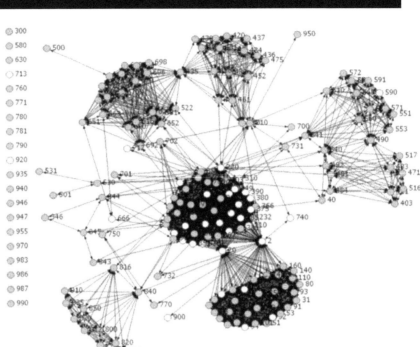

Notes: White circle = democracy; gray circle = nondemocracy. Adapted from p. 350 of Maoz, Z. (2012). Preferential attachment, homophily, and the structure of international networks, 1816-2003. *Conflict Management and Peace Science, 29*(3), 341–369.

far-flung colonies and could take advantage of this privileged network position. A recent study by Edward Kick, Laura McKinney, Steve McDonald, and Andrew Jorgenson (2011) found that these colonial trade patterns continue to influence the structure of current world networks of trade, armament transfers, membership in intergovernmental organizations, and exchange of ambassadors, and that former and current cores of (colonial) empires (France, Germany, Italy, the Netherlands, United Kingdom, and United States) maintain a central position in that network. They also found that even though this core has become more exclusive over time, different groups (blocks) of countries have become more connected. Mark Manger, Mark Pickup, and Tom A.B. Snijders (2012) discovered a similar pattern for preferential trade agreements: Rich countries form such ties among each other and with middle-income countries, whereas the least-developed countries rarely conclude such agreements and therefore remain peripheral.

The analysis of a global hierarchy is not restricted to nations or states; it can also be applied to cities, for instance. Cities serve as global centers for airline connections, financial services, commercial goods, or information flow (Alderson, Beckfield, &

FIGURE 8.11 ● Inter-City Passenger Flow

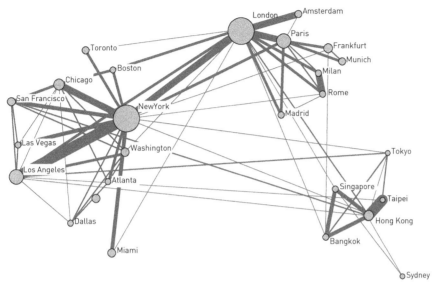

Notes: Only the 30 most important cities in terms of total volume of passengers and links with 500,000 passengers are shown. Adapted from p. 2384 of Derudder, B., & Witlox, F. (2005). An appraisal of the use of airline data in assessing the world city network: A research note on data. *Urban Studies, 42*(13), 2371–2388.

Sprague-Jones, 2010; Derudder, Witlox, Faulconbridge, & Beaverstock, 2008; Friedmann, 1995; Sassen, 2001; Smith & Timberlake, 2001). Much like states or nations, cities are not only defined by their attributes, such as the size of their population and their economies, but also by their relations with each other. Those networks can be dynamic: For example, the network of flight connections between cities' airports reacts quickly to changes in the movement of businesspeople, migrants, and tourists or in the flow of goods, and it is therefore a sensitive barometer for the importance of different cities. Analyzing the airline connections between world cities from 1970s to 1990s, David Smith and Michael Timberlake (2001) found that major cities in western Europe and North America continue to dominate the hierarchical network structure. East Asian cities have ascended quickly to occupy central positions, but few cities in Latin America, Africa, or South Asia are centrally located.

Airline connections might be more sensitive to population growth than to shifts in power, however, and overestimate the importance of cities in the rapidly urbanizing developing countries. Analyses of networks of headquarters and branches of multinational corporations located in 6,000 cities across the world (Alderson et al., 2010) seem to indicate that the city network has become more stratified and unequal. Contrary to Thomas Friedman's assertion that the world has become flat thanks to the development of infrastructure and communication that erases spatial barriers, Alderson et al. (2010) reported that globalization does result in the dispersion of production but not in decentralization of command and control. Quite the contrary: World cities in the core countries in North America and western Europe (New York, London, Paris, Berlin, Bonn, Cologne, and Amsterdam) are becoming more central, whereas peripheral cities in Africa, Latin America, and Asia are increasingly marginal and isolated.

The question of whether the world has become more or less equal, thus, depends very much on what network the researcher chooses to measure and whether he or she focuses on the movement of human beings (from international or domestic migrants, to tourists, to victims of human trafficking), the transfer of goods, information flow, or one of many other interdependencies among different geographical spaces.

End-of-Chapter Questions

1. Why do congresspersons co-sponsor bills? Does co-sponsorship affect the chance that the bill gets passed? If so, how?

2. How does the two-mode or bipartite network discussed in Chapter 3 relate to the analysis of international relations as proposed by Maoz (2012)? What statistical method discussed in Chapter 4 could be applied in this case?

3. Why do shared donors between presidential candidates matter not only for the candidates but also for the party he or she represents?

4. Compare and contrast the structures of an international relations network with the structures in formal organizations. What are the differences and similarities?

5. What are the three powers exercised in international relations? Give an example of each.

6. How does ties formation in trade networks differ from that in military pact networks among nations? What are the results of the difference?

7. What are the differences between the network of international cities linked by airline passengers and network of cities linked by multinational corporate (MNC) headquarters and branches? What are the reasons for the difference?

• Glossary •

Add Health (National Longitudinal Survey of Adolescent Health): Longitudinal study of a nationally representative sample of adolescents in grades 7–12 in the United States during the 1994–1995 school year. The cohort has been followed into young adulthood with four in-home interviews, the most recent in 2008, when the sample was aged 24–32. Add Health combines longitudinal survey data on respondents' social, economic, psychological, and physical well-being with contextual data on the family, neighborhood, community, school, friendships, peer groups, and romantic relationships, providing unique opportunities to study how social environments and behaviors in adolescence are linked to health and achievement outcomes in young adulthood.

Adjacency matrix: A square matrix used to represent a graph/network. The entry values of the matrix cells commonly denote the tie (relation) between the given row actor and column actor. For an illustration of an adjacency matrix, edgelist, and nodelist, see Figures 1.4 and 1.5.

Alcoholics Anonymous (AA): International mutual aid fellowship founded in 1935 by Bill Wilson and Dr. Bob Smith in Akron, Ohio. AA states that its primary purpose is "to stay sober and help other alcoholics achieve sobriety," and it is credited with helping many alcoholics achieve and maintain sobriety.

Alter: All other actors besides the ego. Often used for only other actors directly connected to the ego.

Archival data: Data stored at various archives, such as letters, patents, published journal articles, and professional vita in electronic repositories, such as e-mail or web servers, or on online data bases, such as that of the Federal Election Commission (FEC).

Atomistic model: Research model that presumes independence between units of analysis. The atomistic model is the opposite of the structural-relational model.

Betweenness centrality: measures the extent to which a node sits on the shortest paths between all other pairs of nodes in a given network. A node with high betweenness centrality is located on many such shortest paths, and therefore could, for instance, intercept the messages passing between many pairs.

Binary/valued graph (network): A social network in which ties are only noted as existing or not existing is called a binary network or graph. When the network also contains information about the intensity or type of relationship, indicated by ordinal or continuous values, it is called a valued network or graph.

Bipartite graph: Also called a *bipartite network* or *two-mode network*. It consists of two different sets of nodes, such as persons and events, or students and classes. For a detailed discussion of bipartite graphs, see Chapter 3.

Bipartite matrix: The adjacency matrix associated with a bipartite network.

Boundary specification problem: Decision on which actors and ties to include in a study.

Cascade: Also called *contagious or cascading effects*. Social influences that are exerted by one social actor to the other actors through social networks. In the context of voting, they refer to the situation in which a social actor's act of voting encourages other actors in the network to vote.

Causality: Also called a *causal explanation*, which is a study of causes and consequences. In social sciences, causality examines some social outcomes and the causes that bring about those social outcomes.

Causality ambiguity: Condition in which the order of cause and consequence is not clearly established. An example is education and income: Whereas education (cause) increases income (consequence), income (cause) also buys education (consequence).

Centrality: Node-level measurement indicating the extent to which an actor occupies the central position of a network. The most common centrality measures are degree centrality, betweenness centrality, and closeness centrality.

Centrality in egocentric network: Although centrality is a measurement used mostly in full networks, it can be used in an egocentric network as well.

Centralization: At the whole network or graph level, centralization measures the extent to which nodes in the graph/network have different centralities. See Chapter 3 on how to calculate centralization.

CES-D Scores (the Center for Epidemiological Studies Depression Scale): Screening measure developed to identify current depressive symptoms related to major or clinical depression in adults and adolescents. The most commonly used version of the CES-D is the 20-item version. Items include depressed mood, feelings of guilt, worthlessness and helplessness, psychomotor retardation, loss of appetite, and sleep difficulties.

Clique: Subgroup in a network in which each and every node is directly connected with all other nodes in the subgroup.

Closeness centrality: measures the steps (or "hops") along network ties a given node needs to take to reach all other nodes in a network. A node with high closeness centrality is defined as one that takes the least number of steps to reach other nodes in a network.

Coercive isomorphism: In its abstract definition, coercive isomorphism refers to a situation in which actors in a network become similar to each other because of their vulnerabilities to external forces, such as governmental regulations. For example, corporations all adopt an Equal Employment Opportunity/Affirmative Action (EEO/AA) office in response to federal regulations.

Cognitive social structure (CSS): Network structure derived from the subjective assessment of relations between all pairs in a given network by each network participant. CSS entails two networks. One is the aggregated version (global network) consisting of all network participants' assessment. This global network is often referred to as a factual network. The other network consists of the individual actors' assessment of their network's structure.

Collective efficacy: "The linkage of mutual trust and the willingness to intervene for the common good" in a neighborhood (Sampson, Raudenbush, & Earls, 1997: 919).

Degree centrality: measures the extent to which a node in a network is connected with other nodes. A central node is defined as one that is connected with most other nodes in the network.

Dendogram: Visualization technique that describes grouping of nodes in step-by-step fashion.

Density: Mathematical measurement for the connectivity of social networks. It measures the extent to which nodes in a given network are connected with each other. For a binary network, it ranges from 0 (meaning no connectivity) to 1 (meaning everybody is connected to everybody else in a network).

Differential association theory: Theory in criminology developed by Edwin Sutherland (1947) proposing that through interaction with others, individuals learn the values, attitudes, techniques, and motives for criminal behavior. The theory predicts that an individual will choose the criminal path when the balance of rewards, influence, or pressure for law-breaking exceeds those for law-abiding.

Directed/undirected network: Social networks can be directed when there is a distinction between senders and receivers, such as e-mail exchanges that involve senders and receivers. Social networks can be also undirected when there is no substantive need to distinguish between senders and receivers, such as in a marriage network (A is married to B, B is also married to A).

Dyad: a pair of actors or nodes.

Edgelist: a dataset in which each line is one tie existing in the network, and which records at least both parties involved in this relationship.

Ego: Actor under discussion in a network, the relevant actor.

Egocentric network studies: Social network design that uses conventional random samples in an open population but poses social network questions (using name generators, resource generators, etc.) to the respondents.

Equity investment: Occurs when one firm buys a direct financial interest in another through a direct stock purchase.

Equity swap: Occurs when two firms mutually purchase each other's stock. Joint ventures, equity investments, and equity swaps are all strategic alliances. Joint ventures require more involvement from partnering firms than equity investments/swaps do.

ERGM (exponential random graph models)/P*: Relatively new statistical method that treats the observed network as the dependent variable, seeking to uncover the explanatory factors that account for the emergence of the observed network. An ERGM explicitly models the interdependence between nodes, and pairs of nodes, in a network. When explaining the dependent variable, i.e. the (observed) matrix, it simultaneously accounts for endogenous processes, exogenous actor effects, and covariate matrices. See Chapter 4 for a complete introduction of this method.

Event-based approach: Sample inclusion rule that is based on an actor's participation in certain events under scope.

Expanding selection: One of the reputational methods; it relies on knowledgeable informants to nominate subjects that are relevant to social network studies.

External validity: Extent to which a result from a given study can be replicated in other research settings.

Fixed list selection: Same as the expanding selection, except that the informants are provided with a roster or list of subjects who are determined to be relevant to the study and are asked to nominate the subjects from the list.

Four-firm concentration ratio: Measure of the output accounted for by the largest four firms in an industry out of the total output in the industry. It is basically an index of monopoly in an industry—the higher the ratio, the higher the level of monopoly.

Framingham Heart Study: Long-term, ongoing cardiovascular study on residents of the town of Framingham, Massachusetts. The study began in 1948 with 5,209 adult subjects from Framingham, and it is now on its third generation of participants. Much of the now-common knowledge concerning heart disease, such as the effects of diet, exercise, and common medications such as aspirin, is based on this longitudinal study. It is a project of the National Heart, Lung, and Blood Institute, in collaboration with (since 1971) Boston University.

Full or complete network: Identifies in advance the relevant actors, who are often members of a clearly delineated social group (students of one class, all the countries with a population larger than 100,000, etc.). Then it collects data on all possible pairs, for instance, by asking respondents to identify friends from a roster of those relevant actors.

Graph: Visual illustration of a social network, which is made up of nodes (vertices) and lines (edges) connecting those nodes.

Guanxi network: Interpersonal network in China, which has two distinguishing features compared with the Western-style personal network. First it has a long-term orientation, which entails a greater level of trust and higher expectation of mutuality or reciprocity. Second it is multidimensional, encompassing a variety of expressive and instrumental exchanges between Guanxi partners.

Hidden populations: Individuals with rare, sometimes stigmatizing characteristics, such as drug dealers, sex workers, HIV-positive people, illegal immigrants, terrorists, or gang and mafia members.

HIV/AIDS (Human immunodeficiency virus infection / acquired immunodeficiency syndrome): Disease of the human immune system caused by infection with human immunodeficiency virus (HIV). HIV is transmitted primarily via unprotected sexual intercourse, contaminated blood transfusions, hypodermic needles, and from mother to child during pregnancy, delivery, or breastfeeding. Since its discovery, AIDS has caused an estimated 36 million deaths worldwide, and approximately 35.3 million people were living with HIV globally as of 2012.

Homophily: Situation characterized with greater likelihood of similar individuals to be connected in a network, which is often dubbed as "birds of a feather fly together."

Homophily principle: In the context of international relational networks, the homophily principle predicts that nations will seek out other nations similar to (governance, ideology, etc.) them as partners.

Inbreeding bias: Term coined by James Montgomery (1991) in the context of job recruitment in which employees like to recruit others who are like them to be co-workers.

Informant bias: Discrepancy between self-reported and actual behavior.

Interlocking board: Interorganizational bonding that locks in two or more organizations by sharing the same board of directors between two or more organizations.

Internal network organization: Organizational structure that replaces hierarchical commands with market arm's length transactions to regulate relations between different intraorganization departments within the same organization.

International nongovernmental organizations (INGOs): NGOs operating at an international scope.

Interviewer effects: Any survey administered by a human interviewer creates a social context in which the respondent's answer may depend on the appearance and behavior of the interviewer. Patterns in the respondent's answer due to this social context are ascribed to such interviewer effects.

Jaccard's coefficient: Reliability measure in test-retest to indicate the extent to which an experiment produces reliable results. It ranges from 0% to 100%; the closer the index is to 100%, the higher the reliability.

Joint venture: Two or more legally distinct firms pool a portion of their resources within a jointly owned legal organization that serves a limited purpose for its parents.

Legal cynicism: Cultural frame whereby people perceive the law as illegitimate, unresponsive, and ill-equipped to ensure public safety.

Level of analysis: In analyzing social network data, researchers need to determine their level of analysis such as individual nodes, dyadic pairs, or entire network.

Longitudinal data: Data administered to the same research subjects that are collected over multiple time periods.

Matrix: Mathematic representation of a social network, in which rows and columns indicate nodes and values in the matrix cells represent the ties between their corresponding nodes.

Multidimensional scaling (MDS): Visualization technique that displays the similarities or dissimilarities between nodes in a network. Its input matrix should be a valued undirected matrix.

Multiple name generators: Studies that use a battery of name generators (important matters, lending money, repairing houses, seeking information, etc.).

Name generator: Survey instrument that is used to elicit contacts of the respondents. It may ask respondents for the name of friends, of individuals they asked for help or discussed important matters with, etc.

Name interpreter: In egocentric network studies, name interpreter denotes those questions that capture alters' (or egos' contacts) characteristics, such as gender, race, education, and relations with other alters.

National Health and Social Life Survey (NHSLS): Also known as *The Sex Survey*. It is the most representative U.S. sex survey and reflects the practices of the general U.S. adult population in the 1990s. The study collected information on sexual practices with spouses/co-habitants and other sexual partners and collected background information about the partners.

N-clique: Subgroup in a network in which each and every node is connected with all other nodes in the group via the shortest path, with no longer than *N* steps.

Neighborhood: Collective of both people and institutions occupying a spatially defined area influenced by ecological, cultural, and sometimes political forces.

Network: Also called a *graph* (in particular, in mathematics and related fields). It consists of a set of nodes and an adjacency matrix or edgelist that defines the relations among the nodes.

Network autocorrelation: Network terminology for a phenomenon where people who are closely related to each other tend to be similar on salient individual behavioral and attitudinal dimensions.

Network-behavior panel data: Type of network data in which complete networks as well as changeable attributes are measured over time.

Network constraint: An index based on the number of structural holes an ego node has. The higher the number of holes, the lower the network constraint. Conversely, the lower the number of holes, the higher the network constraint.

Node: Also called an *actor*, a *vertex*, or *points*. It is one of the basic elements in social network analysis that often denotes individuals but sometimes also social groups, such as political parties, work groups, communities, or nations and states.

Nodelist: Collection of social network actors or nodes in a network dataset.

Nominalist strategies: In contrast to the realist strategy, researchers establish the sample inclusion criterion *a priori*.

Nongovernmental organizations (NGOs): NGOS are nonprofit, nongovernmental, legal, voluntary organizations. The United States has about 1.5 million NGOs, operating in the fields of development, environment, or human rights.

Normative isomorphism: Situation in which actors in a network become similar to each other because of their vulnerabilities to normative pressures. For example, a teenager may start smoking because his or her friends do.

One-mode network: Network that consists of only one type of nodes in its nodelist. Compare with *two-mode network*.

Partial treatment group design: Design that imitates conventional experimental design, in which there are control and experimental groups. Partial treatment group design uses naturally networked settings, such as classrooms, or social clubs as control and experimental groups. It randomly selects a few subjects to receive external intervention from the experimental group. Any differences between the experimental group subjects who did not receive external intervention and control group subjects can be attributed to the spillover effects or contagious effects from those experimental group subjects who received external intervention to their group peers who did not receive the intervention.

Partisanship homophily: Tendency for U.S. congresspersons to recruit others from the same party to co-sponsor a bill.

Permutation: Mathematical method that describes a complete rearrangement of a set of numbers. For a given set of number N, a complete rearrangement of the number has $N!$ sets.

Poison pill: Defensive strategy used by a corporation to fend off hostile takeovers by bidders. It involves offering discounts on shares to existing board members, which will increase the cost of bid, forcing the bidders to come back and negotiate with the board.

Politically heterogeneous social networks: Networks in which members hold conflicting political views.

Popularity: In the context of a friendship network, popularity indicates the number of times one is named as a friend among network members.

Positional approach: Sample inclusion in social network analysis based on an actor's formal position or affiliation with certain organizations.

Positional generator: Similar to name generator, but it imposes respondents with a set of occupations, asking them to nominate contacts in those occupations. A positional generator helps researchers to identify the level of social resources accessible to respondents via their networks.

Power as access: In the context of a social network refers to the ability to tap into the resources flowing in a network by gaining access to the network. For example, a group of families sets up a loan system to help each other in case of an emergency. Becoming part of the group provides access power as member families have access to the emergency loans.

Power as brokerage: It is a power that arises when one social actor is connected to two disconnected social actors. For example, when China is connected with the United States and North Korea, which are disconnected from each other, China has brokerage power to negotiate between the two parties. See also *betweenness centrality*.

Power as exit: Power that arises when a given social actor can exit from a network with great ease. For example, a power structure can be easily measured with "who can easily exit the negotiation" between two parties in a negotiation (e.g., car buyers and car dealers).

Preferential attachment (PA)/bandwagon effects: In the context of an international relational network, the PA

or bandwagon effect predicts that nations will seek out other nations that are in the center of a network to form partnerships.

Preprimary period: Time frame of a year prior to the general election of a U.S. president.

Prestige: Degree centrality measurement in directed graphs/networks. A node with high prestige is defined as one receiving many ties but sending out few relations.

QAP (quadratic assignment procedure): Statistical method in social network analysis originally developed by David Krackhardt (1988). It tries to account for the emergence of an observed matrix with one of multiple matrices as explanatory factors.

QAP correlation: Correlation using QAP to examine the relationship between two matrices.

QAP regression: Regression using QAP to explain an observed matrix with a set of explanatory matrices.

Realist strategies: In boundary specification of full network design, researchers rely on the subjective perceptions of the respondents to determine who to include in the sample.

Receiver: Also called a *target*. It is the recipient of a directed tie, who may be the passive partner in the relationship. In matrix, it occupies the column positions.

Reciprocated ties: In directed networks, a reciprocated tie is a tie that leads from A to B and from B back to A. For example: John names Amy as a friend, and Amy also names John as a friend.

Relations: Also called *ties*, *links*, *connections*, *lines*, *edges*, or – for directed relations only – *arcs* or *arrows*. It is another basic element in social network analysis that signifies the relations between nodes. Relations can be binary (1: presence, 0: absence) or valued/weighted. Relations can be also directed (friendship nomination) or undirected (marriage). Some scholars suggest adding signs (+/–) to the relations between nodes to distinguish between positive and negative ties.

Reliability: Extent to which the same survey instruments, when applied to the same set of informants in multiple time periods, yield identical results.

Reputational approach: Sample inclusion in network studies based on nominations of knowledgeable informants. It includes snowball sampling and sampling using fixed list or expanding selection.

Reputational power: One's ability to reconstruct the informal network structure, such as friendship network or advice-seeking networks, among a group of co-workers (Krackhardt, 1992).

Resource generator: Captures respondents' social resources by asking them to report their contacts, who can provide certain forms of facilitation.

Sampling units: When designing social network research, the first step consists of identifying the unit of analysis in the study, which can be individuals or groups of individuals, such as organizations, parties, communities, or states.

Second boundary determination issue: Decision about which contacts or alters of the ego (respondent) to elicit in egocentric network studies.

Sender: Also called a *source*. It refers to the actor that "sends" a directed tie, and who may be the initiator or active partner in the relationship. In matrix presentation, senders occupy the row positions.

Sexually transmitted diseases (STDs): Also referred to as *sexually transmitted infections (STIs)* and *venereal diseases (VDs)*. These are illnesses that have a significant probability of transmission between humans by means of sexual behavior, including vaginal intercourse, anal sex, and oral sex. Some STIs can also be contracted by using intravenous drug needles after their use by an infected person, as well as through contact with contaminated blood or through childbirth or breastfeeding.

Small-world phenomenon: Also called the *theory of six degrees of separation*. Originally proposed by Stanley Milgram (1967), it states that everybody is connected to everybody else within the United States through an average of five intermediary steps.

Social ability model: Theoretical model that posits that delinquent behavior is learned through social interactions with others and the peer group in particular.

Social capital: Capital captured through social relations, or resources, embedded in one's network that can be mobilized to facilitate one's individual actions. Social capital can also refer to public goods such as generalized trust and norms that facilitate collective outcomes.

Social cohesion: Social forces that draw and bind people together.

Social comparison theory: Theory maintaining that the happiness of individuals depends on a comparison of themselves with others close to them.

Social inability model: Theoretical model that maintains that deviant behavior occurs when bonding or attachment to the family and the school fails to constrain adolescents from doing so.

Socialization process: Process through which the referrers of the new employees socialize them into their new roles, avoiding the initial shock or hard landing commonly experienced by new employees.

Strategic alliance: Broadly defined as two or more organizations joining hands to deal with the main strategic opportunities or challenges they are facing. It includes a great variety of formats (see Figure 5.14 for details).

Strength of weak ties: Mark Granovetter discovered in 1973 that job seekers obtain useful information from their weak tie contacts, rather than from their close tie friends, because those weak tie contacts produce fresh, nonredundant information. He dubbed this phenomenon "the strength of weak ties".

Stress indicator: Indicator that measures the discrepancy between the generated multidimensional scaling (MDS) and the original data. Often dubbed as "badness of fit" as the low value in the indicator suggests a good fit of the MDS in representing the original data.

Structural equivalence: Pair of, or a dyad of, nodes that has the same pattern in its connections with other nodes in a given network.

Structural hole theory: Concept developed by Robert Burt (1992) to refer to a network configuration in which an ego node is connected to two or more alter nodes that are disconnected from each other (e.g., Robert in Figure 5.3). According to Burt, the structural hole provides two benefits to the ego node crossing the hole: information and control benefits.

Structural-relational model: Approach that presumes interdependence between units of analysis, which is an assumption fundamental to social network analysis.

Subjective well-being (SWB): Positive evaluation of one's life associated with good feelings.

The forbidden triad: Idea introduced by Mark Granovetter (1973) in which a triadic relationship exists where there are strong ties between actors A and B, and A and C, but where no tie exists between B and C. This is considered as an unbalanced structure.

Triadic closure: Situation that transcends relations from one pair to other pairs. For example, in a friendship network, there is the tendency of "friends of friends to be friends."

Triadic structure: Network structure consisting of three actors.

Valued network: Social network in which lines or edges connecting the nodes have values not restricted to 0 or 1, such as 0, 1, 2, ...

Vertical integration: Occurs when one firm acquires another firm in a different industry. It can be **forward vertical integration**, in which a given firm acquires a client firm to expand their market (e.g., Apple uses forward vertical integration to acquire Apple Authorized Stores to sell Apple products). It also can be **backward vertical integration**, in which a given firm acquires a supplier to ensure supplies of critical inputs for its production (e.g., the famous Ford River Rouge Complex illustrates the backward vertical integration, in which Ford acquired many of its part suppliers).

• References •

Ackland, R. (2013). *Web social science: Concepts, data and tools for social scientists in the digital age*. London, England: Sage Ltd.

Adamic, L. A., & Adar, E. (2003). Friends and neighbors on the Web. *Social Networks, 25*(3), 211–230.

Adamic, L. A., & Glance, N. (2005). The political blogosphere and the 2004 US election: Divided they blog. In *Proceedings of the 3rd international workshop on link discovery* (pp. 36–43). New York, NY: ACM.

Adams, J., & Moody, J. (2007). To tell the truth: Informant accuracy in sexual networks. *Social Networks, 29*(1), 44–58.

Akers, R. L. (1998). *Social learning and social structure: A general theory of crime and deviance*. Lebanon, NH: Northeastern University Press.

Alderson, A. S., Beckfield, J., & Sprague-Jones, J. (2010). Intercity relations and globalisation: The evolution of the global urban hierarchy, 1981–2007. *Urban Studies, 47*(9), 1899–1923.

Alexander, M. C., & Danowski, J. (1990). Analysis of an ancient network: Personal communication and the study of social structure in a past society. *Social Networks, 12*(4), 313–335.

Allison, P. (1999). *Multiple regression: A primer*. Thousand Oaks, CA: Pine Forge Press.

Anderson, C. J., & Paskeviciute, A. (2005). Macro-politics and micro-behavior: Mainstream politics and the frequency of political discussion in contemporary democracies. *The Social Logic of Politics*, 228–248.

Antonucci, T. C., & Akiyama, H. (1991). Social relationships and aging well. *Generations: Journal of the American Society on Aging, 15*, 39–44.

Aral, S. O. (1999). Sexual network patterns as determinants of STD rates: Paradigm shift in the behavioral epidemiology of STDs made visible. *Sexually Transmitted Diseases, 26*(5), 262–264.

Aral, S. O. (2001). Sexually transmitted diseases: Magnitude, determinants and consequences. *International Journal of STD & AIDS, 12*(4), 211–215.

Aseltine, R. H. Jr. (1995). A reconsideration of parental and peer influences on adolescent deviance. *Journal of Health and Social Behavior, 36*, 103–121.

Assassination of Archduke Franz Ferdinand [Course blog]. Retrieved June 7, 2016, from https://blogs.cornell.edu/info2040/2015/09/14/assassination-of-archduke-franz-ferdinand/

Atchley, R. C. (1991). The influence of aging and frailty on perception and expression of the self: Theoretical and methodological issues. In J. E. Birren, J. E. Lubben, J. C. Rowe, & D. E. Deutchman (Eds.), *The concept and measurement of quality of life in the frail elderly* (pp. 207–225). New York, NY: Elsevier.

Athey, N. C., & Bouchard, M. (2013). The BALCO scandal: The social structure of a steroid distribution network. *Global Crime, 14*, 216–237.

Auerbach, D. M., Darrow, W. W., Jaffe, H. W., & Curran, J. W. (1984). Cluster of cases of the acquired immune deficiency syndrome: Patients linked by sexual contact. *American Journal of Medicine, 76*(3), 487–492.

Babbie, E. R. (2009). *The practice of social research*. Belmont, CA: Thomson/Wadsworth.

Baerveldt, C., Van Rossem, R., Vermande, M., & Weerman, F. (2004). Students' delinquency and correlates with strong and weaker ties: A study of students' network in Dutch high schools. *Connections, 26*, 11–28.

Bailey, S., & Marsden, P. V. (1999). Interpretation and interview context: Examining the General Social Survey name generator using cognitive methods. *Social Networks, 21*, 287–309.

Barabási, L. (2003). *Linked: How everything is connected to everything else and what it means*. New York, NY: Plume Books.

Barabási, L., & Albert, R. (1999). Emergence of scaling in random networks. *Science, 286*(5439), 509–512.

Barbera, P. (2014). Birds of the same feather tweet together. Bayesian ideal point estimation using Twitter data. *Political Analysis*. Epub ahead of print. doi:10.1093/pan/mpu011

Barrington, C., Latkin, C., Sweat, M. D., Moreno, L., Ellen, J., & Kerrigan, D. (2009). Talking the talk, walking the walk: Social network norms, communication patterns, and condom use among the male partners of female sex workers in La Romana, Dominican Republic. *Social Science & Medicine, 68*(11), 2037–2044.

Battin, S. R., Hill, K. G., Abbott, R. D., Catalano, R. F., & Hawkins, D. (1998). The contribution of gang membership to delinquency beyond delinquent friends. *Criminology, 36*, 93–116.

Bauman, K., & Ennet, J. (1996). On the importance of peer influence for adolescent drug use: Commonly neglected considerations. *Addiction, 9*, 184–198.

Barusch, A. S., & Spaid, W. M. (1989). Gender differences in caregiving: Why do wives report greater burden? *Gerontologist, 29*(5), 667–676.

Bearman, P. S. (1991). The social structure of suicide. *Sociological Forum, 6*(3), 501–524.

Bearman, P. S., & Moody, J. (2004). Suicide and friendships among American adolescents. *American Journal of Public Health, 94*(1), 89–95.

Bearman, P. S., Moody, J., & Stovel, K. (2004). Chains of affection: The structure of adolescent romantic and sexual networks. *American Journal of Sociology, 110*(1), 44–91.

Beauchamp, M. A. (1965). An improved index of centrality. *Behavioral Science, 10*(2), 161–163.

Beckfield, J. (2003). Review of the transformation of the welfare state: The silent surrender of public responsibility. *Social Forces, 82*(1), 410–411.

Bellair, P. E. (1997). Social interaction and community crime: Examining the importance of neighbor networks. *Criminology, 35*(4), 677–704.

Berardo, R., & Scholz, J. T. (2010). Self-organizing policy networks: Risk, partner selection, and cooperation in estuaries. *American Journal of Political Science, 54*(3), 632–649.

Bergin, A. E., & Lambert, M. J. (1971). The evaluation of therapeutic outcomes. In A. E. Bergin & S. L. Garfield (Eds.), *Handbook of psychotherapy and behavior change:*

An empirical analysis (pp. 217–270). New York, NY: Wiley.

Berkman, L. F., & Glass, T. (2000). Social integration, social networks, social support, and health. *Social Epidemiology, 1*, 137–173.

Berkman, L. F., Glass, T., Brissette, I., & Seeman, T. E. (2000). From social integration to health: Durkheim in the new millennium. *Social Science & Medicine, 51*(6), 843–857.

Berkman, L. F., & Syme, S. L. (1979). Social networks, host resistance, and mortality: A nine-year follow-up study of Alameda County residents. *American Journal of Epidemiology, 109*(2), 186–204.

Berlusconi, G. (2013). Do all the pieces matter? Assessing the reliability of law enforcement data sources for the network analysis of wire taps. *Global Crime, 14*(1), 61–81.

Bernard, R. H., & Killworth, P. (1977). Informant accuracy in social network data II. *Human Communications Research, 4*, 3–18.

Bernard, R. H., Killworth, P., & Sailer, L. (1980). Summary of research on informant accuracy in network data, and on the reverse small world problem. *Connections, 4*(2), 11–25.

Bernard, R. H., Killworth, P., Sailer, L., & Kronenfeld, D. (1984). The problem of informant accuracy: The validity of retrospective data. *Annual Review of Anthropology, 13*, 495–517.

Bian, Y. (1994). *Work and inequality in urban China*. New York, NY: SUNY Press.

Bian, Y. (1997). Bringing strong ties back in: Indirect ties network bridges and job searches in China. *American Sociological Review, 62*, 266–285.

Bond, R. M., Fariss, C. J., Jones, J. J., Kramer, A. D. I., Marlow, C., Settle, J. E., & Fowler, J. H. (2012). A

61-million-person experiment in social influence and political mobilization. *Nature, 489*, 295–298.

Borgatti, S. P. (2006). Identifying sets of key players in a network. *Computational & Mathematical Organization Theory, 12*(1), 21–34.

Borgatti, S. P., & Everett, M. (1992). Graph colorings and power in experimental exchange networks. *Social Networks, 14*, 287–308.

Borgatti, S. P., & Everett, M. (1999). Models of core/periphery structures. *Social Networks, 21*, 375–395.

Borgatti, S. P., Everett, M., & Freeman, L. (2002). *UCINET for Windows: Software for social network analysis*. Harvard, MA: Analytic Technologies.

Borgatti, S. P., Everett, M. G., & Johnson, J. C. (2013). *Analyzing social networks*. London, England: Sage Ltd.

Borgatti, S. P., Mehra, A., Brass, D., & Labianca, G. (2009). Network analysis in the social sciences. *Science, 323*(5916), 892–895.

Bourdieu, P. (1986). The forms of capital. In J. Richardson, ed., *Theory and research for the sociology of education* (pp. 241–258). New York, NY: Greenwood Press.

Box-Steffensmeier, J. M., Christenson, D. P., & Hitt, M. P. (2013). Quality over quantity: Amici influence and judicial decision making. *American Political Science Review, 107*(3), 446–460.

Boyd, D. M., & Ellison, N. B. (2007). Social network sites: Definition, history, and scholarship. *Journal of Computer-Mediated Communication, 13*(1), 210–230.

Brass, D. J., & Burkhardt, M. E. (1992). Centrality and power in organizations. In N. Nohria & R. G. Eccles (Eds.), *Networks and* organizations: Structure, form, and action (pp. 191–215). Boston, MA: Harvard Business School Press.

Brewer, D. D. (2000). Forgetting in the recall-based elicitation of personal and social networks. *Social Networks, 22*(1), 29–43.

Brewer, D. D., & Webster, C. (1999). Forgetting of friends and its effects on measuring friendship networks. *Social Networks, 21*(4), 361–373.

Brickman, P., Coates, D., & Janoff-Bulman, R. (1978). Lottery winners and accident victims: Is happiness relative? *Journal of Personality and Social Psychology, 36*(8), 917–927.

Bright, D. A., & Delaney, J. J. (2013). Evolution of a drug trafficking network: Mapping changes in network structure and function across time. *Global Crime, 14*(2–3), 238–260.

Brooks-Gunn, J., Duncan, G. J., & Aber, J. L. (Eds.). (1997). *Neighborhood poverty. Vol. I: Context and consequences for children*. New York, NY: Russell Sage Foundation.

Browning, C. R., Feinberg, S. L., & Dietz, R. D. (2004). The paradox of social organization: Networks, collective efficacy, and violent crime in urban neighborhoods. *Social Forces, 83*(2), 503–534.

Bursik, R. J. Jr. (1988). Social disorganization and theories of crime and delinquency: Problems and prospects. *Criminology, 26*(4), 519–552.

Bursik, R. J. Jr., & Grasmick, H. G. (1993). *Neighborhoods and crime: The dimensions of effective community control*. New York, NY: Lexington Books.

Burt, R. S. (1978). Cohesion versus structural equivalence as a basis for network subgroups. *Sociological Methods and Research, 7*(2), 189–212.

Burt, R. S. (1982). *Toward a structural theory of action*. New York: Academic Press.

Burt, R. S. (1992). *Structural holes: The social structure of competition*. Cambridge, MA: Harvard University Press.

Burt, R. S. (1997). The contingent value of social capital. *Administrative Science Quarterly, 42*(2), 339–365.

Burt, R. S. (1998). The gender of social capital. *Rationality and Society, 10*(1), 5–46.

Cacioppo, J. T., Fowler, J. H., & Christakis, N. A. (2009). Alone in the crowd: The structure and spread of loneliness in a large social network. *Journal of Personality and Social Psychology, 97*(6), 977–991.

Cairns, R. B., Cairns, B. D., Nekerman, H. J., Gest, S. D., & Gariepy, J. (1988). Social networks and aggressive behavior: Peer support or peer rejection? *Developmental Psychology, 24*, 815–823.

Calvo, E., & Murillo, M. V. (2013). When parties meet voters: Assessing political linkages through partisan networks and distributive expectations in Argentina and Chile. *Comparative Political Studies, 46*(7), 851–882.

Campbell, D. E. (2006). *Why we vote: How schools and communities shape our civic life*. Princeton, NJ: Princeton University Press.

Campbell, K. E., & Lee, B. (1991). Name generators in surveys of personal networks. *Social Networks, 13*(3), 203–221.

Caplan, G. (1974). *Support systems and community mental health: Lectures on concept development*. New York, NY: Behavioral Publications.

Carley, K. (2004). *Estimating vulnerabilities in large covert networks*. Paper presented at the 2004 International Symposium on Command and Control Research and Technology.

Carpenter, M., Li, M., & Jiang, H. (2012). Social network research in organizational contexts: A systematic review of methodological issues and choices. *Journal of Management, 38*(4), 1328–1361.

Chadwick, A. (2013). *The hybrid media system: Politics and power*. London, England: Oxford University Press.

Child, J. (2005). *Organization: Contemporary principles and practice*. Chichester, West Sussex, England: Wiley.

Child, J., & Faulkner, D. (1998). *Strategies of cooperation: Managing alliances, networks, and joint ventures*. New York, NY: Oxford University Press.

Cho, W. K. T., & Fowler, J. H. (2010). Legislative success in a small world: Social network analysis and the dynamics of congressional legislation. *The Journal of Politics, 72*(1), 124–135.

Christakis, N. A., & Fowler, J. H. (2007). The spread of obesity in a large social network over 32 years. *New England Journal of Medicine, 357*(4), 370–379.

Christakis, N. A., & Fowler, J. H. (2008). The collective dynamics of smoking in a large social network. *New England Journal of Medicine, 358*(21), 2249–2258.

Christakis, N. A., & Fowler, J. H. (2009). *Connected: The surprising power of our social networks and how they shape our lives*. New York, NY: Little, Brown.

Chung, S. (1996). Performance effects of cooperative strategies among investment banking firms:

A loglinear analysis of organizational exchange networks. *Social Networks, 18*, 121–148.

Claes, M., & Simard, R. (1992). Friendship characteristics of delinquent adolescents. *International Journal of Adolescence and Youth, 3*, 287–301.

Cohen, A. K. (1955). *Delinquent boys: The culture of the gang*. New York, NY: Free Press.

Cohen, S., Doyle, W. J., Skoner, D. P., Rabin, B. S., & Gwaltney, J. M. (1997). Social ties and susceptibility to the common cold. *Journal of the American Medical Association, 277*(24), 1940–1944.

Cohen, S., & Janicki-Deverts, D. (2009). Can we improve our physical health by altering our social networks? *Perspectives on Psychological Science, 4*(4), 375–378.

Cohen, S., & Lemay, E. P. (2007). Why would social networks be linked to affect and health practices? *Health Psychology, 26*(4), 410–417.

Cole, S., Hawkley, L. C., Arevalo, J. M., Sung, C. Y., Rose, R. M., & Cacioppo, J. T. (2007). Social regulation of gene expression in human leukocytes. *Genome Biology, 8*(9), R189.

Coleman, J. S. (1988). Social capital and the creation of human capital. *American Journal of Sociology, 94*, 95–120.

Collins, C., & Jones, R. (1997). Emotional distress and morbidity in dementia carers: A matched comparison of husbands and wives. *International Journal of Geriatric Psychiatry, 12*(12), 1168–1173.

Coromina, L., & Coenders, G. (2006). Reliability and validity of egocentered network data collected via Web. A meta-analysis of multilevel multitrait multimethod studies. *Social Networks, 28*, 209–231.

Cranmer, S. J., & Desmarais, B. A. (2011). Inferential network analysis with exponential random graph models. *Political Analysis, 19*(1), 66–86.

Curtis, R., Friedman, S. R., Neaigus, A., Jose, B., Goldstein, M., & Ildefonso, G. (1995). Street-level drug markets: Network structure and HIV risk. *Social Networks, 17*(3), 229–249.

Dahl, R. A. (1961). *Who governs? Democracy and power in an American city*. New Haven, CT: Yale University Press.

Davis, A., Gardner, B. B., & Gardner, M. (1941). *Deep South: A social anthropological study of caste and class*. Chicago, IL: University of Chicago Press.

Davis, G. F., & Greve, H. R. (1997). Corporate elite networks and governance changes in the 1980s. *American Journal of Sociology, 103*(1), 1–37.

Davis, G. F., Yoo, M., & Baker, W. E. (2003). The small world of the American corporate elite, 1982-2001. *Strategic Organization, 3*, 301–326.

Davis, J. A., & Leinhardt, S. (1972). The structure of positive interpersonal relations in small groups. In J. B. Morris, Z. Anderson, & B. Anderson (Eds.), *Sociological theories in progress* (Vol. 2). Boston, MA: Houghton Mifflin.

de la Haye, K., Robins, G., Mohr, P., & Wilson, C. (2010). Obesity-related behaviors in adolescent friendship networks. *Social Networks, 32*(3), 161–167.

Demiroz, F., & Kapucu, N. (2012). Anatomy of a dark network: The case of the Turkish Ergenekon terrorist organization. *Trends in Organized Crime, 15*(4), 271–295.

Derudder, B., & Witlox, F. (2005). An appraisal of the use of airline data in assessing the world city network: A research note on data. *Urban Studies, 42*(13), 2371–2388.

Derudder, B., & Taylor, P. (2005). The cliquishness of world cities. *Global Networks, 5*(1), 71–91.

Derudder, B., Witlox, F., Faulconbridge, J., & Beaverstock, J. (2008). Airline data for global city network research: Reviewing and refining existing approaches. *GeoJournal, 71*(1), 5–18.

Desmarais, B. A., Harden, J. J., & Boehmke, F. J. (2015). Persistent policy pathways: Inferring diffusion networks in the American states. *American Political Science Review, 109*(02), 392–406.

Desmarais, B. A., La Raja, R. J., & Kowal, M. S. (2015). The fates of challengers in U.S. House elections: The role of extended party networks in supporting candidates and shaping electoral outcomes. *American Journal of Political Science, 59*(1), 194–211.

Desmarais, B. A., Moscardelli, V. G., Schaffner, B. F., & Kowal, M. S. (2015). Measuring legislative collaboration: The Senate press events network. *Social Networks, 40*, 43–54.

Diesner, J., & Carley, K. (2004). *Using network text analysis to detect the organizational structure of covert networks*. Paper presented at the North American Association for Computational Social and Organizational Science (NAACSOS) Conference. Pittsburgh, PA.

Diesner, J., Frantz, T. L., & Carley, K. M. (2005). Communication networks from the Enron email corpus: It's always about the people, Enron is no different. *Computational & Mathematical Organization Theory, 11*(3), 201–228.

DiMaggio, P., & Garip, F. (2012). Network effects and social inequality.

Annual Review of Sociology, 38, 93–118.

Ding, Y. (2011). Scientific collaboration and endorsement: Network analysis of coauthorship and citation networks. *Journal of Informetrics, 5*(1), 187–203.

Dombroski, M., Fischbeck, P., & Carley, K. M. (2003). *Estimating the shape of covert networks*. Presented at the 8th International Command and Control Research and Technology Symposium, National Defense War College, Washington, DC.

Doreian, P. (1989). Network autocorrelation models: Problems and prospects. In D. A. Griffith (Ed.), *Spatial statistics: Past, present, future* (pp. 369–389). Ann Arbor: Michigan Document Services.

Doreian, P., & Woodard, K. (1992). Fixed list versus snowball selection of social networks. *Social Science Research, 21*, 216–233.

Doreian, P., & Woodard, K. (1994). Defining and locating cores and boundaries of social networks. *Social Networks, 16*(4), 267–293.

Dowdle, A., Limbocker, S., Yang, S., Stewart, P. A., & Sebold, K. (2013). *The invisible hands of political parties in presidential elections: Party activists and political aggregation from 2004 to 2012*. New York, NY: Palgrave McMillian.

Durkheim, E. (1949). *The division of labor in society* (G. Simpson, Trans.). New York, NY: Free Press.

Easterlin, R. A. (1974). Does economic growth improve the human lot? Some empirical evidence. In M. Abramovitz, P. A. David, & M. Warren (Eds.), *Nations and households in economic growth* (pp.89–125). New York, NY: Academic Press.

Eilstrup-Sangiovanni, M., & Jones, C. (2008). Assessing the dangers of

illicit networks: Why al-Qaida may be less threatening than many think. *International Security, 33*(2), 7–44.

Eisenberg, M. E., Neumark-Sztainer, D., Story, M., & Perry, C. (2005). The role of social norms and friends' influences on unhealthy weight-control behaviors among adolescent girls. *Social Science & Medicine, 60*(6), 1165–1173.

Elliott, D., & Menard, S. (1996). Delinquent friends and delinquent behavior: Temporal and developmental patterns. In J. D. Hawkins (Ed.), *Delinquency and crime: Current theories* (pp. 28–67). Cambridge, MA: Cambridge University Press.

Ellison, N., Vitak, J., Gray, R., & Lampe, C. (2014). Cultivating social resources on social network sites: Facebook relationship maintenance behaviors and their role in social capital processes. *Journal of Computer-Mediated Communication, 19*(4), 855–870.

Emirbayer, M. (1997). Manifesto for a relational sociology. *American Journal of Sociology, 103*, 281–317.

Entwisle, B., Faust, K., Rindfuss, R. R., & Kaneda, T. (2007). Networks and contexts: Variation in the structure of social ties. *American Journal of Sociology, 112*(5), 1495–1533.

Erdos, P., & Renyi, A. (1959). On random graphs. I. *Publicationes Mathematicae, 6*, 290–297.

Erickson, B. H. (2004). The distribution of gendered social capital in Canada. In H. Flap & B. Volker (Eds.), *Creation and returns of social capital: A new research program* (pp. 27–51). New York, NY: Routledge.

Erickson, G. D. (1975). The concept of personal network in clinical practice. *Family Process, 14*(4), 487–498.

Everett, M. G., & Borgatti, S. P. (1999). The centrality of groups and classes. *Journal of Mathematical Sociology, 23*(3), 181–201.

Faulkner, R. R., & Cheney, E. R. (2013). The multiplexity of political conspiracy: Illegal networks and the collapse of Watergate. *Global Crime, 14*, 197–215.

Faust, K. (1997). Centrality in affiliation networks. *Social Networks, 19*, 157–191.

Fava, M., & Paolo, C. (2008). Major depressive disorder and dysthymic disorder. In T. Stern, J. Rosenbaum, J. Biederman, M. Fava, & S. Rauch, Eds., *The MGH textbook of comprehensive clinical psychiatry*. Philadelphia, PA: Mosby-Elsevier.

Feld, S. L., & Carter, W. C. (2002). Detecting measurement bias in respondent reports of personal networks. *Social Networks, 24*(4), 365–383.

Feldman-Savelsberg, P., Ndonko, F. T., & Yang, S. (2005). How rumor begets rumor: Collective memory, ethnic conflict, and reproductive rumors in Cameroon. In G. Fine, A. V. Campion-Vincent, & C. Heath (Eds.), *Rumor mills: The social impact of rumor and legend* (pp. 141–159). New York, NY: Transaction.

Ferligoj, A., & Hlebec, V. (1999). Evaluation of social network measurement instruments. *Social Networks, 21*(2), 111–130.

Fernandez, R. M., Castilla, E. J., & Moore, P. (2000). Social capital at work: Networks and employment at a phone center. *American Journal of Sociology, 105*(5), 1288–1356.

Fiori, K. L., Antonucci, T. C., & Cortina, K. S. (2006). Social network typologies and mental health among older adults. *The Journals of Gerontology Series B: Psychological*

Sciences and Social Sciences, 61(1), 25–32.

Fischer, C. S. (1982). What do we mean by "friend"? An inductive study. *Social Networks, 3*(4), 287–306.

Fowler, J. H. (2006). Connecting the Congress: A study of cosponsorship networks. *Political Analysis, 14*(4), 456–487.

Fowler, J. H. (2006). Legislative cosponsorship networks in the US House and Senate. *Social Networks, 28*, 454–465.

Fowler, J. H., & Christakis, N. A. (2009). Dynamic spread of happiness in a large social network: Longitudinal analysis of the Framingham Heart Study social network. *British Medical Journal, 338*, 23–27.

Fowler, J. H., Heaney, M. T., Nickerson, D. W., Padgett, J. F., & Sinclair, B. (2011). Causality in political networks. *American Politics Research, 39*(2), 437–480.

Fowler, J. H., & Jeon, S. (2008). The authority of Supreme Court precedent. *Social Networks, 30*, 16–30.

Frank, O. (1981). A survey of statistical methods for graph analysis. In S. Leinhardt (Ed.), *Sociological methodology* (pp. 110–155). San Francisco, CA: Jossey-Bass.

Frank, O., & Strauss, D. (1986). Markov graphs. *Journal of the American Statistical Association, 81*, 832–842.

Fratiglioni, L., Paillard-Borg, S., & Winblad, B. (2004). An active and socially integrated lifestyle in late life might protect against dementia. *Lancet Neurology, 3*(6), 343–353.

Freeman, L. (1977). A set of measures of centrality based upon betweeness. *Sociometry, 40*, 35–41.

Freeman, L. (1979). Centrality in social networks: I. Conceptual clarification. *Social Networks, 1*, 215–239.

Freeman, L. (1992). Filling in the blanks: A theory of cognitive categories and the structure of social affiliation. *Social Psychology Quarterly, 55*(2), 118–127.

Freeman, L. (2004). *The development of social network analysis: A study in the sociology of science*. Vancouver, BC, Canada: Empirical Press.

Freeman, L., Romney, K., & Freeman, S. (1987). Cognitive structure and informant accuracy. *American Anthropologist, 89*(2), 310–325.

Freeman, L., & Webster, C. (1994). Interpersonal proximity in social and cognitive space. *Social Cognition, 12*(3), 223–247.

Friedman, S. R., Neaigus, A., Jose, B., Curtis, R., Goldstein, M., Ildefonso, G., Rothenberg, R. B., & Des Jarlais, D. C. 1997). Sociometric risk networks and risk for HIV infection. *American Journal of Public Health, 87*(8), 1289–1296.

Friedmann, J. (1995). The world city hypothesis: A decade of research and analysis. In P. L. Knox & P. Taylor (Eds.), *World cities in a world system*. Cambridge, MA: Cambridge University Press.

Fritsch, M., & Kauffeld-Monz, M. (2010). The impact of network structure on knowledge transfer: An application of social network analysis in the context of regional innovation networks. *The Annals of Regional Science Springer, 44*(1), 21–38.

Gaag, M. van der, & Snijders, T. A. B. (2004). Proposals for the measurement of individual social capital. In H. Flap & B. Volker (Eds.), *Creation and returns of social capital:*

A new research program (pp. 199–219). New York, NY: Routledge.

Gabasova, E. (2016, January 25). Star Wars social networks: The Force Awakens [Blog]. Retrieved June 7, 2016, from http://evelinag.com/blog/2015/12-15-star-wars-social-network/index.html

Galaskiewicz, J. (1985). *Social organization of an urban grants economy: A study of business philanthropy and nonprofit organizations*. Orlando, FL: Academic Press.

Galaskiewicz, J., & Zaheer, A. (1999). Networks of competitive advantage. In S. Andrews & D. Knoke (Eds.), *Research in the sociology of organizations* (pp. 237–261). Stamford, CT: JAI Press.

Gerich, J., & Lehner, R. (2006). Video computer-assisted self-administered interviews for deaf respondents. *Field Methods, 18*(3), 267–283.

Ghoshal, S., & Bartlett. C. A. (1990). The multinational corporation as an interorganizational network. *The Academy of Management Review, 15*(4), 603–625.

Giordano, P. C., Cernkovich, S. A., & Pugh, M. D. (1986). Friendships and delinquency. *American Journal of Sociology, 91*, 1170–1202.

Gogineni, A., Stein, M. D., & Friedmann, P. D. (2001). Social relationships and intravenous drug use among methadone maintenance patients. *Drug and Alcohol Dependence, 64*(1), 47–53.

González-Bailón, S., Borge-Holthoefer, J., & Moreno, Y. (2013). Broadcasters and hidden influentials in online protest diffusion. *American Behavioral Scientist, 57*(7), 943–965.

Gottfredson, M. R., & Hirschi, T. (1990). *A general theory of crime*.

Stanford, CA: Stanford University Press.

Grannis, R. (1998). The importance of trivial streets: Residential streets and residential segregation 1. *American Journal of Sociology, 103*(6), 1530–1564.

Granovetter, M. (1973). The strength of weak ties. *American Journal of Sociology, 78*, 1360–1380.

Granovetter, M. (1985). Economic action and social structure: The problem of embeddedness. *The American Journal of Sociology, 91*(3), 481–510.

Groh, D. R., Jason, L. A., & Keys, C. B. (2008). Social network variables in Alcoholics Anonymous: A literature review. *Clinical Psychology Review, 28*(3), 430–450.

Guardo, M. D., & Harrigan, K. (2012). Mapping research on strategic alliances and innovation: A co-citation analysis. *The Journal of Technology Transfer, 37*(6), 789–811.

Gulati, R. (1995). Social structure and alliance formation patterns: A longitudinal analysis. *Administrative Science Quarterly, 40*, 619–652.

Gulati, R. (1998). Alliances and networks. *Strategic Management Journal, 19*, 293–317.

Hafner-Burton, E. M., Kahler, M., & Montgomery, A. H. (2009). Network analysis for international relations. *International Organization, 63*, 559–592.

Hafner-Burton, E. M., & Montgomery, A. H. (2006). Power positions: International organizations, social networks, and conflict. *Journal of Conflict Resolution, 50*(1), 3–27.

Hall, R. L. (1992). Measuring legislative influence. *Legislative Studies Quarterly, 17*(2), 205–231.

Hanneman, R. A., & Riddle, M. (2005). *Introduction to social network methods.* Riverside, CA: University of California, Riverside. Retrieved from http://faculty.ucr.edu/~hanneman/

Hansell, S., & Wiatrowski, M. D. (1981). Competing conceptions of delinquent peer relations. In G. F. Jensen (Ed.), *Sociology of delinquency: Current issues* (pp. 93–108). Beverly Hills, CA: Sage.

Hargens, L. L. (2000). Using the literature: Reference networks, reference contexts, and the social structure of scholarship. *American Sociological Review, 65*(6), 846–865.

Harris, J. K. (2014). *An introduction to exponential random graph modeling.* Thousand Oaks, CA: Sage.

Haunschild, P. R. (1993). Interorganizational imitation: The impact of interlocks on corporate acquisition activity. *Administrative Science Quarterly, 38*, 564–592.

Havassy, B. E., Hall, S. M., & Wasserman, D. A. (1991). Social support and relapse: Commonalities among alcoholics, opiate users, and cigarette smokers. *Addictive Behaviors, 16*(5), 235–246.

Hawkley, L. C., Masi, C. M., Berry, J. D., & Cacioppo, J. T. (2006). Loneliness is a unique predictor of age-related differences in systolic blood pressure. *Psychology and Aging, 21*(1), 152–164.

Haynie, D. L. (2001). Delinquent peers revisited: Does network structure matter? *American Journal of Sociology, 106*(4), 1013–1057.

Heckathorn, D. D. (1997). Respondent-driven sampling: A new approach to the study of hidden populations. *Social Problems, 44*(2), 174–199.

Helfstein, S., & Wright, D. (2011). Covert or convenient? Evolution of terror attack networks. *Journal of Conflict Resolution, 55*(5), 785–813.

Helleringer, S., & Kohler, H.-P. (2007). Sexual network structure and the spread of HIV in Africa: Evidence from Likoma Island, Malawi. *Aids, 21*(17), 2323–2332.

Hirschi, T. (1969). *Causes of delinquency.* Oakland: University of California Press.

Hlebec, V., & Ferligoj, A. (2002). Reliability of social network measurement instruments. *Field Methods, 14*(3), 288–306.

Hoeve, M., Dubas, J. S., Eichelsheim, V. I., van der Laan, P. H., Smeenk, W., & Gerris, J. R. (2009). The relationship between parenting and delinquency: A meta-analysis. *Journal of Abnormal Child Psychology, 37*, 749–775.

Hoffmann, J. P., Su, S., & Pach, A. (1997). Changes in network characteristics and HIV risk behavior among injection drug users. *Drug and Alcohol Dependence, 46*(1–2), 41–51.

Holland, P. W., & Leinhardt, S. (1981). An exponential family of probability distributions for directed graphs. *Journal of the American Statistical Association, 76*(373), 33–50.

Holmberg, S. D. (1996). The estimated prevalence and incidence of HIV in 96 large US metropolitan areas. *American Journal of Public Health, 86*(5), 642–654.

Holme, P., Edling, C. R., & Liljeros, F. (2004). Structure and time evolution of an Internet dating community. *Social Networks, 26*(2), 155–174.

Holzer, H. J. (1987). *Hiring procedures in the firm: Their economic determinants and outcomes.* Washington, DC: National Bureau of Economic Research.

Ingersoll-Dayton, B., Morgan, D., & Antonucci, T. C. (1997). The effects of positive and negative social exchanges on aging adults. *The Journals of Gerontology Series B: Psychological Sciences and Social Sciences, 52*(4), S190–S199.

Inkpen, A. C. (1995). *The management of international joint ventures: An organizational learning perspective.* London, England: Routledge.

Jelalian, E., & Mehlenbeck, R. (2002). Peer-enhanced weight management treatment for overweight adolescents: Some preliminary findings. *Journal of Clinical Psychology in Medical Settings, 9*(1), 15–23.

Jones, M., & Fischer, C. (1978). A procedure for surveying personal networks. *Sociological Methods and Research, 7*(November), 131–148.

Jung, D. F., & Lake, D. A. (2011). Markets, hierarchies, and networks: An agent-based organizational ecology. *American Journal of Political Science, 55*(4), 972–990.

Kahn, R. L., & Antonucci, T. C. (1980). Convoys over the life course. Attachment, roles, and social support. In P. B. Baltes & O. G. Brim (Eds.), *Life-span development and behavior* (pp. 254–283). New York, NY: Academic Press.

Kalleberg, A. L., Knoke, D., Marsden, P. V., & Spaeth, J. L. (1996). *Organizations in America: Analyzing their structures and human resource practices.* Thousand Oaks, CA: Sage.

Kandel, D. B., & Davies, M. (1991). Friendship networks, intimacy, and illicit drug use in young adulthood: A comparison of two competing theories. *Criminology, 29*(3), 441–470.

Kasarda, J. D., & Janowitz, M. (1974). Community attachment in mass society. *American Sociological Review, 39*(3), 328–339.

Keefe, P. (2006, March 12). Can network theory thwart terrorists? *The New York Times.*

Keister, L. A. (2000). *Chinese business groups: The structure and impact of interfirm relations during economic development.* New York, NY: Oxford University Press.

Keister, L. A. (2009). Interfirm relations in China group structure and firm performance in business groups. *American Behavioral Scientist, 52*(12), 1709–1730.

Keller, F. B. (2015). Networks of power. Using social network analysis to understand who will rule and who is really in charge in an authoritarian regime. theory, method, and application on Chinese communist elites (1982-2012). Doctoral dissertation, New York University.

Keller, F. B. (2016a). Moving beyond factions: Using social network analysis to uncover patronage networks among Chinese elites. *Journal of East Asian Studies, 16*(1), 17–41.

Keller, F. B. (2016b). Analyses of elite networks. In H. Best, M. Cotta, J.-P. Daloz, J.n Higley, U. Hoffmann Lange, J. Pakulski, & E. Semenova (Eds.), *The Palgrave handbook of political elites.* London, England: Palgrave Macmillan.

Kelly, J. F., Stout, R. L., Magill, M., & Tonigan, J. S. (2011). The role of Alcoholics Anonymous in mobilizing adaptive social network changes: A prospective lagged mediational analysis. *Drug and Alcohol Dependence, 114*(2), 119–126.

Kelly, J. G., Snowden, L. R., & Munoz, R. F. (1977). Social and community interventions. *Annual Review of Psychology, 28*(1), 323–361.

Kenis, P., & Knoke, D. (2002). How organizational field networks shape interorganizational tie-formation rates. *Academy of Management Review, 27*, 275–293.

Kent, D. (1978). *The rise of the Medici: Faction in Florence, 1426-1434.* Chicago, IL: University of Chicago Press.

Kick, E. L., McKinney, L. A., McDonald, S., & Jorgenson, A. (2011). A multiple-network analysis of the world system of nations, 1995-1999. In J. Scott & P. Carrington (Eds.), *The handbook of social network analysis.* London, England: Sage Ltd.

Kiecolt-Glaser, J. K., Dura, J. R., Speicher, C. E., Trask, O. J., & Glaser, R. (1991). Spousal caregivers of dementia victims: Longitudinal changes in immunity and health. *Psychosomatic Medicine, 53*(4), 345–362.

Kirk, D. S., & Papachristos, A. V. (2011). Cultural mechanisms and the persistence of neighborhood violence. *American Journal of Sociology, 116*(4), 1190–1233.

Kirkland, J. H., & Gross, J. H. (2014). Measurement and theory in legislative networks: The evolving topology of congressional cooperation. *Social Networks, 36*, 97–109.

Klofstad, C. (2011). *Civic talk: Peers, politics, and the future of democracy.* Philadelphia, PA: Temple University Press.

Klovdahl, A. S. (1985). Social networks and the spread of infectious diseases: The AIDS example. *Social Science & Medicine, 21*(11), 1203–1216.

Knoke, D. (1990). *Political networks: The structural perspective.* Cambridge, MA: Cambridge University Press.

Knoke, D. (2001). *Changing organizations: Business networks in the new political economy.* Boulder, CO: Westview Press.

Knoke, D. (2011). Policy networks. In J. Scott & P. J. Carrington (Eds.), *The SAGE Handbook of Social Network Analysis* (pp. 210–222). London, England: Sage Ltd.

Knoke, D. (2012a). *Economic networks.* Cambridge, England: Polity.

Knoke, D. (2012b). Social networks and terrorism. In M. Safar & K. A. Mahdi (Eds.), *Social networking and community behavior modeling: Qualitative and quantitative measures* (pp. 232–246). Hershey, PA: IGI Global.

Knoke, D. (2013). "It takes a network": The rise and fall of social network analysis in U.S. Army counterinsurgency doctrine. *Connections, 33*(1), 1–10.

Knoke, D., & Burt, R. (1983). Prominence. In R. S. Burt & M. J. Miner (Eds.), *Applied network analysis: A methodological introduction* (pp. 195–222). Beverly Hills, CA: Sage.

Knoke, D., & Kuklinski, J. H. (1982). *Network analysis.* Beverly Hills, CA: Sage.

Knoke, D., & Laumann, E. O. (1982). The social organization of the national health policy domain. In P. V. Marsden & N. Lin (Eds.), *Social structure and network analysis* (pp. 255–270). Beverly Hills, CA: Sage.

Knoke, D., Pappi, F. U., Broadbent, J., & Tsujinaka, Y. (1996). *Comparing policy networks: Labor politics in the U.S., Germany, and Japan.* New York, NY: Cambridge University Press.

Knoke, D., & Yang, S. (2008). *Social network analysis.* Thousand Oaks, CA: Sage.

Kogovšek, T., & Ferligoj, A. (2005). Effects on reliability and validity of egocentered network measurements. *Social Networks, 27,* 205–229.

Kop, W. J., Berman, D. S., Gransar, H., Wong, N. D., Miranda-Peats, R., White, M. D., Shin, M., Bruce, M., Krantz, D. S., & Rozanski, A. (2005). Social network and coronary artery calcification in asymptomatic individuals. *Psychosomatic Medicine, 67*(3), 343–352.

Koplan, J. P., Liverman, C. T., & Kraak, V. A. (Eds.). (2005). *Preventing childhood obesity: Health in the balance.* Washington, DC: National Academies Press.

Koschade, S. (2006). A social network analysis of Jemaah Islamiyah: The applications to counterterrorism and intelligence. *Studies in Conflict & Terrorism, 29*(6), 559–575.

Krackhardt, D. (1987). QAP partialling as a test of spuriousness. *Social Networks, 9,* 171–186.

Krackhardt, D. (1990). Assessing the political landscape: Structure, cognition, and power in organizations. *Administrative Science Quarterly, 35,* 342–369.

Krackhardt, D. (1992). The strength of strong ties: The importance of philos in organizations. In N. Nohria & R. G. Eccles (Eds.), *Networks and organizations* (pp. 226–240). Boston, MA: Harvard Business School Press.

Krackhardt, D. (1994). Constraints on the interactive organization as an ideal type. In C. Heckscher & A. Donnellan (Eds.), *The post-bureaucratic organization* (pp. 211–222). Newbury Park, CA: Sage.

Krackhardt, D., & Brass, D. J. (1994). Intra-organizational networks: The micro side. In S. Wasserman & J. Galaskiewicz (Eds.), *Advances in the social and behavioral sciences from social network analysis* (pp. 209–230). Newbury Park, CA: Sage.

Krackhardt, D., & Kilduff, M. (1999). Whether close or far: Perceptions of balance in friendship networks in organizations. *Journal of Personality and Social Psychology, 76,* 770–782.

Krackhardt, D., & Porter, L. W. (1985). When friends leave: A structural analysis of the relationship between turnover and stayers' attitudes. *Administrative Science Quarterly, 30*(2), 242–261.

Krackhardt, D., & Porter, L. W. (1986). The snowball effect—Turnover embedded in communication-networks. *Journal of Applied Psychology, 71*(1), 50–55.

Kramarz, F., & Skans, O. N. (2014). When strong ties are strong: Networks and youth labour market entry. *The Review of Economic Studies, 81*(3), 1164–1200.

Krebs, V. E. (2002). Mapping networks of terrorist cells. *Connections, 24*(3), 43–52.

Krohn, M. D. (1986). The web of conformity: A network approach to the explanation of delinquent behavior. *Social Problems, 33,* 601–613.

Krohn, M. D., Massey, J. L., & Zielinski, M. (1988). Role overlap, network multiplexity, and adolescent deviant behavior. *Social Psychology Quarterly, 51*(4), 346–356.

Krohn, M. D., & Thornberry, T. P. (1993). Network theory: A model for understanding drug abuse among African-American and Hispanic youth. In M. R. De La Rosa & J.-L. Recio Adrados (Eds.), *Drug abuse among minority youth: Advances in research and methodology* (NIDA Research Monograph 130, pp. 102–128). Washington, DC: U.S. Department of Health and Human Services.

Kronenfeld, D. B., & Kronenfeld, J. (1972). Toward a science of design for successful food service. *Institutions and Volume Feeding Management, 70,* 38–44.

Kruskal, J. B., & Wish, M. (1978). *Multidimensional scaling*. Beverly Hills, CA: Sage.

Kubrin, C. E., & Weitzer, R. (2003). New directions in social disorganization theory. *Journal of Research in Crime and Delinquency, 40*(4), 374–402.

Kumbasar, E., Romney, K., & Batchelder, W. (1994). Systematic biases in social perception. *American Journal of Sociology, 100*(2), 477–505.

Kurtz, G., & Lucas, G. (1977). *Star wars. Episode IV: A new hope* [Motion picture]. U.S.: 20th Century Fox. (Subsequent movies premiered in 1980, 1983, 1999, 2002, 2005, and 2015, including several TV series based off of the *Star Wars* brand.)

Lakon, C. M., Ennett, S. T., & Norton, E. C. (2006). Mechanisms through which drug, sex partner, and friendship network characteristics relate to risky needle use among high risk youth and young adults. *Social Science & Medicine, 63*(9), 2489–2499.

Lane, P. J., Salk, J. E., & Lyles, M. A. (2001). Absorptive capacity, learning, and performance in international joint ventures. *Strategic Management Journal, 22*(12), 1139–1161.

LaPierre, R. T. (1934). Attitudes vs. actions. *Social Forces, 13*, 230–237.

Latkin, C. A., Knowlton, A. R., Hoover, D., & Mandell, W. (1999). Drug network characteristics as a predictor of cessation of drug use among adult injection drug users: A prospective study. *American Journal of Drug and Alcohol Abuse, 25*(3), 463–473.

Latkin, C. A., Mandell, W., Vlahov, D., Knowlton, A., Oziemkowska, M., & Celentano, D. (1995). Personal network characteristics as antecedents to needle-sharing and shooting gallery attendance. *Social Networks, 17*(3), 219–228.

Laumann, E. O., Gagnon, J. H., Michael, R. T., & Michaels, S. (1994). *The social organization of sexuality: Sexual practices in the United States*. Chicago, IL: University of Chicago Press.

Laumann, E. O., Marsden, P. V., & Prensky, D. (1989). The boundary-specification problem in network analysis. In R. Burt & M. Minor (Eds.), *Applied network analysis* (pp. 18–34). Newbury Park, CA: Sage.

Laumann, E. O., & Youm, Y. (1999). Racial/ethnic group differences in the prevalence of sexually transmitted diseases in the United States: A network explanation. *Sexually Transmitted Diseases, 26*(5), 250–261.

Layard, R. (2006). Happiness and public policy: A challenge to the profession. *The Economic Journal, 116*(510), C24–C33.

Lee, M. (2011). Ethics of social network analysis. In G.A. Barnett, & J. G. Golson (Eds.) *SAGE encyclopedia of social networks* (pp. 590–592). Thousand Oaks, CA: Sage.

Levy, S. J., & Pierce, J. P. (1990). Predictors of marijuana use and uptake among teenagers in Sydney, Australia. *Substance Use & Misuse, 25*(10), 1179–1193.

Lewis, K., Kaufman, J., Gonzalez, M., Wimmer, A., & Christakis, N. (2008). Tastes ties and time: A new social network dataset using Facebook.com. *Social Networks, 30*(4), 330–342.

Lin, N. (2001). *Social capital: A theory of social structure and action*. New York, NY: Cambridge University Press.

Lin, N., Cook, K., & Burt, R. S. (Eds.). (2001). *Social capital: Theory and research*. New York, NY: Aldine de Gruyter.

Lin, N., & Dumin, M. (1986). Access to occupations through social tie. *Social Networks, 8*, 365–385.

Lin, N., Fu, Y., & Hsung, R.-M. (2001). The position generator: Measurement techniques for investigations of social capital. In N. Lin, K. Cook, & R. Burt (Eds.), *Social capital: Theory and research* (pp. 57–81). Hawthorne, NY: Aldine de Gruyter.

Lubbers, M. J., & Snijders, T. A. B. (2007). A comparison of various approaches to the exponential random graph model: A reanalysis of 102 student networks in school classes. *Social Networks, 29*, 489–507.

Luce, D., & Perry, A. D. (1949). A method of matrix analysis of group structure. *Psychometrika, 14*, 95–116.

Lucioni, R. (2013, December 7). Political polarisation: United States of amoeba. *Economists*. Retrieved from http://www.renzolucioni.com/articles/senate-voting-relationships/

Lueg, C., & Fisher, D. (2003). *From usenet to coWebs: Interacting with social information spaces*. New York, NY: Springer.

Luo, Y. (2000). *Partnering with Chinese firms: Lessons for international managers*. Aldershot, England: Ashgate.

Lusher, D., Koskinen, J., & Robins, G. (2012). *Exponential random graph models for social networks: Theory methods and applications*. New York, NY: Cambridge University Press.

Lyons, R. (2011). The spread of evidence-poor medicine via flawed social-network analysis. *Statistics, Politics, and Policy, 2*(1).

Malchodi, C. S., Oncken, C., Dornelas, E. A., Caramanica, L., Gregonis, E., & Curry, S. L. (2003). The effects of peer counseling on smoking cessation and reduction. *Obstetrics & Gynecology, 101*(3), 504–510.

Malm, A., & Bichler, G. (2011). Networks of collaborating criminals:

Assessing the structural vulnerability of drug markets. *Journal of Research in Crime and Delinquency, 48*(2), 271–297.

Manger, M. S., Pickup, M. A., & Snijders, T. A. B. (2012). A hierarchy of preferences: A longitudinal network analysis approach to PTA formation. *Journal of Conflict Resolution, 56*(5), 853–878.

Maoz, Z. (2012). Preferential attachment, homophily, and the structure of international networks, 1816-2003. *Conflict Management and Peace Science, 29*(3), 341–369.

Marsden, P. V. (1987). Core discussion networks of Americans. *American Sociological Review, 52*(1), 122–131.

Marsden, P. V. (2002). Egocentric and sociocentric measures of network centrality. *Social Networks, 24*(4), 407–422.

Marsden, P. V. (2011). Survey methods for network data. In J. Scott & P. J. Carrington (Eds.), *The SAGE handbook of social network analysis* (pp. 370–388). London, England: Sage Ltd.

Marsden, P. V., & Campbell, K. E. (1990). Recruitment and selection processes: The organizational side of job searches. *Social Mobility and Social Structure*, 59–79.

Marsden, P. V., & Lin, N. (1982). *Social structure and network analysis*. Beverly Hills, CA: Sage.

Maurer, I., Bartsch, V., & Ebers, M. (2011). The value of intraorganizational social capital: How it fosters knowledge transfer, innovation performance, and growth. *Organization Studies, 32*, 157–185.

McCarty, C., & Govindaramanujam, S. (2005). A modified elicitation of personal networks using dynamic visualization. *Connections, 26*(2), 61–69.

McChrystal, S. A. (2011). It takes a network: The new front line of modern warfare. *Foreign Policy*, (March–April), 1–6.

McCormick, T. H., Salganik, M. J., & Zheng, T. (2010). How many people do you know? Efficiently estimating personal network size. *Journal of the American Statistical Association, 105*(489), 59–70.

McCrady, B. S. (2004). To have but one true friend: Implications for practice of research on alcohol use disorders and social network. *Psychology of Addictive Behaviors, 18*(2), 113.

McKnight, A. J., & McPherson, K. (1986). Evaluation of peer intervention training for high school alcohol safety education. *Accident Analysis & Prevention, 18*(4), 339–347.

McPherson, M., Smith-Lovin, L., & Brashears, M. E. (2006). Social isolation in America: Changes in core discussion networks over two decades. *American Sociological Review, 71*(3), 353–375.

McPherson, M., Smith-Lovin, L., & Cook, J. M. (2001). Birds of feature: Homophily in social networks. *Annual Review of Sociology, 27*, 415–444.

Metz, T., & Jäckle, S. (2016). Hierarchical, Decentralized, or Something Else? Opposition Networks in the German Bundestag. Legislative Studies Quarterly, 41(2), 501–542.

Milgram, S. (1967). The small world problem. *Psychology Today, 1*, 61–67.

Mills, C. W. (1956). *The power elite*. New York, NY: Oxford University Press.

Mintz, B., & Schwartz, M. (1985). The power structure of American business. *Administrative Science Quarterly, 32*(3), 482–484.

Mittelman, M. S., Ferris, S. H., Shulman, E., Steinberg, G., Ambinder, A., Mackell, J. A., & Cohen, J. (1995). A comprehensive support program: Effect on depression in spouse-caregivers of AD patients. *Gerontologist, 35*(6), 792–802.

Mizruchi, M. S. (1996). What do interlocks do? An analysis, critique, and assessment of research on interlocking directorates. *Annual Review of Sociology, 22*, 271–298.

Montgomery, J. D. (1991). Social networks and labor market outcomes: Towards an economic analysis. *American Economic Review, 81*(5), 1408–1418.

Moody, J. (2004). The structure of a social science collaboration network: Disciplinary cohesion from 1963 to 1999. *American Sociological Review, 69*, 213–238.

Moos, R. H. (2007). Theory-based active ingredients of effective treatments for substance use disorders. *Drug and Alcohol Dependence, 88*(2), 109–121.

Morenoff, J. D., Sampson, R. J., & Raudenbush, S. W. (2001). Neighborhood inequality, collective efficacy, and the spatial dynamics of urban violence. *Criminology, 39*(3), 517–558.

Morimoto, S. A., & Yang, S. (2013). What friendship entails: An empirical analysis of graduate students' social networks. *Sociological Spectrum, 33*, 99–116.

Myers, C. A., & Shultz, G. P. (1951). *The dynamics of a labor market: A study of the impact of employment changes on labor mobility, job satisfactions, and company and union policies*. Upper Saddle River, NJ: Prentice-Hall.

Natarajan, M. (2006). Understanding the structure of a large heroin distribution network: Quantitative analysis of qualitative data. *Journal of Quantitative Criminology, 22,* 171–192.

Neblett, R. C., Davey-Rothwell, M., Chander, G., & Latkin, C. A. (2011). Social network characteristics and HIV sexual risk behavior among urban African American women. *Journal of Urban Health, 88*(1), 54–65.

Newman, M. E. (2010). *Networks: An introduction* (p. 39). New York, NY: Oxford University Press.

Nickerson, D. (2008). Is voting contagious? Evidence from two field experiments. *American Political Science Review, 102,* 49–57.

Nohria, N., & Ghoshal, S. (1997). *The differentiated network: Organizing multinational corporations for value creation.* San Francisco, CA: Jossey-Bass.

Oliver, J. E. (2003). Suburbanization and sense of community. In D. Levison & K. Christensen (Eds.), *The encyclopedia of community.* Thousand Oaks, CA: Sage.

Ouellet, F., Boivin, R., Leclerc, C., & Morselli, C. (2013). Friends with (out) benefits: Co-offending and re-arrest. *Global Crime, 14,* 141–154.

Padgett, J. F., & Ansell, C. K. (1993). Robust action and the rise of the Medici, 1400-1434. *American Journal of Sociology, 98*(6), 1259–1319.

Paik, A., & Sanchagrin, K. (2013). Social isolation in America: An artifact. *American Sociological Review, 78,* 339–360.

Palmer, D., & Barber, B. M. (2001). Challengers, elites, and owning families: A social class theory of corporate acquisitions in the 1960s. *Administrative Science Quarterly, 46,* 87–120.

Palmer, D., Jennings, P. D., & Zhou, X. (1993). Late adoption of the

multidivisional form by large U.S. corporations: A further exploration of the institutional, political, and economic accounts. *Administrative Science Quarterly, 37*(1), 100–131.

Papachristos, A. V. (2009). Murder by structure: Dominance relations and the social structure of gang homicide. *American Journal of Sociology, 115*(1), 74–128.

Parigi, P., & Sartori, L. (2014). The political party as a network of cleavages: Disclosing the inner structure of Italian political parties in the seventies. *Social Networks, 36,* 54–65.

Patterson, G. R., & Dishion, T. J. (1985). Contributions of families and peers to delinquency. *Criminology, 23,* 63–79.

Pattillo-McCoy, M. (1999). *Black picket fences: Privilege and peril among the Black middle class.* Chicago, IL: University of Chicago Press.

Paxton, S. J., Schutz, H. K., Wertheim, E. H., & Muir, S. L. (1999). Friendship clique and peer influences on body image concerns, dietary restraint, extreme weight-loss behaviors, and binge eating in adolescent girls. *Journal of Abnormal Psychology, 108*(2), 255–266.

Penninx, B. W. J. H., Van Tilburg, T., Kriegsman, D. M. W., Deeg, D. J. H., Boeke, A. J. P., & van Eijk, J. Th. M. (1997). Effects of social support and personal coping resources on mortality in older age: The Longitudinal Aging Study Amsterdam. *American Journal of Epidemiology, 146*(6), 510–519.

Pfeffer, J., & Salancik, G. (1978). *The external control of organizations.* New York, NY: Harper & Row.

Pinquart, M., & Sörensen, S. (2000). Influences of socioeconomic status, social network, and competence on

subjective well-being in later life: A meta-analysis. *Psychology and Aging, 15*(2), 187–223.

Podolny, J. M., & Page, K. L. (1998). Network forms of organization. *Annual Review of Sociology, 24,* 57–76.

Podolny, J. M., & Stuart, T. (1995). A role-based ecology of technological change. *American Journal of Sociology, 100*(5), 1224–1260.

Poole, K. T., & Rosenthal, H. (1997). *Congress: A political-economic history of roll call voting.* New York, NY: Oxford University Press.

Potterat, J. J., Muth, S. Q., Rothenberg, R. B., Zimmerman, H. P., Green, D. L., Taylor, J. E., Bonney, M. S., & White, H. A. (2002). Sexual network structure as an indicator of epidemic phase. *Sexually Transmitted Infections, 78*(supplementary 1), i152–i158.

Potterat, J. J., Phillips-Plummer, L., Muth, S. Q., Rothenberg, R. B., Woodhouse, D. E., Maldonado-Long, T. S., Zimmerman, H. P., & Muth, J. B. (2002). Risk network structure in the early epidemic phase of HIV transmission in Colorado Springs. *Sexually Transmitted Infections, 78*(1), i159–i163.

Potterat, J. J., Rothenberg, R. B., & Muth, S. Q. (1999). Network structural dynamics and infectious disease propagation. *International Journal of STD/AIDS, 10*(3), 182–185.

Powell, W. W. (1990). Neither market nor hierarchy: The network forms of organization. *Research in Organizational Behavior, 12,* 295–336.

Powell, W. W., Koput, K. W., & Smith-Doerr, L. (1996). Interorganizational collaboration and the locus of innovation: Networks of learning in biotechnology. *Administrative Science Quarterly, 41*(1), 116–145.

Pruchno, R. A., & Resch, N. L. (1989). Husbands and wives as caregivers: Antecedents of depression and burden. *Gerontologist, 29*(2), 159–165.

Putnam, R. D. (1993). *Making democracy work: Civic traditions in modern Italy*. Princeton, NJ: Princeton University Press.

Qin, J., Xu, J. J., Hu, D., Sageman, M., & Chen, H. (2005). Analyzing terrorist networks: A case study of the global salafi jihad network. *Intelligence and Security Informatics*, 287–304.

Rapoport, A. (1953). Spread of information through a population with sociostructural bias: I. Assumption of transitivity. *Bulletin of Mathematical Biophysics, 15*, 523–533.

Rapoport, A. (1957). Contribution to the theory of random and biased nets. *Bulletin of Mathematical Biology, 19*, 257–277.

Rees, A., & Schultz, G. (1970). *Workers in an urban labor market*. Chicago, IL: University of Chicago Press.

Rice, R. (1994). Network analysis and computer-mediated communication systems. In S. Wasserman & J. Galaskiewicz (Eds.), *Advances in social network analysis* (pp. 167–203). Thousand Oaks, CA: Sage.

Rice, R., Borgman, C., Bednarski, D., & Hart, P. J. (1989). Journal-to-journal citation data: Issues of reliability and validity. *Scientometrics, 15*(3–4), 257–282.

Rice, R., Donohew, L., & Clayton, R. (2003). Peer network, sensation seeking, and drug use among junior and senior high school students. *Connections, 26*(2), 32–58.

Robins, G. (2015). *Doing social networks research: Network research design for social scientists*. Thousand Oaks, CA: Sage.

Robins, L. N., Davis, D. H., & Goodwin, D. W. (1974). Drug use by U.S. Army enlisted men in Vietnam: A follow-up on their return home. *American Journal of Epidemiology, 99*(4), 235–249.

Rodríguez, J. A. (2005). *The March 11th terrorist network: In its weakness lies its strength*. Paper presented at the XXV International Sunbelt Conference, Los Angeles, CA.

Romney, K., & Weller, S. (1984). Predicting informant accuracy from patterns of recall among individuals. *Social Networks, 6*(1), 59–77.

Romney, K., Weller, S., & Batchelder, W. (1987). Culture as consensus: A theory of culture and informant accuracy. *American Anthropologist, 88*(2), 313–338.

Rosenquist, J. N., Fowler, J. H., & Christakis, N. A. (2011). Social network determinants of depression. *Molecular Psychiatry, 16*(3), 273–281.

Rothenberg, R. B., Sterk, C., Toomey, K. E., Potterat, J. J., Johnson, D., Schrader, M., & Hatch, S. (1998). Using social network and ethnographic tools to evaluate syphilis transmission. *Sexually Transmitted Diseases, 25*(3), 154–160.

Rountree, P. W., & Warner, B. D. (1999). Social ties and crime: Is the relationship gendered? *Criminology, 37*(4), 789–813.

Ruan, D. (1998). The content of the General Social Survey discussion networks: An exploration of General Social Survey discussion name generator in a Chinese context. *Social Networks, 20*(3), 247–264.

Ruan, D., Freeman, L., Dai, X., Pan, Y., & Zhang, W. (1997). On the changing structure of social networks in urban China. *Social Networks, 19*(1), 75–89.

Rutledge, T., Reis, S. E., Olson, M., Owens, J., Kelsey, S. F., Pepine, C. J., Mankad, S., et al. (2004). Social networks are associated with lower mortality rates among women with suspected coronary disease: The National Heart, Lung, and Blood Institute-Sponsored Women's Ischemia Syndrome Evaluation study. *Psychosomatic Medicine, 66*(6), 882–888.

Sabidussi, G. (1966). The centrality index of a graph. *Psychometrika, 31*, 581–603.

Sageman, M. (2004). *Understanding terror networks*. Philadelphia: University of Pennsylvania Press.

Sageman, M. (2008). The next generation of terror. *Foreign Policy*, (March/April), 37–42.

Sampson, R. J., & Groves, W. B. (1989). Community structure and crime: Testing social-disorganization theory. *American Journal of Sociology, 94*, 774–802.

Sampson, R. J., Raudenbush, S. W., & Earls, F. (1997). Neighborhoods and violent crime: A multilevel study of collective efficacy. *Science, 277*(5238), 918–924.

Sassen, S. (2001). Cities in the global economy. In R. Paddison (Ed.), *Handbook of urban studies*. New York, NY: Sage.

Schacter, S. (1968). Social cohesion. In *International Encyclopedia of the Social Sciences* (Vol. 2, pp. 542–546). New York, NY: Macmillan and Free Press.

Schwartz, D. M., & Rouselle, T. D. (2009). Using social network analysis to target criminal networks. *Trends in Organized Crime, 12*(2), 188–207.

Scott, J. G. (2012). *Social network analysis* (3rd ed.). London, England: Sage Ltd.

Scott, R. W., &. Davis, G. F. (2006). *Organizations and organizing: Rational, natural and open systems perspectives.* Upper Saddle River, NJ: Pearson Prentice.

Seeman, T. E. (2000). Health promoting effects of friends and family on health outcomes in older adults. *American Journal of Health Promotion, 14*(6), 362–370.

Seidman, S. B. (1983). Network structure and minimum degree. *Social Networks, 5*(3), 269–287.

Settle, J. E., Bond, R. M., & Levitt, J. (2011). The social origins of adult political behavior. *American Politics Research, 39*(2), 239–263.

Shalizi, C. R., & Thomas, A. C. (2011). Homophily and contagion are generically confounded in observational social network studies. *Sociological Methods & Research, 40*(2), 211–239.

Shaw, C., & McKay, H. (1942). *Juvenile delinquency and urban areas.* Chicago, IL: University of Chicago Press.

Shaw, W. S., Patterson, T. L., Semple, S. J., Ho, S., Irwin, M. R., Hauger, R. L., & Grant, I. (1997). Longitudinal analysis of multiple indicators of health decline among spousal caregivers. *Annals of Behavioral Medicine, 19*(2), 101–109.

Sherman, S. G., Latkin, C. A., & Gielen, A. C. (2001). Social factors related to syringe sharing among injecting partners: A focus on gender. *Substance Use & Misuse, 36*(14), 2113–2136.

Siegel, D. A. (2009). Social networks and collective action. *American Journal of Political Science, 53*(1), 122–138.

Siegel, D. A. (2011). When does repression work? Collective action in social networks. *Journal of Politics, 73*(4), 993–1010.

Slez, A., & Martin, J. L. (2007). Political action and party. Formation in the United States Constitutional Convention. *American Sociological Review, 72*(1), 42–67.

Smångs, M. (2010). Delinquency, social skills and the structure of peer relations: Assessing criminological theories by social network theory. *Social Forces, 89*, 609–631.

Smith, D. A., & Timberlake, M. F. (2001). World city networks and hierarchies, 1977-1997: An empirical analysis of global air travel links. *American Behavioral Scientist, 44*(10), 1656–1678.

Smith, K. P., & Christakis, N. A. (2008). Social networks and health. *Annual Review of Sociology, 34*, 405–429.

Snijders, T. A. B. (2011). Network dynamics. In J. Scott and P. J. Carrington (Eds.), *The SAGE handbook of social network analysis* (pp. 501–513). London, England: Sage Ltd.

Snijders, T. A. B., Bunt, G. G. van de, & Steglich, C. E. G. (2010). Introduction to actor-based models for network dynamics. *Social Networks, 32*, 44–60.

Snijders, T. A. B., & Koskinen, J. (2012). Longitudinal models. In D. Lusher, J. Koskinen, & G. Robins (Eds.), *Exponential random graph models for social networks: Theory, methods and applications* (pp. 130–140). New York, NY: Cambridge University Press.

Sparrow, M. K. (1991). The application of network analysis to criminal intelligence: An assessment of the prospects. *Social Networks, 13*(3), 251–274.

Spencer, L., & Pahl, R. (2006). *Rethinking friendship: Hidden solidarities today.* Princeton, NJ: Princeton University Press.

Steglich, C., Snijders, T. A. B., & Pearson, M. (2010). Dynamic networks and behavior: Separating selection from influence. *Sociological Methodology, 40*(1), 329–393.

Stohl, C., & Stohl, M. (2007). Networks of terror: Theoretical assumptions and pragmatic consequences. *Communication Theory, 17*(2), 93–124.

Stover, G. N., & Northridge, M. E. (2013). The social legacy of HIV/AIDS. *American Journal of Public Health, 103*(2), 199.

Sutherland, E. H., & Cressey, D. R. (1974). *Criminology* (9th ed.). Philadelphia, PA: Lippincott.

Sutherland, E. H., Cressey, D. R., & Luckenbill, D. F. (1992). *Principles of criminology* (11th ed.). Lanham, MD: AltaMira Press. (Originally published by E. W. Sutherland & D. R. Cressey, 1934; Sutherland's differential association theory was developed in the 4th ed., 1947, Philadelphia, PA: Lippincott.)

Taylor, P. (2004). Regionality in the world city network. *International Social Science Journal, 56*(181), 361–372.

Thoits, P. A. (1986). Social support as coping assistance. *Journal of Consulting and Clinical Psychology, 54*(4), 416–423.

Torfason, M. T., & Ingram, P. (2010). The global rise of democracy: A network account. *American Sociological Review, 75*(3), 355–377.

Trogdon, J. G., Nonnemaker, J., & Pais, J. (2008). Peer effects in adolescent overweight. *Journal of Health Economics, 27*(5), 1388–1399.

Tsai, W. (2000). The formation of intraorganizational linkages. *Strategic Management Journal, 21*(9), 925–939.

Tsai, W. (2001). Knowledge transfer in intraorganizational networks: Effects of network position and absorptive capacity on business unit innovation and performance. *The Academy of Management Journal, 44*(5), 1002.

Tsvetovat, M., & Carley, K. M. (2005). *Structural knowledge and success of anti-terrorist activity: The downside of structural equivalence* (Paper 43). Pittsburgh, PA: Institute for Software Research.

Ugander, J., Karrer, B., Backstrom, L., & Marlow, C. (2011). *The anatomy of the Facebook social graph*. Manuscript submitted for publication. arXiv:1111.4503.

Useem, M. (1979). The social organization of the American business elite and participation of corporation directors in the governance of American institutions. *American Sociological Review, 44*(4), 553–572.

Useem, M. (1984). *The inner circle: Large corporations and the rise of business political activity in the U.S. and U.K.* New York, NY: Oxford University Press.

Uzzi, B. (1996). The sources and consequences of embeddedness for the economic performance of organizations: The network effect. *American Sociological Review, 61*, 674–698.

Valente, T. W. (2003). Social network influences on adolescent substance use: An introduction. *Connections, 25*(2), 11–16.

Valente, T. W., Gallaher, P., & Mouttapa, M. (2004). Using social networks to understand and prevent substance use: A transdisciplinary perspective. *Substance Use & Misuse, 39*(10–12), 1685–1712.

Valente, T. W., & Vlahov, D. (2001). Selective risk taking among needle exchange participants: Implications for supplemental interventions.

American Journal of Public Health, 91(3), 406–411.

Van Praag, B., & Kapteyn, A. (1973). Further evidence on the individual welfare function of income: An empirical investigation in the Netherlands. *European Economic Review, 4*(1), 33–62.

VanderWeele, T., & An, W. (2013). Social networks and causal inference. In S. L. Morgan (Ed.), *Handbook of causal analysis for social research* (p. 357). New York, NY: Springer Science.

von Sydow, K., Lieb, R., Pfister, H., Höfler, M., & Wittchen, H.-U. (2002). What predicts incident use of cannabis and progression to abuse and dependence? A 4-year prospective examination of risk factors in a community sample of adolescents and young adults. *Drug and Alcohol Dependence, 68*(1), 49–64.

Wallerstein, I. (1974). *The modern world-system. Vol. I: Capitalist agriculture and the origins of the European world-economy in the sixteenth century*. New York, NY: Academic Press.

Wang, P. (2013). ERGM extensions: Models for multiple networks and bipartite networks. In D. Lusher, J. Koskinen, & G. Robins (Eds.), *Exponential random graph models for social networks: Theory, methods and applications* (pp. 115–128). New York, NY: Cambridge University Press.

Warr, M., & Stafford, M. C. (1991). The influence of delinquent peers: What they think or what they do? *Criminology, 29*, 851–866.

Wasserheit, J. N., & Aral, S. O. (1996). The dynamic topology of sexually transmitted disease epidemics: Implications for prevention strategies. *Journal of Infectious Diseases, 174*(Supplement 2), S201–S213.

Wasserman, S., & Faust, K. (1994). *Social network analysis: Methods*

and applications. New York, NY: Cambridge University Press.

Wasserman, S., & Pattison, P. (1996). Logit models and logistic regressions for social networks. I: An introduction to Markov graphs and p*. *Psychometrika, 60*, 401–425.

Watts, D. J. (2003). *Six degrees: The science of a connected age*. New York: W.W. Norton.

Weerman, F. M. (2011). Delinquent peers in context: A longitudinal network analysis of selection and influence effects. *Criminology, 49*(1), 253–286.

Wegener, B. (1991). Job mobility and social ties: Social resources, prior job, and status attainment. *American Sociological Review, 56*(1), 60–71.

Wenzel, S., Holloway, I., Golinelli, D., Ewing, B., Bowman, R., & Tucker, J. (2012). Social networks of homeless youth in emerging adulthood. *Journal of Youth & Adolescence, 41*(5), 561.

White, H. (2011). Scientific and scholarly networks. In J. Scott & P. J. Carrington (Eds.), *The SAGE handbook of social network analysis* (pp. 271–286). London, England: Sage Ltd.

White, H., Boorman, S., & Breiger, R. (1976). Social structure from multiple networks. I. Blockmodels of roles and positions. *American Journal of Sociology, 81*(4), 730–780.

White, K., & Watkins, S. C. (2000). Accuracy, stability and reciprocity in informal conversational networks in rural Kenya. *Social Networks, 22*(4), 337–355.

White, M. J., Kim, A., & Glick, J. E. (2005). Mapping social distance: Ethnic residential segregation in a multiethnic metro. *Sociological Methods and Research, 34*, 173–203.

Wijk, R. V., Jansen, J. J. P., & Lyles, M. A. (2008). Inter- and intra-organizational knowledge transfer:

A meta-analytic review and assessment of its antecedents and consequences. *Journal of Management Studies, 45*(4), 830–853.

Wilson, W. J. (1987). *The truly disadvantaged: The inner city, the underclass, and public policy*. Chicago, IL: University of Chicago Press.

Yan, E., & Ding, Y. (2012). Scholarly network similarities: How bibliographic coupling networks, citation networks, co-citation networks, topical networks, coauthorship networks, and co-word networks relate to each other. *Journal of the American Society for Information Science & Technology, 63*(7), 1313–1326.

Yang, S. (2008). Bureaucracy versus high performance: Work reorganization in the 1990s. *The Journal of Socio-Economics, 37*(5), 1825–1845.

Yang, S. (2013). Networks: An introduction by M.E.J. Newman. *The Journal of Mathematical Sociology, 37*(4), 250–251.

Yang, S., Limbocker, S., Dowdle, A., Stewart, P. A., & Sebold, K. (2015). Party cohesion in presidential races: Applying social network theory to the preprimary multiple donor networks of 2004 and 2008. *Party Politics, 21*, 638–648.

Yoshino, M. Y., & Rangan, S. (1995). *Strategic alliances: An entrepreneurial approach to globalization*. Boston, MA: Harvard Business School Press.

Youm, Y., & Laumann, E. O. (2002). Social network effects on the transmission of sexually transmitted diseases. *Sexually Transmitted Diseases, 29*(11), 689–697.

Youtie, J., Kay, L., & Melkers, J. (2013). Bibliographic coupling and network analysis to assess knowledge coalescence in a research center environment. *Research Evaluation, 22*(3), 145–156.

Zajac, E. J., & Westphal, J. D. (1996). Who shall succeed? How CEO/board preferences and power affect the choice of new CEOs. *Academy of Management Journal, 39*, 64–90.

Zarit, S. H., Todd, P. A., & Zarit, J. M. (1986). Subjective burden of husbands and wives as caregivers: A longitudinal study. *Gerontologist, 26*(3), 260–266.

Zimmerman, G. M., & Messner, S. F. (2010). Neighborhood context and the gender gap in adolescent violent crime. *American Sociological Review, 75*(6), 958–980.

• Index •

Lightning Source UK Ltd.
Milton Keynes UK
UKHW030957241020
372152UK00004B/77